KING'S LYNN

The Custom House, built in 1683.

KING'S LYNN

Paul Richards

Phillimore

1990

Published by
PHILLIMORE & CO. LTD.
Shopwyke Hall, Chichester, Sussex

ISBN 0 85033 603 1

Printed and bound in England by
STAPLES PRINTERS ROCHESTER LIMITED
Love Lane, Rochester, Kent.

To my Parents
and
Michelle and Alison

Contents

List of Illustrations ix
Acknowledgements xi
Preface xiii

1. The Making of the Town 1
2. The Port of Lynn 18
3. Town Industries 32
4. An English Market Town 46
5. The Merchants of Lynn 59
6. Townspeople 73
7. Religion and Society 88
8. Class and Culture 103
9. The City State 116
10. Lynn since the Coming of the Railways 135

Bibliography 155
Index 159

A Neo-Gothic window of the Lynn Savings Bank (1858),
displaying the town crest.

List of Illustrations

Frontispiece: The Custom House

1.	The Wash and the rivers of the Fenland in the Middle Ages	2
2.	The pattern of occupation between 1050 and 1750	2
3.	Hampton Court	5
4.	The Gildhall	7
5.	The old market cross in 1600	11
6.	William Raistrick's plan of Lynn, 1725	14
7.	Map of Lynn in 1846	15
8.	Part of Lynn's waterfront, about 1730	20
9.	The 'Lynn and Wells Mail' in the late 1830s	22
10.	The tower at Clifton House	25
11.	The Purfleet before the erection of the Custom House	26
12.	Lynn harbour in 1841	30
13.	Shipbuilding on the River Nar	33
14.	Thomas Philip Bagge (1773-1829)	37
15.	The Kettle Mills in the early 19th century	40
16.	The Greyfriars Tower and adjacent windmill	40
17.	Street names and locations of crafts in medieval Lynn	43
18.	Aickman's Iron Foundry, 1827	43
19.	The Tuesday Market Place about 1800	48
20.	The west side of the Tuesday Market Place, 1842	49
21.	An aerial view of the Saturday Market Place	50
22.	The Lynn Bank, opened in 1782	57
23.	The door of 27 King Street	57
24.	Walter Coney's house, Saturday Market Place	60
25.	William Atkin, mayor in 1619	63
26.	Memorial to Thomas Greene and his wife, St Nicholas' chapel	63
27.	Sir John Turner (1631-1711)	66
28.	Charles Turner's house, in the Tuesday Market Place	66
29.	The doorway of the Browne family mansion, Nelson Street	68
30.	Fanny Burney (1752-1840)	70
31.	Timber-framed house, St Ann's Street	74
32.	John Cross	74
33.	The Purfleet, or 'great drain' of Lynn	79
34.	North Place	79
35.	The Lynn and West Norfolk Hospital, built 1835	82
36.	St James' Workhouse	85
37.	The sole surviving piece of the Augustinian friary	89
38.	The Red Mount Chapel	93
39.	St Margaret's church from the south, about 1680	96
40.	The interior of St Margaret's before 1741	96
41.	The Wesleyan Methodist chapel opened in 1813	98
42.	St John's church, built 1846	101
43.	*The Lattice House*	106

44.	John Green, 1818	108
45.	The town theatre, built in 1813	110
46.	The Athenaeum, opened in 1854	113
47.	The town walls	118
48.	The doorway to the Trinity Gildhall, 1624	120
49.	The hanging of the Hamond children in 1708	124
50.	The East Gate	124
51.	The first known map of Lynn, about 1588	126
52.	Peace celebrations, 1814	131
53.	Lord George Bentinck, M.P. for Lynn 1828-48	133
54.	High Street looking south, in the late 19th century	137
55.	Aerial view of Lynn, early 1960s	138
56.	The Fisher Fleet at North End	141
57.	The Alexandra Dock shortly after its opening	141
58.	Frederick Savage and traction engine	143
59.	Peace Festival Procession, 19 July 1919	147
60.	Lynn's bus station between the wars	149
61.	True's Yard in the 1930s	149
62.	The proclamation of the mart, 1908	153

Acknowledgements for Illustrations

The author would like to thank the following for permission to reproduce illustrations: The Society for Medieval Archaeology, 1, 2, 17; King's Lynn Museums (Norfolk Museums Service), 11, 15, 18, 27, 39, 47 and 50; R. Bradfer-Lawrence, 13, 14, 20 and 28; Norwich City Library, 16; Lynn News, 21; King's Lynn Borough Council, 25, 30 and 53; Ron Carter, 34 and 61; Aerofilms, 55; Arthur Johnson, 58; Jim Dawson, 60. He acknowledges also the help given by the staff of the public library in King's Lynn (Norfolk Library Service) in the selection of illustrations for reproduction.

Acknowledgements

I am grateful to the staff of the Public Library at King's Lynn for supporting my research over several years and to Ray Wilson and Alison Gifford most of all. The staff of King's Lynn Museums have also been most helpful. I thank the Borough Council of King's Lynn and West Norfolk for allowing me access to the town records. My wish to draw and to photograph in St Margaret's and St Nicholas' at King's Lynn was welcomed by Canon Michael Yorke. The staff of the Norfolk Record Office and City Library at Norwich have been both co-operative and courteous.

Too many citizens to mention have kindly assisted me in various ways to enrich this book. My sincere thanks go to them. Diana Bullock and Michael Begley read the script, with good advice and encouragement the inevitable result. I am glad Dorothy Owen agreed to comment on my attempt to compress her interpretation of the town's origins. Alan Carter first stimulated my interest in local history and I remain sad at his too-early death. I am indebted also to other historians of the borough, past and present.

I have been fortunate in having such a willing and able photographer as Jim Tuck, whose work is seen throughout the book. Susan Richards and Richard Wilkins have applied their skill to provide me with some excellent drawings. Typing has always been efficiently undertaken by Beverley Setchell. Alison Gifford has not only used her expertise to produce the index, but long kept up my spirits to finish the book.

Staff at Phillimore & Company have kept faith in the book despite my inability to go faster, and I appreciate all their guidance. I am, of course, totally responsible for its structure and content.

Gateway through the southern range of the Benedictine priory, reopened in 1975.

Preface

The first nine chapters of this book tackle key themes in the history of King's Lynn (hereafter 'Lynn', as in local parlance) from its foundation about 1100 until the arrival of the railways in 1846. The approach adopted has, I hope, some logic. At the outset the making and remaking of Lynn over 750 years of building is discussed, to outline its physical history. Chapter Two describes the overseas and coastal trade of the port of Lynn which generated the wealth necessary for the development of the town; wool, corn, fish, wine, timber and coal were the staples which filled the ships. The industries and markets largely dependent on Lynn's river and sea commerce are the subjects of Chapters Three and Four, respectively. The town's maritime economy determined the shape and character of local society and politics that preoccupy subsequent chapters; Lynn's merchant rulers in private and public life are highlighted, and the life and labour of the townspeople are investigated. In 1537 'Bishop's' Lynn became 'King's' Lynn, as this important English 'city state' finally threw off the shackles of its ecclesiastical lords, the bishops of Norwich.

At the head of the great Ouse rivers, connecting it with a hinterland comprising England's richest counties, and facing Europe across the North Sea, Lynn was also well situated to trade with London and other parts of Britain. It has been described aptly as 'The Warehouse on the Wash'. Then the advent of a faster and more direct transport system soon robbed Lynn of all these geographical advantages. The railways and new docks together, however, sparked the town's first industrial revolution, as local factories began to supply English farmers with machinery, artificial manure and animal feed. Yet Lynn's lack of an industrial hinterland in a nation increasingly reliant on exchanging manufactures for imported foodstuffs accelerated its relative decline in Britain's urban hierachy. The town's second industrial revolution was planned after 1945 by local and central governments to save it from stagnation, though the repercussions for the integrity of this ancient borough have been profound, despite the preservation of historic buildings and streets. The final chapter of the book reflects on Lynn's modern history by discussing familiar themes.

This book does not attempt to squeeze as many 'facts' as possible between its covers, but is concerned to make sense of one of England's most fascinating urban histories, that of a town that has made a critical contribution to national economic and political development. Lynn deserves much more research and writing. I trust that this volume will stimulate further work by students of all ages and kinds. That the book will be enjoyed by the general reader is my greatest wish.

Paul Richards
Lynn
February 1990

14th-century window at 9 King Street.

Chapter One

The Making of the Town

Early-medieval Lynn

In the course of the 11th century growing numbers of seaborne traders brought furs, cloth, millstones and other merchandise into the 'linn', or estuarine lake, at the south-eastern corner of the Wash. Salt, fish and wool attracted these English and European ships. At the Norman Conquest Lynn had a small population. The Domesday Book of 1086 gives no indication of any substantial settlement, but the large number of saltworkings recorded reveals not only the insatiable demand for salt to cure fish and meat, but a substantial salt-exporting trade. Domesday Book suggests, moreover, that this trade had been even bigger before 1086. Salt making had surely been tempting migrants to the eastern shore of the linn for a considerable period.

The sandy shores of the linn between high- and low-water-marks were ideal for the salters. Salt-impregnated sand was heaped into huge containers. Salt water from adjoining watercourses was channelled through these containers to pick up more salt and boiled in pans over peat fires until the salt had crystallised. Waste discarded from the salt workings, or salterns, raised the level of the land so that the high-tide mark was pushed towards the sea. By this process parts of the linn were claimed, the original shore bank running now through the Walks, or parkland, half a mile to the east of the River Ouse. Natural banks were enlarged and strengthened by these salt-tippings to form the framework of the streets of medieval Lynn.

The linn was the eastern shore of the Gaywood estate, the property of the bishops of Norwich. Herbert de Losinga was said to have paid William II at least 1,000 marks for the see, and was obliged by the Pope to found monastic houses as penance for this act of simony. One of these monasteries was the Benedictine priory at Lynn. It is clear from Herbert's charter of 1101, however, that there was already a small town at Lynn. It said that he had been 'requested' to build the church at Lynn 'in honour of the Holy Mary Magdalene and St Margaret and all holy virgins'. He endowed the Benedictine monks of Norwich with this church and lordship over the market and fair as well as the land between the Millfleet and Purfleet. This endowment included the churches of Gaywood and Mintling, and a new mill that the monks had made under his 'instructions', all on the Gaywood estate of which Lynn was the offshoot, the new Priory Church of St Margaret becoming a second parish church.

Losinga's Lynn expanded to the north and east of the Saturday Market Place, where the fair 'held on the feast of St Margaret' and 'the sand market' had been established before 1101. St James Street must have been built up early because the first chapel of ease to St Margaret's church, that of St James, was erected at its eastern end by the 1130s (it was 'founded in the soc' of the Norwich monks). Traffic between Lynn and Gaywood must have flowed along this thoroughfare. By the mid-12th century houses faced the waterfront from the east side of Queen Street, and building had taken place on the south bank of the Purfleet. The Purfleet was bridged where it was crossed by the High Street, and again at Baxters Plain, indicating the early growth of New Conduit and Tower Streets. The Millfleet was bridged in 1250, linking Bishop's Lynn with the independent township of South Lynn. Excavations in the 1960s suggested that All Saints and Friar Streets formed the east bank of the Nar, or Friar Fleet.

Bishop's Lynn grew northwards from the Saturday Market Place, rather than east or

1

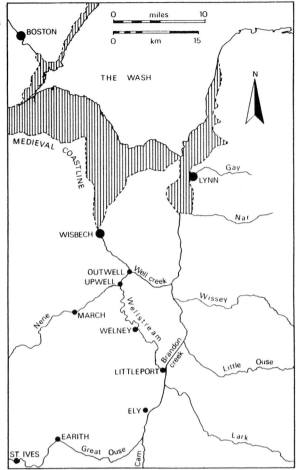

1. The medieval shoreline of the Wash, and the rivers of the Fenland following the diversion of the Great Ouse in the 13th century.

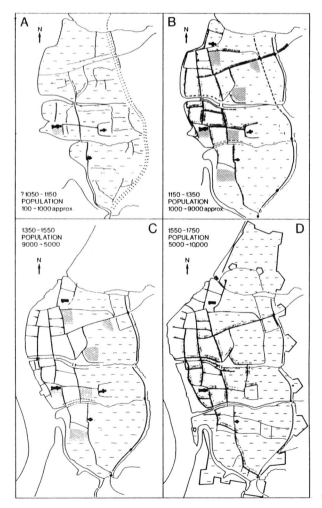

A

? 1050 – 1150
POPULATION
100 – 1000 approx.

B

1150 – 1350
POPULATION
1000 – 9000 approx.

1350 – 1550
POPULATION
9000 – 5000

C

1550 – 1750
POPULATION
5000 – 10,000

D

2. Sketch maps of Lynn indicating the changing pattern of occupation between 1050 and 1750.

south, because of the attraction of the Purfleet, a good harbour. Building began on the north bank of this waterway before the 1140s. Bishop Turbe, however, founded a chapel in this 'Newland', 'which we have recently provided for settlement', implying that it was already occupied; the witness list to Turbe's charter of the 1140s included men who were soon to endow Norfolk monasteries with property between the Purfleet and River Gaywood. St Nicholas chapel, also a chapel of ease of St Margaret's, was sited on higher ground to the north-east of the Tuesday Market Place. It was given to the monks of Norwich, but the Newland itself, of great economic potential, remained under the direct control of the bishops.

Losinga or his successor had almost certainly established a second market at Lynn before Turbe formally founded the Newland by charter. Why should they have done so? William D'Albini was granted a half share of the tolls of the market and 'the port of Lynn' by a charter of Henry I, dated about 1106. D'Albini never claimed tolls collected from the merchants operating near St Margaret's church, south of the Purfleet, so the grant refers to the Newland. His territory lay on the north bank of the River Gaywood, so he was in a position to start a town to compete with that of the bishops. Had Losinga launched a second town about the Tuesday Market Place to prevent him doing so? To achieve this goal Losinga would have needed to offer D'Albini the concessions recorded in the charter. Thus Lynn sprang from the economic and geographical advantages of settlement at this corner of the Wash, and politics dictated that there should be two markets, or centres of urban growth.

The Tuesday Market Place was the hub of a second town, laid out on a grander scale than the first. The south side of the market-place was probably further south than at present, on the line of Norfolk Street, or Damgate. The frontage of this causeway was being rapidly built up about 1200, all the way to the East Gate. Merchants constructed substantial houses on the east side of King Street before 1200. The Newland Survey of about 1270, a record of rentals in this part of Lynn, tells of an ordered street pattern and considerable urban development. How far the Newland was a town 'planned' by the bishops is difficult to say, but Lynn's street pattern was probably shaped by natural features reinforced by human activity.

What did medieval Lynn look like? It was a timber town, that has long been destroyed by fire and redevelopment, yet the archaeological survey of Lynn in the 1960s, supported by documentary evidence, reveals much. Most early secular buildings were raised on a framework of oak posts set in pits, but stone or brick foundation walls were common by 1250. The Great Fire of 1331 prompted greater use of brick and tile, but thatch and timber houses were cheaper and continued to be erected until brick became widely available. Oak from Norfolk and fir from the Baltic lands were the most common woods for the frames of houses, warehouses and wharves, while various softwoods were used for flooring and wattle and daub infilling of the walls. Some Norfolk flint and carstone were used also, and sometimes Scandinavian igneous rock brought to the port as ballast.

The width of plots at Lynn ranged from 15 to 24 feet. Most tenements were at right angles to the street, often with a short street range cutting across the main house, parallel to the frontage, making an 'L' shape. Houses were entered by passages from the street through these front ranges, which were sometimes distinct properties. Halls were open to the roof so that the smoke from the hearth could escape. Its warmth would have drawn much of the daily activity of the household into the hall. At one or both ends of the halls unheated chambers on two storeys would have been used for butteries, pantries and extra sleeping accommodation. Portable braziers may have been used to heat them. Kitchens were often built away from the house to reduce the risk of fire.

Some merchants built stone houses running parallel to the street, as the discovery in 1976 of an early-medieval property in King Street reveals. From the outside No. 32 appears to be a three-storey 19th-century house; Nos. 30 and 28 are definitely timber-framed and late-medieval. The interiors of Nos. 30 and 32 tell a different story, however, indicating they were once one building. Here the gable ends of a stone hall-house constructed in the late 12th century are well preserved, both with Romanesque arcading on each of the two floors, although the original building was probably open to the roof. This house was erected parallel to the street on a building line distinct from the present one. Its dimensions were approximately forty by twenty feet. The house was divided by a thick rubble wall about 1300, and about 1400 its southern half, No. 30, was rebuilt with No. 28 as a timber-framed structure.

Nos. 30 and 32 King Street contain the oldest secular building in Lynn, standing on what was probably the most valuable piece of real estate in Newland. The stone house stood almost certainly on the south-west corner of the Tuesday Market Place, beside the ancient route from Norfolk to Lincolnshire via Norfolk Street and the ferry. Another Norman-style stone house on the east side of Queen Street was demolished, unfortunately, in 1977, and there had been a third on the east side of King Street before 1914, while documentary evidence shows the existence of three other big stone houses to the east of the Tuesday Market Place. These were those the bishop of Norwich built for himself west of St Nicholas' chapel, and for his steward where Lloyds Bank now stands, and a third called Boyland Hall, probably on the site of Fells Warehouse in Market Lane, where foundations of a large early-medieval building were found by archaeologists in the 1970s.

By far the largest buildings in medieval Lynn were religious. Losinga's Priory Church of St Margaret was much smaller than the present building, but it took several decades to complete, the two towers not being added before 1150. Only the lower part of the south-west tower remains of this Norman church. It was rebuilt on a larger scale in the 13th century in Early English style, at the prompting of Bishop de Grey. The only substantial part of this church to survive is the chancel. St Nicholas' chapel was also rebuilt and enlarged in the early 13th century, but only the tower survived further rebuilding in the 15th century. Of the other chapel of ease to St Margaret's, St James', most was demolished in the late 16th century, the transepts being turned into a workhouse, which collapsed in 1854. All Saints church at South Lynn can be said to be the borough's oldest, although it was rebuilt in both the 13th and 15th centuries.

By 1250, all English towns of any size had been invaded by the urban shock troops of the medieval Church, the friars, men dedicated to the welfare of the poor. Because they were forced to build on the edges of towns coming into full growth, the friaries, or remains of them, act as signposts of the extent of urban development at this period. Nothing survives of the extensive complex of the Blackfriars, or Dominicans, except street names, the final vestiges being destroyed when the railway station was made in the 1840s. The arched brick gateways belonging to the Augustinians and the Whitefriars, or Carmelites, are late-medieval structures. Most impressive of all the friary fragments in Lynn is the brick tower of the church of the Greyfriars, built by the Franciscans. It escaped destruction after the Dissolution of the Monasteries because of its usefulness as a seamark. The arcading to the south of this tower is the remains of a late-medieval building relocated from the Tuesday Market Place.

Religious buildings dominated the townscape of medieval Lynn much more than they do today. The contrast with the hovels of the urban masses was particularly stark. The excavation of the Marks and Spencer site in the 1960s indicated that these were mostly timber and thatch huts, perhaps with small enclosures. They must have been extremely insanitary, uncomfortable and overcrowded.

Late-medieval Lynn
During the 14th and 15th centuries the bank of the Ouse was slowly moved westwards by the 'claiming' of land from the wide and slow-flowing river. How far this process was

deliberately engineered is uncertain. A combination of human and natural forces seems the most likely explanation; townspeople dumping rubbish at designated spots into a river depositing silt. Commercial and domestic buildings were erected along the waterfront. This process began at the western sides of the two market-places, taking place later along the west sides of Nelson, Queen and King Streets, where the houses of Lynn's merchants had previously faced the Ouse across the street. The unique line of late-medieval houses and warehouses running along the Ouse today was, therefore, built on land claimed from the sea. At Thoresby College in Queen Street a slate can be seen, only a few yards west of the street, marking the site of the quay in about 1300.

One such house is Hampton Court, in Nelson Street. It began before 1350 with the

3. Hampton Court, in Nelson Street.

construction of a stone-and-brick house at right-angles to the street. This is the present southern range of the property. At each end of the hall, or main part of the house, were rooms on two storeys providing storage space and extra accommodation. Only the hall was heated. The east and west ranges were erected in brick in the late 15th century by the Ampfles family, whose merchant mark is carved in the right-hand spandrel of the Nelson Street entrance. The eastern, street, range has a timber-framed and jettied upper floor, which probably served as living quarters for the tenants of the shops below. The western range was a riverside warehouse with open arcades for the reception of goods. By the 17th century further silting had ensured that this building had lost its function.

Another quadrilateral complex, known as the Hanseatic Warehouse, faces Hampton Court from the north side of St Margaret's Lane. Built in the 1480s for German merchants on land bought by the king, the original warehouse is a jettied timber building, now infilled with brick on both storeys. Its western end abutted on the Ouse. The street range has been removed by later building, but the riverside range is well preserved, an extension made about 1600 and probably used as a refectory. The long courtyard is dominated to the north by a massive three-storey brick warehouse, built after the refectory. To the west is another warehouse, Marriott's Barn, standing parallel to the Ouse, its stone lower half emphasising the need to resist the tide. The Germans may have added the brick second storey in the 16th century.

Lynn's 15th-century commercial prosperity is most solidly embodied in the Trinity Gildhall in the Saturday Market Place, the old building having been destroyed by fire in 1421. The new hall was erected on a different site, near the old hall, at right-angles to the street. It is raised on a stone undercroft, used as wine cellars directly accessible from the market-place. Entry to the Gildhall was, as today, up a staircase to a door in the west wall. The body of the hall is brick, with dressed stone for windows and doors, but flint and stone squares give the façade a distinct chequer pattern. The magnificent south window has seven lights, with a transom, or horizontal line of stone, a few feet from its base. Wooden shutters in this lower part allowed some ventilation.

Opposite the Gildhall, in Queen Street, stands Thoresby College, finished in 1510. This, a quadrangular building of Oxbridge character, was founded by a merchant, Thomas Thoresby, to provide a home for 16 priests.

An important medieval building in King Street passed into corporation hands after the dissolution of Lynn's religious gilds in 1547. This is the 15th-century St George's Gildhall, because of the destruction of the merchant gildhalls at London and York during the Second World War the largest and oldest in England. One of the doors at pavement level led to the undercroft, where wine and other commodities were stored, the other gave access to the quayside through a long passage under the floor of the hall. The hall itself was entered up stairways built against the north and south walls, the passages to them serving as light wells. When the hall was erected its west end would have been close to the riverbank; 'claiming' of land encouraged the building of warehouses there, producing a long string of buildings.

The *Tudor Rose* (11 St Nicholas' Street) was a new building typical of the smaller 'L'-shaped merchant houses of 15th-century Lynn. Jettied timber-framed street ranges, with brick infilling, accommodated a shop below and living space above. The main part of the house was the hall to the rear, often of stone as well as brick. Access to it was from a side passage. A number of long buildings parallel to the street containing shops, but no domestic quarters, seem to have been built. One 15th-century timber-framed and jettied building with a crown-post roof in St James' Street encompasses several shops. A similar development was *The Lattice House*, in Chapel Street. Here two halls were built behind the street range about 1500.

4. The Gildhall of the Holy Trinity was built in the 1420s and the porch added in 1624. To the right is the town gaol of 1784.

The amount of investment in ecclesiastical building testifies to the growing wealth generated by trade in the 15th century. Papal permission for a new St Nicholas' chapel was granted in 1374, but work on this elegant brick and stone structure was not completed until 1429. Because of subsidence the north-west tower of St Margaret's was rebuilt in the 1450s; a central lantern similar to that at Ely Cathedral was erected in the 1480s and a spire was added to the south-west tower. A charnel chapel built at the north-west corner of St Margaret's in the 1320s was a partial solution to the overcrowding of the churchyard.

The Benedictine monks of St Margaret's priory seem to have drained their resources in building projects. To boost their income the prior decided to found the Chapel of Our Lady on the Red Mount, an artificial mound raised as part of the town defences. It replaced a smaller chapel built here by the Gild of Our Lady. The prior's intention was to make a wayside chapel for pilgrims on their way to the shrine at Walsingham, thousands of whom passed through Lynn. The chapel is two-and-a-half storeys in rough red brick, within which are three small stone chambers. The middle chamber is a vestry and the upper and lower ones are chapels, the upper one perhaps being an addition. It has a fine fan-vaulted roof. After its closure in 1537 the chapel was used as an observatory, water tower, gunpowder store and stables.

Medieval towns spent much time and money on building defences. Lynn's defences to the east followed the old sea bank rather than hugging the built-up area, a decision influenced by the natural protection provided to north, west and south by the rivers Gaywood, Ouse and Nar. They formed a 'D'-shaped enceinte a mile north to south and half a mile east to west. The construction of ditches, banks and walls to the east of the town was encouraged by the civil wars of the mid-12th and mid-13th centuries, Henry III granting murage for four years, significantly, in 1266, the year after the Battle of Evesham. These defences were improved in the mid-14th century because of fears of a French invasion. Fragments of the stone and brick wall still standing in Kettlewell Lane probably date from the 1330s. Extra security was provided by the building of nine bastions or towers at intervals around the 'D', including at the mouths of the fleets.

The four main entrances to Lynn were dominated by wooden towers, or bretasks, built on artificial mounds. These, apart from that at the mouth of the Purfleet, were replaced by stone and brick gates. Nothing remains of Dowshill Gate, on the north edge of the town, by the River Gaywood. The East Gate stood at the east end of Littleport Street before its demolition in 1800. It had been rebuilt in the 1440s and was repaired in 1541, when it was adorned with the arms of Henry VIII. The South Gate has survived. Here the bretask was superseded by a stone and brick gate about 1350, rebuilt about 1450. This structure was given an ashlar front in 1520, disguising what is a major brick building of its time, once equipped with a portcullis and drawbridge. Distinguished visitors to the town were entertained in the room above the entry. Pedestrian passages were driven through the building in the 19th century. The North Guannock gate was one of two which lay between the South Gate and the Red Mount; it still survives despite reconstruction. There must have been a gate on this site from early in Lynn's history if the main exit from the Saturday Market Place was due east, to the old sea bank here. Once alternative routes were established, however, it was redundant.

The end of the medieval town

The development of the town made possible by the commercial prosperity of 15th-century Lynn had slowed by 1500. Population loss was one obvious cause of urban decay, and there is evidence of it in 'An Act for the re-edifying of void grounds within the town of Lynn', for which the corporation successfully petitioned parliament in 1535. The preamble talks of 'divers and many messuages and tenements of old time builded within the said town' being 'a long time' in 'great decay and desolation'. Unfortunately no facts or figures are mentioned, but it is obvious how this urban blight was affecting buildings which formed part of Lynn's flood defences. High tides were pushing the sea through broken houses and walls in several places, causing 'great hurt and damage' to nearby properties. The act gave the mayor power to proclaim that the corporation would possess and repair the decayed buildings after a year if the owners did not do so. Decay was not just eating into the riverside streets. The east part of the town around St James' chapel had contracted, as was noted in 1577: 'St James End Strete conteyneth many old fletes and lanes decayed whose names not knownen'.

Lynn was one of many English towns experiencing decline, as an Act of Parliament of 1541 'to re-edify houses' in no fewer than 36 confirms. In York, Hull, Lincoln, Ipswich, Yarmouth, Lynn and other important provincial centres 'many beautiful houses of habitation' had fallen into ruin. Mayors were empowered to take possession of decaying properties. The explanation of this urban crisis is too complicated to explore here, but the drift of the cloth industry from town to country to escape the restrictions and expense of craft gilds, was a key factor in Norwich, Lincoln, Northampton and Coventry. Urban populations were also reduced by outbreaks of plague in 1518-19 and bad harvests in the 1520s.

Lynn's economy must have been affected by the Reformation of the 1530s, when its monasteries were dissolved by Henry VIII, although the number of monks had been falling for decades. The Benedictine priory and the four friaries were closed and plundered for building materials. The Chapel of Our Lady on the Red Mount was desecrated and loads of bricks and tiles removed. Thoresby College escaped demolition because it was sold as a house to the town clerk for £100. The Chapel of Our Lady on the Millfleet bridge was also converted into a house. The end of the heavy pilgrim traffic to Walsingham should also be remembered in any assessment of the impact of the Reformation on demand for local goods and services. The consequences for the townscape of medieval Lynn were severe, as Richards observed in 1812:

> Moreover, we must reckon among the most striking and memorable effects which the Reformation had upon Lynn the very visible and degrading change it produced in the aspect of appearance of the town, reducing it, as it evidently did, to a most mean and paltry object, compared to what it was previously to that event. For the demolition and disappearance of so many stately edifices, which had long been the pride and boast of the inhabitants, must have been a most strange, humiliating and transforming effect upon the place, both with respect to its external aspect, or as it appeared from the adjacent country, and also as it looked within, to those who passed through its streets, or observed it internally. It must have looked somewhat like a town that had undergone a close and successful siege, and which had been left half demolished and ruined by a victorious and exasperated enemy.

Tudor and Stuart Lynn

Medieval Lynn was largely remade between 1550 and 1650 when brick buildings slowly replaced timber structures. Bricks and stones from the friaries continued to be used. In 1570 Alderman Kynne was sold 100 loads of stone from the Greyfriars at 4d. a load. A more permanent and plentiful supply of bricks came from new kilns at Gaywood, West Lynn, Tilney and Terrington. Bricks were also sent by barge from Ely and Cambridge. The corporation bought 1,000 for £5 at Stourbridge Fair in 1613. Timber was still required in large quantities for windows, doors, floors, roofs and panelling, and oak and elm were brought from the borough's estate at Snettisham and from elsewhere in Norfolk and Suffolk. Scandinavian deal was cheaper, however, and imported in large quantities. Thatching was forbidden as a fire risk, so tiles were increasingly used, many imported from Holland.

The remaking of Lynn involved the alteration of existing houses (still with their medieval 'L' plan) as much as building anew. The street fronts of many houses were changed dramatically by building walls up to the first-floor jetty. The brick chimney stack was the harbinger of a domestic revolution. Heating at several levels was now possible, and floors were inserted into open halls. There was greater specialisation of room use. Household comfort was also improved by the spread of glazed windows, often with small diamond panes. Parker has written a detailed account of how Hampton Court and Thoresby College were transformed into modern homes. At the former the quadrangle was closed by the construction of a northern range of brick complete with a massive chimney stack, no doubt serving the business of the resident baker, John Hampton. Five ogee Dutch gables were part of the complete rebuilding of the brick front wall of Thoresby College.

Lynn's Tudor and Stuart merchants were not slow to invest in the rebuilding of their warehouses in brick. Some of the best-preserved examples are to be found at Clifton House in Queen Street. Between the warehouses and the house itself stands a brick tower dating from the 1580s, from where merchants could watch for ships. Friends were entertained in its heated rooms. Pictorial evidence shows similar towers elsewhere at Lynn.

Many warehouses abutted on the River Ouse, so it was possible to build watergates, or openings in their gable ends, to permit small boats to deliver cargoes under cover at high tide. A series of watergates along the waterfront is visible in the western prospect of the town drawn in 1725. During invasion scares the corporation instructed merchants to lock and bar their watergates.

Two important Lynn houses dating from the first half of the 17th century show how the new and high-status dwelling was now being built parallel to the street rather than following the traditional plan. Both buildings are also symmetrical in plan. The Greenland Fishery of 1605 in South Lynn is particularly interesting because of its combination of 'old' and 'new' builds in this period of transition. The house has a typically medieval timber structure, but the gable ends are of brick, with big chimney stacks. The hall on the first floor was heated by fireplaces at each end of the room, and was lit by several windows in the east wall, overlooking the street, although only one of the three oriel windows appears to be original. Access to the house was by a central passage. A door leading to what was probably the kitchen took the visitor up the stairs, built into the southern chimney stack, to the hall and attic, where the bedrooms were. The roof was raised soon after 1605 to provide more comfortable attic accommodation. The second house is St Nicholas House, in St Nicholas Street. This was a double-piled house of rough red brick. Its street range was rebuilt about 1800, leaving the other with its Dutch gable bearing the date 1645.

Modernisation affected most levels of housing. The 'L'-shaped 15th-century *Tudor Rose*, adjacent to St Nicholas House and connected to it by a gallery still visible from the street, had four windows with diamond lattice casements inserted on the first floor and its doorway adorned with classical columns about 1600. A huge brick chimney stack was built between the hall and front shop of 30 King Street, to heat both. It was, no doubt, occupied by a comfortably-off tradesman. Modest brick houses dating from the 17th century survive in Bridge Street, but it seems certain that the poorest families inhabited traditional timber structures.

This was an important period for public building. The corporation acquired new property and civic responsibilities once the monasteries and gilds had been suppressed, and its merchant members used their powers to promote the economic and social interests of the town. Building programmes funded from the taxation of commerce began. The most ambitious was the redevelopment of the common staithe to the west of the Tuesday Market Place, with new warehouses and other facilities. Building along the west side of the square itself in the 1620s included a custom house and cottages. A classical porch was added to

5. The old market cross in 1660.

the Trinity Gildhall, the headquarters of the corporation, in stone and flint chequer to match the hall. Above the door a zealous official embedded the arms of Elizabeth I from the Chapel of St James. Those of Charles II were added above them in 1664.

The Custom House built in 1620 was always too small, despite being 'butified' in 1667. St George's Gildhall was used as a second custom house after 1656, but it soon proved inadequate. Sir John Turner proposed to the corporation the erection of an 'Exchange' for merchants in 1683. He was granted a plot adjacent to the Purfleet bridge for Bell's excellently-proportioned structure of Ketton stone. The building, described as 'ornamentall and of great use and convenience as an Exchange for the meeting of merchants', was opened in 1685, with a life-sized statue of Charles II above the main door on the north side, facing Turner's house. The upper floor of the Exchange was let to H.M. Customs and the lower left open for merchants to deal in, but most merchants found it too far from the Tuesday Market Place, and the Customs occupied the whole building by 1717. Despite alterations, the Custom House has withstood the tides for over 300 years, and remains Lynn's most elegant and famous piece of architecture.

The *Duke's Head* in the Tuesday Market Place was built just after the Custom House, a coaching inn Turner wanted for the accommodation of merchants using his 'Exchange'. It replaced a medieval inn on the same site. Red brick was chosen for this, Bell's most imposing Renaissance mansion to have survived. The inn was constructed around a courtyard with wooden galleries and stairs giving access to the rooms, almost all panelled in oak. As well as the several parlours, bars and dining-rooms, there was a cock room with deal furniture 'for fighting cocks'. Coaches passed through to a second courtyard equipped with 25 stalls for horses.

Georgian Lynn

The building of Bell's majestic market cross in 1710, replacing the Tudor cross, was one stage in the transformation of the Tuesday Market Place in the 18th century. This new structure was octagonal, with a wooden dome and a first-floor balcony supported by 16 Ionic columns. Radiating from it were timber stalls for tradesmen. Earlier, in 1703, another big classical mansion was erected on the site of the 1620 Custom House. No doubt Bell was commissioned to design this house by Charles Turner; unfortunately it was destroyed by fire in 1768. A new mansion was built on the site for George Hogge, and serves today as Barclays Bank although the façade was remade in 1957. A French nobleman, de la Rochefoucauld, visited Lynn in 1784 with Arthur Young and thought that the Tuesday Market Place was 'large and handsome', with 'some fine buildings looking onto it', of which Hogge's house was a 'large and beautiful' example. Mr. Hogge was 'a very wealthy merchant', and when 'we were there' he had an experience which was 'as pleasant as it was unusual' — the sight of 25 of his vessels, ready to sail. In the north-west corner of the market-place stands the mansion built by the Bagges, whose commercial and domestic worlds revolved around two inner courtyards. Only the front range now survives.

The streets leading into the Tuesday Market Place were also redeveloped during the century, most notably King Street. St George's Chambers (No. 27) is the finest mansion in the street, its front cased in limestone. Other handsome houses in the street are of red or yellow brick, with good doorways.

The Saturday Market Place was dominated by St Margaret's church, described by Mackerell in 1737 as 'a very large, stately and magnificent pile'. On the night of 8 September 1741, however, it was battered by a violent storm. The spire on the south-west tower fell into the nave and the central lantern was rendered unsafe. Shocked townspeople responded to the mayor's public appeal for rebuilding, inspired by generous donations of £1,000 from George II and Robert Walpole, but an Act of Parliament was nevertheless required to raise £3,500 by a rate on the inhabitants of the parish. Matthew Brettingham was called from work at Holkham Hall to direct operations. The nave and transepts were rebuilt, the roof was given a plaster ceiling and a gallery was constructed around the nave, but Brettingham's church was smaller and less impressive than its predecessor. The north aisle was much narrower, allowing the market-place to be extended, and the lantern was not replaced despite the arguments of shipowners that it was an important seamark.

The largest secular building in the vicinity of the Saturday Market Place is the Assembly Room and Card Room, a Georgian extension of the Town Hall. It was erected by Thomas King and William Tuck, and cost £1,300. The 60,000 Ely bricks ordered by the chamberlain in 1766 were presumably for this yellow-brick building. It was completed by 1767. The old Town Hall served as an anteroom for those attending the fashionable balls there. When Beatriffe visited Lynn in 1795 he found them 'capacious' and 'handsomely fitted up', despite thinking the glass doors linking all three rooms to be 'mean'.

In 1784 the corporation commissioned another building, the two-and-a-half storey gaol. Of white brick, it was the work of William Tuck, and cost £500. Five years earlier the old shambles and the charnel chapel housing the grammar school were both demolished, and a new shambles erected with the grammar school above.

St Margaret's House, in St Margaret's Place, deserves mention. The Hanseatic Warehouse behind this mansion was bought from its German owners in 1751 by Edward Everard. Parts of the east wing of the medieval building were incorporated into the new house. The houses along the west side of Nelson Street were remodelled rather than rebuilt, only No. 15 being completely new. This three-storey mansion of yellow brick, with its impressive Tuscan doorway, was erected for Samuel Browne about 1750. A single-storey counting house is attached. The west side of Queen Street, leading north from the Saturday Market Place, has a fine series of Georgian houses. Clifton House, with the initials S T and date 1708 on the rainwater head facing the street, is the grandest. Beloe thought that Simon Tayler employed Bell to rebuild the house. The doorway leading to the main entrance in the southern wall is distinguished by Baroque 'barley sugar' columns. The whole was a modern and luxurious abode for a rich vintner, it having extensive cellars under the neighbouring King's Staithe Square.

Beyond the high-status buildings of the riverside streets, little of Georgian Lynn remains because of redevelopment. Some modest late 18th-century houses survive south of the Millfleet in All Saints, Friar and Southgate Streets, showing that the middling orders of town society were enjoying better living conditions, but more traditional timber-and-thatch structures still housed many labouring families, as pictorial evidence tells. Yet Lynn was becoming safer and healthier as it was rebuilt in brick and the streets were lit, paved and cleaned by the corporation.

One of the most significant town improvements of the 18th century was the landscaping of the green belt between the built-up area and the medieval defences. About 1750 Charles Turner and William Mixon promoted a scheme to landscape a large portion of the green belt, following the fashion of aristocrats implementing similar plans on their country estates. By the end of the century, visitors were impressed by it:

> The new walk or mall, from the bars by the workhouse to Guanock Gates, is about 340 yards long, and eleven yards wide between the quick hedges. At convenient distances on each side of the walk, a recess is left in the hedge in a semicircular form, where benches are fixed, and twenty people may sit down at a time. Upon a gentle ascent on the right, is a plantation and shrubbery, laid out in a pleasing taste by the late Charles Turner Esq. On the bottom of this winds a pretty lively stream of water, which after passing through Lady Bridge, empties itself into the Ouse. At the end of Mr Turner's shrubbery is a small plantation of lime trees and Scotch firs intermixed, whence there is a good view of Lynn, and the adjacent villages, where wood, water, modern buildings, and ancient ruins, are so happily blended as to form a most charming prospect.

Civic pride only partly explains the preoccupation of Lynn's 18th-century rulers with the physical state of their town. In a world being opened up by the new turnpikes, towns competed for custom from merchants, gentry and even tourists. The comments of visitors to Lynn throughout the century leave no doubt of its appeal. In 1722 Daniel Defoe declared Lynn to be 'a beautiful well built and well situated town'. The town's first historian, Benjamin Mackerell of Norwich, called it 'beautiful' and 'large' in 1738, and the *Universal British Directory* of 1797 said it was 'a large, rich and populous town'. Contemporary estimates of the number of houses are interesting: Mackerell thought that there were 'about 2360' houses; *The General Gazetteer or Compendious Geographical Dictionary* of 1782 said there were '2000 good brick houses'.

Lynn in the first half of the 19th century

Early in the new century William Richards noted how dwellings of 'small' rent 'had lately sprung up in certain alleys' as well as on the town's outskirts. By the term 'alleys' he referred to the development of the infamous courts, or yards, of Lynn, in which merchants and tradesmen had formerly stored goods, burned rubbish and gardened. These plots offered the house-building land so much in demand at the time. Of the 3,000 houses in Lynn in 1831, about a thousand were situated in 160 yards, reached by narrow passages from the main streets. Over 4,000 of the town's 13,400 citizens were huddled together here. Norfolk

6. William Raistrick's plan of Lynn (1725). The green belt between the built-up area and the town defences gave Lynn the air of a garden city.

Street, for example, was linked to 29 yards, accommodating 750 people in 170 cottages — a population larger than that of the street proper. These yards were often named after the tradesmen who built or worked in them, or after adjacent taverns. Not surprisingly, the yards were unsanitary as well as overcrowded, and in a horrific state. These black spots were conveniently hidden from the gaze of rich inhabitants and visitors alike, however. Elected to parliament while on a tour of North America, Lord Stanley visited his new constituency later in 1848. After an enjoyable perambulation under the guidance of Richard Bagge, this young aristocrat judged the ancient borough to be 'a fine old place, with its churches, public walks and gardens'.

Suburban growth south of Lynn from the 1820s can be ascribed to the lack of adequate building space in the old town, and to the desire of the middling classes to escape its noise, squalor and overcrowding. The population of South Lynn leapt from 701 to 4,772 between 1801 and 1851. The entry into Lynn from the south was soon impressing observers of the early-Victorian town. Burnett asserts that few similar boroughs could boast of such an approach as London Road, with its 'handsome' and 'elegant' houses. To contemporaries,

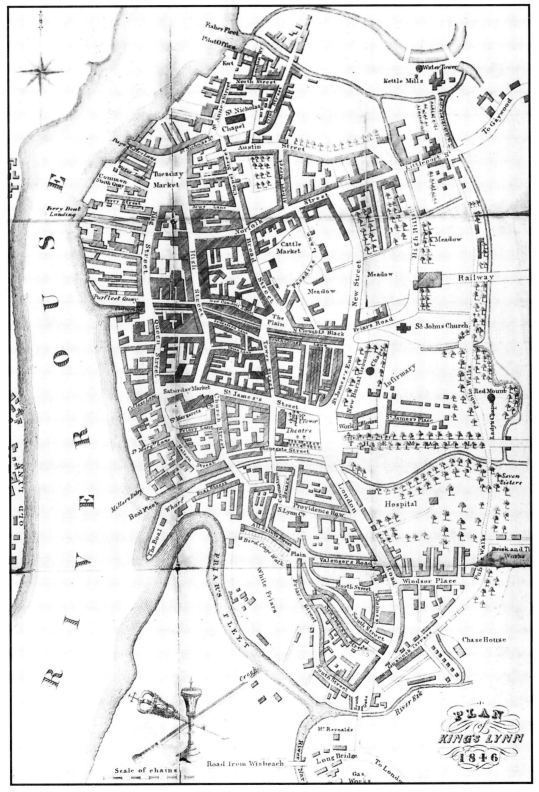

7. Map of Lynn in 1846 showing the new streets that were 'springing up' in the second quarter of the 19th century. The railway station had just been built.

London Road exemplified the modernisation of an ancient borough faced with the challenge of an Age of Expansion. Of the 1,384 houses built in Lynn between 1821 and 1851, half appeared in All Saints' parish, to the south of the Millfleet. White's directory of 1845 lists 19 bricklayers and builders, 22 joiners and builders, and 18 brick and tile dealers operating in Lynn, testimony to the amount of building work taking place.

Not all citizens approved of the growth of the town, as William Armes' attitude to Checker Street demonstrates. Friar Street had backed onto pleasant gardens where house-wives purchased vegetables until 'on a fatal day, a millionaire and a lawyer looked wistfully upon the spot' holding 'sundry consultations' before 'the fences were broken down, the ground was planned for the new Checker Street, and the contractors' carts of bricks and lime soon cut up and obliterated the kitchen garden'. Who were the millionaire and the lawyer? According to Hillen, the new street was named after a Mr. Checker of Gaywood, who was a fellmonger. This tradesman must have been 'the millionaire' behind the contractor responsible for the actual building of the terraced housing.

The development of London Road pulled Lynn's suburban growth towards the South Gate, as Wood's plan of the town in 1830 indicates, but the location of the railway station immediately to the east of the old town encouraged building in this district, too. Between Norfolk Street and St John's Terrace, to the south, were fields. In 1846 all this land was sold by the corporation, with a smaller area sold by the Bagge family, to the Lynn and Ely Railway Company for a total of £25,000. The first railway station was rapidly constructed in wood at right-angles to Blackfriars Road for £1,800 by John Sugars. The company sold land to the west of the station to Henry Barnett of London's Lombard Street in 1849. He seems to have promoted the making of Portland Street, then sold surplus plots to W. S. Simpson of Ely, the contractor for the Lynn to Downham railway in 1846.

The Lynn and West Norfolk General Hospital was opened in 1835. This was the largest and most important civic building in Lynn for 150 years, if its later extensions are included. The hospital was built on corporation land off London Road by John Sugars after a neo-classical design, using yellow brick. The poor and aged who escaped illness might be selected for one of the almshouses founded by philanthropists. Henry Framlingham's endowment in Broad Street about 1700 was rebuilt in Tudor style on London Road in 1848. Just to the north was St James' burial ground (now St James' Park), started in 1802 to relieve full churchyards. More space was soon needed, and in 1850 All Saints' parish opened a small burial ground at Hardwick, to the south of the town. It was to become the borough cemetery.

Religious building is of the greatest significance in the history of Lynn in the first half of the 19th century, especially building by the Nonconformists. The Methodists were the most numerous group of these. The Wesleyans graduated from a small chapel in Blackfriars Street to an impressive building in Tower Street, unfortunately demolished about 1960. Subscriptions raised over £4,000 for this spacious chapel, designed and built in 1812 by the Lynn contractor Samuel Newham. Even the Baptist minister William Richards admitted that it was 'magnificent' and 'capacious'. Of all the chapels built in 19th-century Lynn only the Baptist chapel of 1841 could match it in size. This Baptist chapel, a neo-classical edifice in grey and red brick, still stands in Blackfriars Street on a site the minister described as 'the best' in town. Buildings belonging to the Quakers, Unitarians and Independents, or Congregationalists, have all been swept away by the redevelopment of the 1960s.

The increase of Lynn's population left the Anglicans seriously short of church sittings. St John the Evangelist, known as the 'Poor Man's Church' because the sittings were free, was built in the Walks in the 1840s to rectify this. Lord Bentinck, Daniel Gurney and Richard Bagge fattened an appeal which raised over £5,000; another £1,000 was granted by the Church Building Society. Lynn's Ecclesiastical Building Society, of clergy and other professions, all fascinated by the architecture of the Middle Ages, influenced its Early English design by the famous Salvin. Opening day witnessed a long procession of civic dignitaries, clergy, builders and workmen to it from the Town Hall.

The resources had already been found for a new town theatre, needed after St George's Gildhall was sold as a warehouse in 1812 and its theatre thus lost. Although the financial contribution of Norfolk's landed class to the project was substantial, the corporation took the lead. A committee was appointed to direct the building of the new playhouse on corporation land at Tower Fields. Of the nine plans despatched to the committee, that of Samuel Newham was accepted, and the foundation stone was laid in July 1813. Unfortunately this was the signal for several years of financial wrangling between Newham and the corporation, because the cost of the theatre rose to over £6,000. The outcome, however, was a building of some architectural distinction amongst provincial theatres.

Between 1811 and 1851 Lynn's population doubled from 10,000 to 20,000, as migrants flowed in looking for work. Over these 40 years the number of houses in the borough increased from 2,323 to 3,994, growing most quickly in the 1830s and 1840s, when new streets were 'springing into existence'. Two local improvement Acts of Parliament in 1803 and 1806 are signs of commercial traffic becoming too heavy for the old streets. Obstacles were unceremoniously removed, like part of the north transept of St Margaret's, the Greyfriars gateway in St James' Street, and the Chapel of Our Lady on the Millfleet bridge.

A final 'improvement' should be mentioned. In 1824 there was a public meeting at the Town Hall to launch a 'Gas Light Company' selling the message that Lynn should 'keep pace with the improvements of the age'. Shareholders were to be allowed a maximum of ten £20 shares. There was not the interest or capital readily available to promote such a company, however. The Malam family intervened, investing over £14,000 in a gasworks outside the South Gate. The seven miles of piping in 1825 had been extended to 14 miles by 1854. Street lamps increased in number from 175 to 235 between 1834 and 1850. Nevertheless the family was not popular. In 1841 over 200 consumers complained of the high gas prices and threatened to return to oil and candles. Finally, in 1856, the Malams were taken over by the Lynn Gas and Coke Company (Limited), which had a capital of £10,000.

The town wall at Kettlewell Lane.

Chapter Two

The Port of Lynn

The hinterland: rivers and roads

Before about 1250 the port of Lynn was at the head of only the small west-Norfolk Rivers Gay and Nar, and several smaller rivers or fleets, of which the Purfleet provided the town's main harbour. The River Ouse joined the Nene at Upwell and flowed into the Wash through Wisbech. To relieve silting in the Wisbech estuary the Well Creek was excavated to divert some of the waters of the Nene and Ouse to the sea at Lynn. At about the same time the course of the Ouse was diverted to flow past Ely, and Brandon Creek was dug to allow the Great Ouse to meet the Little Ouse and River Wissey further to the north and east, and to open a more direct route for the combined streams to Lynn.

Lynn was well placed even before these changes to the river system. Other cuts had linked the Fenland rivers from the 12th century, when Ely and Cambridge men sent corn to Lynn by boat. In 1227 Huntingdon merchants complained of the threat to their market because St Ives, owned by the abbot of Ramsey, was closer to Lynn by river. Reclamation by lay and ecclesiastical landowners increased the population and agricultural productivity of the Fens in the early Middle Ages, and in 1250 Matthew Paris made his famous observation that the Fens had recently been transformed from a haunt of 'devils' to fertile meadows and fields. Lynn's hinterland soon encompassed England's 12 most populous and richest counties.

Gras and Darby stress how Lynn was the natural outlet for huge amounts of corn, wool, hides and ale transported by water. Wine, fish, salt, cloth and building materials were returned up river by its merchants, who regularly visited St Ives, Ely and Cambridge. Ely, Ramsey, Peterborough and other Fenland religious houses had property and agents in the Wash port. The estates of the bishops of Ely constituted an inland economy of some size and dynamism by 1200. Produce was carted from the bishops' manors to markets in all the principal East Anglian towns, yet the river connections to Lynn tended to channel the commercial operations of the bishops through the port. At Lynn the bishops' men sold corn and wool to European as well as English merchants and bought the timber and other commodities needed on the Ely estates. No better example of Lynn's dependence on its hinterland for its commercial prosperity could be provided.

Although Lynn gained from the 13th-century diversions of the Fenland rivers, the increased flow of the Ouse accentuated the problems of navigation and drainage in its hinterland. The Great Ouse was becoming too big. It flowed more slowly and dropped more silt, stopping the Fenland waters from running out to sea quickly enough. High tides ran fast up-river because of the wide estuary below Lynn, the old riverbanks were not strong enough to contain them, and the marshland suffered floods, at least 12 major inundations in the later Middle Ages and after. In 1613, for example, the sea swamped the land immediately to the west of the Ouse estuary, isolating villages, destroying reclamation work and killing sheep and cattle. Boats from Lynn rescued the Marshlanders.

The Bedford Level Corporation, composed of landowners, employed Cornelius Vermuyden to drain the Fens and reclaim tens of thousands of fertile acres. The Dutchman made two cuts, or canals, of about twenty miles, from Earith to Denver; these were the 'Old' and 'New' Bedford Rivers, dug before and after the Civil War. They shortened the course of the Ouse and accelerated the passage of water to the sea, while new land could be cultivated.

William Dugdale's diary of his travels through the area in 1657 is a record of the economic consequences of Vermuyden's work. Onions, peas, hemp, flax, oats, wheat, coleseed and woad were all being grown; Thorney was surrounded with Fens, but 'the Fens now environing it are by the Adventurers draynings, more so drye, that there are of all sorts of corne and grasse, now growing thereon, the greatest plenty imaginable'.

Fenland landowners were far more pleased with Vermuyden's work than the merchants of Lynn. The 'Lynn Law' of 1630 had supposedly protected their interests, but the construction of Denver Sluice threatened their town's very existence. Unfortunately Vermuyden directed all the waters of the Middle and South Bedford Levels to this single outfall at Denver, where the sluice doors were opened when the level of water on the seaward side fell below a certain height. There was usually so much water trying to escape to the sea, however, that the doors were seldom open long enough before the tides shut them. Vermuyden had stopped the flooding of the Fens, but the threat of flooding inland now loomed larger. Moreover, the dam stopped the tide from swelling up the Ouse, so more silt was dropped in Lynn harbour, making the escape of Fenland water even more difficult.

Just as calamitous for Lynn's merchants was that the Ouse above Denver became slower and shallower, without the gush of tide to carry boats upstream. Boats from Lynn had reached Cambridge within 24 hours and sea-going ships had sailed well inland. Now, in the summer, only small craft were navigable beyond Denver because of the low water, forcing transhipment of loads at the sluice. In 1696 the corporation of Lynn won the support of merchants from Cambridge, Thetford and Bury for an unsuccessful parliamentary bill to remove all drainage sluices. In 1713 Denver sluice 'blew up' following a lethal combination of high tides and a heavy flow of Fenland water. It was fully rebuilt in 1748-50, despite protests.

Although the obstacles to smooth navigation on the Ouse appear to have been increasing from the late 17th century, the extension of inland waterways continued. Bedford was linked to Lynn, over 70 miles away by river, in 1690. Cambridge students sent trunks to London via Lynn because water transport was cheaper than the much shorter overland route. Improvements to the Ouse, Cam, Nar and Lark in the 18th century confirmed the buoyancy of trade. In 1722 Daniel Defoe was impressed by the fact that Lynn enjoyed 'the greatest extent' of inland navigation of any English port outside London, and served six counties 'wholly' and three 'in part' with coal, wine and provisions. Contemporary with him was a local engineer, Badeslade, whose *Treatise on Navigation* emphasised how Lynn's commerce with its hinterland enriched the nation. He quoted 'an ancient authority' who compared the Ouse to 'the milky way' because of its traffic: 'And Lynn sits at the door of this river as it were the turnkey of it'.

To sustain the trade of the port, however, demanded greater and greater effort. Corporation records of the 18th century are full of references to repairs to the banks of the Ouse, clearing the fleets and provision of new quays and cranes. In 1772 the corporation obtained a local Act of Parliament to improve the reliability of pilots, establish new mooring posts and ban fires on ships for repair work and other purposes. The dumping of ballast and rubbish which might block the entrance to the harbour drove Lynn's rulers to distraction, and buoys and beacons were necessary as silting made the two main channels to the port more treacherous.

In 1749 Lynn's M.P., Charles Turner, used an official enquiry to highlight the port's problems. Because of the increase of trade and the size of ships entering the harbour, larger lighters had been made necessary. Unloading from 'lofty' ships into smaller craft was wasteful of coal; corn, flour and salt could not be properly protected. Small lighters were often lost. Large ones had decks and were high enough in the water to resist winds and tides, but were difficult to manoeuvre between the harbour and Denver Sluice. Not only did the crooked channel make navigation awkward, but the breadth of the river demanded

8. Part of Lynn's waterfront, about 1730, lined with warehouses into which small boats could gain access at high tide through watergates. Unusually high tides flooded cellars and houses.

long lines from lighters to horses on the bank. Those responsible for the upkeep of the Ouse banks blamed the lighter teams for damaging them; squabbles over towing rights were not settled until an Act of Parliament of 1790.

During the 18th century the corporation sought the advice of several famous engineers about the improvement of the worsening Ouse navigation: Armstrong, Kinderley, Rennie, Smeaton and Telford. All reached the same conclusion: a canal or cut from St Germans to Lynn would not only save three miles for lighters by eliminating the loop of the river, but would help to scour the bed of the Ouse, to the benefit of both navigation and drainage. Acts of Parliament to effect this plan coincided with the Revolutionary and Napoleonic wars and the subsequent economic slump. Work finally began on the Eau Brink Cut in 1818, the commissioners for the project borrowing some £400,000. The contractors used a steam engine to drain the three-mile-long canal, which was dug by over 1,000 navvies. When the cut opened in the summer of 1821, thousands of spectators witnessed a steam packet from Gravesend and sailing boats use it for the first time. Within two years the faster flow of water through the cut had scoured the Ouse bed several feet deeper, yet the ebb tide deposited more silt on the east side of Lynn's harbour, to the consternation of its merchants. Another Act of Parliament in 1831 awarded compensation, though new landing stages, better placed than the old, were eventually built up by the silting.

The Ouse estuary was wide and shallow and a deterrent to ocean-going ships, which were being constructed larger all the time. The port of Lynn was in danger of being overtaken by Hull and other east-coast towns with deeper harbours. The Estuary Cut, finished in

1853, was absolutely essential for the survival of the Wash port, but controversy about its effects hampered its progress for decades. The corporation feared the direct rush of the tides would cause flooding. The first sod was not cut until 1850, when the chairman of the Estuary Company, Sir William Folkes, led the contractors, workers and citizens in a procession through the town. The Estuary Cut was a far less ambitious scheme than had been promoted by Sir John Rennie, whereby most of the Wash was to be reclaimed, with channels to the ports of Lynn, Boston and Wisbech. His 'Victoria County' had promised 150,000 fertile acres.

The conventional wisdom that England's roads were impassable before the turnpike trusts of the 18th century is mistaken. Speaking at Lynn in 1962, Professor Carus-Wilson reminded us how long-distance overland haulage to and from the Wash ports was important in medieval times. Trains of packhorses were used to transport wool, cloth and other merchandise. A Lancastrian linen-draper who travelled to Lynn's February Mart in Elizabethan times used carts. Wool, cloth and groceries were amongst loads carried by road between Lynn and Norwich about 1600. Carrier services linking Lynn and London, 98 miles to the south, are listed in the *Merchant and Trader's Necessary Companion* of 1715. A large quantity of Irish calf and goat skins was brought to Lynn from Manchester 'by landcar' in 1714. In 1716 a Mr. Thompson, from St Neots, complained to the Custom House that farmers 'near' him sending malt by wagon were less harassed by excisemen than he, who hired lighters to reach Lynn.

England's highways only appeared inadequate when better communications were demanded by landowners and merchants eager to exploit the growing urban markets of Georgian England. Turnpike trusts were created by Acts of Parliament to engineer road improvements, the trustees taking tolls from the traffic. Between 1760 and 1775 over 450 acts were passed; roads linking Lynn with Norwich, Cambridge and Wisbech were the subject of turnpike acts in 1765, 1786, 1806, 1823 and 1826. Other routes inland from the east and south gates were covered by acts of 1771, 1791, 1811 and 1831.

Lynn merchants jogged the landowners of the town's hinterland into action, as the turnpike projects of 1765 and 1771 reveal. In 1764 the Town Clerk, Scarlet Browne, and the mayor, James Robertson, tried to persuade James Johnstone to co-operate with the corporation and subscribe to the turnpike trust. The Wisbech turnpike would go through his estate, Browne informed him, and open 'good and convenient communication' from northern and western counties into East Anglia. It was 'very necessary work', which had been 'long wished for', and the tolls should bring good profits. The corporation itself subscribed £1,000 to the new highway. The wealthy citizens of Lynn met at the *Duke's Head* to consider the best way to implement the act of 1771 to widen and repair roads from the South Gate to Stoke Ferry, Downham, Narborough and East Winch. Philip Case, Edward Everard, George Hogge and other trustees borrowed £4,490 from Gurney's Bank at Norwich, at five per cent interest, to remake these roads.

Many farmers and merchants did not want to risk water transport, or were not well placed to use it, and were prepared to bear road carriage costs. In the early 19th century wagons belonging to Swann & Son left Lynn's Tuesday Market Place for London every day, with passengers as well as goods. The two-day journey was broken at Cambridge to connect with other cross-country wagons. Accidents on this road were not uncommon, according to one of Swann's regular passengers, William Armes. Mack and Co. also ran wagons to the metropolis in 1845, although goods could then be switched to railway trucks at Bishops Stortford.

Stage-coaches were rapidly developed from the 1750s. In 1793 Lynn boasted two lines to London: *The Sun* left the *Duke's Head* on Tuesdays, Thursdays and Sundays, indoor passengers being charged 25s. for the 98 miles. The other coach left from the *Crown Inn* in

9. The 'Lynn and Wells Mail' in the late 1830s.

Church Street. This service seems to have been the *Lynn Union*, driven after 1821 by the legendary Tom Cross. A third stage-coach, called *The Lord Nelson*, ran to London from *The Globe* by 1822. A Royal Mail coach linked Lynn to London in the 1830s, with mailcarts taking the post on to north Norfolk coastal towns. It was probably little faster than the alternative coaches, for 10 m.p.h. was about their maximum, and 12 hours a good time for the journey.

Despite the romance attached to the age of the stage-coach almost as soon as it had ended, the reality was harsh. Discomforts of all kinds were experienced by passengers, not least in the frosts and snow of winter. Drivers took risks and sometimes upset their coaches; 'the cattle' were often driven until they dropped. Coach travel was not cheap and was far from ideal. One Baptist minister, William Richards, complained to a friend in 1818 about how late the London coaches always arrived in the town, while in December 1839 another, Thomas Wigner, left London at seven a.m. and arrived in Lynn at 10 p.m. accompanied by the ubiquitous William Armes, whose cigar had made Wigner ill.

Several cross-country coaches started from or passed through Lynn, calling at the principal inns. In 1836 there were almost daily services to the major towns of the eastern counties. But by 1845 the competition of the railways was beginning to destroy the stage-coach network. A sign of the times was *The Victoria*, a service in 1845 from Lynn to Northampton and nearby Blissworth railway station, for connections to Birmingham, London and Leeds, whereas there had formerly been a service from Yarmouth to Birmingham.

Overseas trade: the Middle Ages

Before the Black Death of 1348-9 decimated their populations, England and Europe had had rapidly expanding economies, as the trade across the North Sea reveals. The early 'take-off' of Boston and Lynn emphasises the strategic advantages of the Wash. When King John collected a tax of a fifteenth of the value of all imports and exports in 1203, these twin ports provided more than any others save London and Southampton. Merchants from all parts of Europe travelled to Lynn, exchanging timber, furs, wine and cloth for corn, wool, salt and fish. Europe's growing urban populations were hungry for the wool and foodstuffs of the islanders to the west, England being in a colonial relationship to them; only London could rival the size of the cities of Germany, Flanders and Italy.

By the early 14th century the English economy had developed considerably. So important had the cloth trade become by 1300 that a royal ulnager was posted in Lynn to tax it there. The Melchbournes and their close associate John Weasenham were three of the kingdom's foremost merchant capitalists, dealing in wool, corn, ale, fish and cloth. They ranked with the de la Poles of Hull and the Cunnings of Bristol as well as London traders like John Lovekin, the fishmonger. They sailed their own ships to all parts of Europe.

Trade between Lynn and the Low Countries was vital to both. Bruges, Ghent and other Flemish towns were the cloth manufacturing centres of Europe and their merchants travelled to Lynn for wool before 1200. The abbeys of Ely, Ramsey, Crowland and Peterborough despatched huge quantities of it to Europe through Lynn, as did other landowners, great and small. Fenland flocks multiplied. In 1267-8, 1,406 sacks of wool, worth £3,440, were exported from Lynn, the bulk of it probably purchased by Flemish merchants though agents from Florence and elsewhere in Italy were operating in the Wash port, too, often reselling the wool as far east as Constantinople. So wealthy were the Bardi and fellow Italian merchants that under Edward III they farmed the English customs in return for making him large loans. Lynn's own merchants were increasingly prominent in the export of wool to Flanders, Gascony and the Baltic. About two thousand sacks a year left the Wash port in the early 14th century, as well as corn, ale and dyestuffs.

English wool exports were lucrative enough from the 12th century to pay for the import of large quantities of wine from the vineyards of south-western France, a region under English control. Official records indicate a heavy trade from Gascony to Lynn by 1266, when Henry III ordered 50 tuns of wine to be sent from the town to Kenilworth Castle. Claret was also taken up-river to Ely, Bury and Cambridge. Between September 1308 and June 1309 at least 22 ships, laden with an average of 93 tuns of wine, left the new town of Libourne for England. Three were Lynn boats. In 1333-4, Lynn merchants chartered 11 ships to bring wine from Gascony. Gascon vintners asserted their presence in London, but left the provincial ports to the English. The leading role of the Wash port in England's wine trade seems confirmed by the appointment of Thomas Melchbourne and John Weasenham as deputy-butlers to the king. They collected 2s. a tun of wine (250 gallons) imported by foreign merchants, and prisage from native ships according to tunnage. These two Lynn merchants were excellently placed to supply wine to Edward III because of their command over the corn and wool trade, both of which were encouraged by the Gascons. Bargains were easily struck in a duchy where cornfields had given way to vineyards.

Because of the prevailing winds, voyages from Lynn to Gascony could take weeks or months, while the return journey was possible in ten days. Threats to the wine trade intensified after the outbreak of the Hundred Years War in 1337. Gascon vineyards were destroyed in the fighting; attacks on English shipping by French warships and pirates were partly forestalled by sailing in convoys, but Edward III taxed the vessels to pay for armed escorts. Nevertheless there were quiet periods in this prolonged conflict which helped trade, such as in 1362 when a group of Bordeaux wine producers chartered *The Grace of God* of Lynn.

Even more important to Lynn's trade than Flanders and France was Northern Europe, and central to it was the Hanseatic League, a union of German towns with the power of a nation state. The Hansa was granted liberties in Lynn in 1271, and they were confirmed by the mayor and burgesses in 1310. Other foreign merchants were obliged to lodge, for security reasons, with burgesses, but not the Germans. They brought furs, beeswax, fish, cereals, pitch, cloth and timber, exporting corn, wool, skins, cloth, salt and lead. Relations with the Germans were not always good, however: English traders were expelled from their depots in Baltic towns in 1367, and Lynn merchants complained of confiscation of goods in the Baltic in 1385.

For so desirable a commodity, little attention has been paid to the import of beeswax into England from Russia. Models, seals, writing tablets and candles were made from it; in some Lynn gilds wax was a currency for paying entry fees and fines. In May 1467 a Hansa ship docked at Lynn with beeswax, sturgeon and wine, sailing two weeks later with cloth. It returned in October with beeswax, linen and eels.

Trade with the northern lands of Scotland, Iceland and Norway began early. Salt, fish and cloth were brought to Lynn by Scots and exchanged for wheat, malt and ale. Provisioning royal expeditions against Scotland was a very profitable business for Lynn's merchants. Icelanders exported cloth, falcons, train oil and fish in exchange for corn, malt, pots, nails and shoes. In the early 15th century the merchants of Lynn sent a fishing fleet to Iceland annually, after being ousted from the Baltic. Trade was disrupted in the 1420s following clashes between English sailors and the agents of the king of Denmark, who claimed the island.

By 1250 Bergen, in Norway, was already the greatest fish market in Europe, and Matthew Paris counted 200 ships in its harbour. Lynn ships sailed for Bergen with corn and cloth, and returned with timber, whetstones, fish, furs and hawks. Twelve falcons sent by the king of Norway to Henry III in 1245 came through Lynn. The Norwegians came to Lynn to buy food: about 1250, 11 Norwegian ships were loading corn there at the same time. Soon the Hansa was as alarmed by the English penetration of Norway as it was of the Baltic, and in 1392 and 1394 Bergen was sacked and the houses of Lynn merchants there destroyed by the pirates known as the Victual Brothers, encouraged by Lübeck. In the 15th century the Hansa finally excluded English merchants from Danzig, Bergen and the entire northern region. Not until 1475 was peace restored between the league and England, by the Treaty of Utrecht, and the league's power was symbolised at Lynn by the building of their new warehouse.

Lynn's trade was becoming more diversified by the late 14th century. Dutch merchants became prominent, having access to a wide hinterland up the Rhine and becoming involved in the salt trade from the Bay of Biscay. Coastal traffic was also important. Ships from Newcastle and Scotland brought fish and coal, taking away corn and ale. Just before 1400 large quantities of raw hides were brought from Newcastle to feed Lynn's leather industry, but this traffic was captured by London. Stone from the famous Holywell quarries in Rutland was taken down the Fenland rivers to Lynn and shipped to Windsor to construct the castle; Derbyshire lead followed a similar route.

Lynn's national standing was diminished by London's increasing domination of foreign trade and the dwindling of wool exports in the later Middle Ages. What Lynn lacked to compensate for these developments was a cloth-manufacturing hinterland of the kind boosting the trade of Bristol, Exeter, Hull, Yarmouth and even Ipswich. Coventry merchants used Lynn to export cloth to northern Europe in the 15th century and the port handled some of the cloth produced in East Anglia, but it did not regain the traffic in the commodity enjoyed when the old textile towns of the East Midlands had flourished. Lynn's role as the gateway to these towns is clear from the activities of the merchants of Picardy. When the goods of Frenchmen in England were confiscated by the crown in 1294, they had more woad, an essential dyestuff, at Lynn than elsewhere.

Overseas trade since the Middle Ages

What kind of port was Lynn about 1600, when its international peak had been reached nearly three hundred years before? It was still among England's leading ports, with 96 ships entering and 159 leaving the harbour in 1604-5; Bristol had no more than 121 ships in and 99 out clearing its port in 1600-1. Lynn accounted for four times the overseas trade of its old rival across the Wash, Boston. Corn brought down-river for export was the motor of the Norfolk port, and it paid for the import of goods for distribution up-river. The cycle of good and bad harvests therefore determined the cycle of boom and slump in Lynn.

Scotland, in particular the merchants of Kirkcaldy, was Lynn's most important foreign trading partner. The Scots exchanged salt, fish, cloth, oats, barley, wheat and some coal for cloth, skins, hemp, lead, corn, malt, beer, peas, beans and re-exported raisins and figs.

Lynn merchants had also returned to Iceland, as Tobias Gentleman mentions in 1614 when praising the seafaring traditions of the port. About 30 ships sailed there from the Wash each spring. Although John Mason imported beef, port and tallow from Carrickfergus in 1614, trade with Ireland was limited because it was too remote and poor.

Trade between England and northern Europe about 1600 was officially monopolised by the chartered companies of London, but merchants from Lynn and other east-coast ports interloped. Their ships fetched timber, pitch, tar, iron, flax, hemp, cloth, glass and rye from the Baltic and Scandinavia, taking hides, cloth, and re-exporting soap, wine, spices and other luxury goods. Baltic goods also reached Lynn through Dutch ports, along with German ones: by 1600 Amsterdam had emerged as Europe's greatest entrepot, and Dutch merchants had settled in Lynn.

France and southern Europe were still good trading regions. There was a light traffic with Normandy, French run; pitch, coal, cloth, hemp and the odd cargo of bones, horns and broken glass were taken from Lynn to Dieppe. Were these strange cargoes recycled to make the second-grade statuettes for the pilgrim market for which Dieppe was famous? Hops, peas,

10. The late 16th-century tower at Clifton House allowed merchants to watch for ships from comfortable rooms. Tudor and Jacobean traders kept 'a day booke' for recording 'all such bargaines and contractes, receiptes and deliveryes as they make'. Overdue debts were written into another book called 'a debt booke' and removed from 'the day booke'. Debts were often paid in the porch of St Margaret's church.

vinegar, bottles, paper, millstones and plaster of Paris were imported from Rouen and Dieppe to Lynn. Lynn merchants, however, were far more interested in the wine and salt of south-west Francer.

The Iberian peninsula also attracted trade from the Norfolk port once the Spanish Company was opened to provincial members. Cargoes from Lynn were often transhipped at Harwich or Gravesend into London vessels bound for Seville or Lisbon. Corn, in particular, timber, cloth, tar, peas and beans were sent south in exchange for salt, wine, figs, raisins, sugar, almonds, liquorice and pepper. The trade to southern Europe emphasises sharply how dependent Lynn's trade was on the harvest: when the harvest was good, trading took place as far away as Marseilles, Genoa and Leghorn, and even at Agadir, in Morocco.

Lynn's overseas trade suffered greatly in the 17th century from civil war at home and the ravages of the Dutch and French. In 1627, trying to be excused crown requisition of ships

11. The Purfleet before the erection of the Custom House, with Sir John Turner's house to the right. An engraving after a drawing by Henry Bell.

and money, the corporation told the government that 34 vessels had been lost in two years to 'the Dunkirkers'. The Dutch wars were even more damaging, but the defeat of the Dutch fleet at the Battle of Lowestoft in 1666 marked a turning point. Lynn was well positioned to ship much of the growing export of corn to Europe in peacetime.

Lynn's trade prospered in the 18th century. In 1784 a French aristocrat visiting Lynn believed the harbour capable of taking 250 ships, and it was 'hearty full' when he saw it. De la Rochefoucauld also tells us that the port sent out 'a large number of ships to the North and some to America' despite the preponderance of the coastal trade. Baltic and Norwegian timber was a great draw, for Lynn merchants were involved in shipbuilding and supplying the building industry. Complaints about the drift of wood on the Ouse and piles of timber obstructing the riverside testify to the extent of the trade. In 1785 Browne and Everard had deals in stock from the Baltic worth over £10,000. Most timber was deposited along the banks of the Nar, just to the south of the harbour; a house for sawing timber by a 'machine with horses' was built at the mouth of this river in the 1730s. When the Revolutionary Wars began in 1793, trade with the Baltic was disrupted, and more Lynn ships sailed to North America for timber.

According to William Richards, 208,000 quarters of corn were shipped from Lynn in 1761, of which 125,000 went abroad. England was beginning to import as well as export corn, however, especially in years of bad harvests such as 1767, when a great deal was shipped up-river by lighter. The Baltic was the chief source of supply. In 1783, for example, William and Thomas Bagge commissioned Samuel Baker to sail *The Chance* to Stralsund to load wheat; the cargo was to be taken to Bristol, or another port if prices there were low.

The merchants of 18th-century Lynn showed few signs of being over-adventurous. A West Indian plantation owner called Crisp Molineux encouraged them to trade with his home islands by sending foodstuffs, bricks and coal for sugar, rum and spices, and some ships were despatched there. Lynn merchants shared the outlay on vessels fitted out for 'adventures' on the Spanish Main, in fact piratical raids against Spanish possessions, some of which seem to have been skippered by Thomas Alderson. Yet there was no sustained enthusiasm for either of these operations, probably because of the high risks and costs compared with European trade, and Custom House returns of the 1730s record only occasional shipments of wine and linen to the West Indies.

The wine traffic grew from the late 17th century — the figures adorned with the sheaf and vine on the Custom House of 1685 are highly symbolic. Mackerell wrote of 'the spacious vaults' for wine in the port 50 years later, and Hillen talked of 'underground Lynn' because of the extensive cellarage along the riverside and market-places. Thousands of gallons were shipped upstream to the port's hinterland, as Defoe noted in 1722. Almost three quarters of the wine brought to English ports in the early 18th century came from Portugal as, following the Methuen Treaty of 1703 and the deterioration of international relations, prohibitive duties were imposed on Spanish and French wines. Most Portuguese wines were unpopular because of their bitterness, however, and the merchants of Lynn found ways of obtaining their beloved claret. Lisbon was capital of an empire in Brazil and Africa, and English foodstuffs were re-exported to the colonists. Of the 65 corn ships sailing from the Wash in the last quarter of 1737 (there were at least 266 during the year October 1737 to September 1738), the 16 biggest cargoes were bound for Lisbon. On 3 October 1737 Samuel Browne's *Elizabeth*, captained by John Mountain, sailed for the Portuguese capital with 1,300 quarters of corn, a typical quantity.

The story of the *Minerva*, of Lynn, reveals the hazards of trade when Europe was at war. This 188-ton brig was built in 1785 for George Hogge, and traded in wine. In September 1796 the *Minerva* and her crew of nine called at Lisbon and Faro to load wine. They set sail for England on 20 October, although unable to buy enough provisions. Caught in a gale for several days, the captain ran for Lisbon for more food and water, docking on 2 November. There the vessel joined a convoy bound for England under the protection of a frigate, and sailed again on 20 November. The convoy was scattered by a storm and on 28 December the brig was 'brought to' by a French privateer, the *Patriot*. The crew was imprisoned near Brest and in June 1797 put ashore near Dartmouth.

The coastal trade

In 1812 William Richards claimed that the French wars had severely damaged Lynn's overseas commerce, and that its trade was 'almost wholly confined' to the coastal traffic in corn and coal. In 1784 de la Rochefoucauld observed how Lynn was far more involved in home than foreign trade, and that coal 'for a large part of England' was sent up-river from it. Most of the ships leaving the harbour in Jacobean times were carrying corn to northern Britain or south to feed the capital.

London, with some half-million inhabitants about 1700, dwarfed all other English towns, and the demands of its food markets increasingly affected the farming of counties to the north and west. Defoe commented in 1714 that England 'depended' on London for the consumption of its food. Much of the capital's needs were transported coastwise from East Anglian ports. The drainage of the Fens after 1650 gave Lynn an even more important role, and fish, butter, beans and hides were despatched to London in large quantities. Feeding London had a high priority for the government. When the city of Cambridge complained to the Privy Council in 1565 about the great amounts of corn going to London through Lynn, it was ignored.

In 1621 about thirteen thousand quarters of grain were sent coastwise from Lynn, over 10,000 of them to the capital. London took half the corn shipped from Lynn by coaster in 1734. Lynn-made starch and soap were sent there also in the early 17th century, and local sand for glass-making. In return the Wash received a vast range of luxury and general cargoes manufactured in the city or collected by its merchants from all over the world. Tobacco from America, Mediterranean wine and dried fruits, furniture, tombstones, haberdashery, apothecary wares, snuff, vinegar and soap are only a sample of the variety of goods arriving in the same ships. The fact that soap was going both ways casts doubts on Jacobean business efficiency!

Lynn was a significant provincial entrepot by 1600, as its extensive coastal trade with smaller ports shows. Fish, malt, peas, beans, iron and salt were amongst the cargoes of ships sailing between the Wash and Dover, Colchester, Dartmouth, Hastings and other harbours along the east and south coasts. Boston received groceries, wine, hops, ale, iron, flax, linen, soap and fish, and sent butter, corn and wool in return. In 1624 Boston shipped coastwise nearly 13,000 stones of wool, of which 8,000 went to Lynn. East Anglian cloth manufacturers bought much of the wool coming into Lynn, which was 'a greate place for wool broking'. In the 1730s Lynn still took half the wool shipped from Boston, although Colchester and Hull were beginning to take an increasing share of it.

Trade with Hull flourished. Corn, flour and malt to feed the growing urban populations of Yorkshire were the most important cargoes from the Ouse to the Humber in the early 19th century; then manufactured goods and hardware from Birmingham began to reach Lynn by canal barge and coaster. Iron and hardware were transported the 50 miles up-river from Lynn to Bury for about 10s. a ton, whereas to bring the same loads to Bury by wagon the 26 miles from Ipswich cost 15s. a ton. Yarn from the West Riding also found its way to Norwich through the ports of Hull and Lynn, from where it was transported by wagon.

The coal trade between Lynn and the north-east of England grew rapidly after 1550, and in the 17th century Lynn's coastal trade was increasingly directed by supplying the demand of the North-East for corn in return for the coal eagerly purchased in the Wash port. London was the most attractive market for the colliers, but Lynn, with its broad hinterland, came next. In 1608 about a thousand ships arrived at Lynn from Newcastle and another 150 from Sunderland, landing over 20,000 tons of coal. By the 1680s this annual tonnage had nearly doubled, and Lynn's merchants were concerned about the colliers of 'strangers and foreigners' crowding the harbour. Lynn vessels were unloaded first, however, and escaped taxation. The landowners of Bedfordshire and Huntingdonshire petitioned parliament against these privileges in 1704, only to be frustrated by Lynn's M.P., Robert Walpole.

Many of the colliers plying between the North-East and Lynn in the mid-18th century were brigantines or brigs, ranging from 150 to 350 tons. Most were built and owned in the North-East, but a good number belonged to Lynn merchants, like the Bagge brothers William and John. The latter sailed to Shields for coal in the spring of 1747, where he encountered double troubles. He wrote to William:

> This is to advise you of my being still in this harbour detained by a hard gail of wind at NNE and thick bad weather. We every day hear of privateers upon the north east coast taking last Wednesday Eltenhams [?] sloop belonging to our place off Hartley. Mr Hog's brig Clampett came in from Leath yesterday in the gail the weather so bad could not deal with Blith . . . I hope the Lynn is arrived by this time. Here is about a hundred sail of large ships loaded waiting for an opportunity and hope we shall gett out with them.

Despite further problems about loading enough of the right kind of coal, John was eventually able to return to Lynn. By 1747 it was unusual for Lynn merchants to sail with their vessels.

The brig *Jane* sailed from Lynn for the North-East in the early 19th century. Six men each owned an eighth of her, the rest being William Green Allen's, who kept the ship's accounts. The annual profit earned by each of the owners ranged from £30 to £50. Expenses for maintenance and repair were considerable, as bills for new sails, ropes, cable and tar all record. In 1810 a new anchor had to be bought for £21; in 1813 about £7 was paid to 'Mr Hogg' for a topmast. Beer and bread had to be provided for the crew, and their wages found: the master alone was paid £6 a month. There was pilotage and other dues to be paid in the north and at Lynn. The *Jane* would have been more profitable if she had been able to take regular cargoes from her home port, but there were only occasional loads of sand for Shields, where glass was made, sometimes tiles, and once a load of hay, so she sailed north in ballast on most voyages.

Once in the North-East the *Jane* could load about a hundred chaldrons of coal. Her cargoes were often bought in Lynn by Mr. Bagge, for around £280, while 'Messrs Everard and Sons' and 'country merchants' were other frequent customers. The unloading of the cargo was checked by meters for the payment of national and local tolls, and most of the coal was taken up-river by lighters. In 1815 the *Jane*'s account book ends; the brig was almost certainly sold to William and Thomas Bagge, who owned her in 1821 when she was lost off Whitby and only three of the crew of eight rescued, leaving five widows and 16 children.

Much of the coal was consumed locally, but far more was transhipped to lighters for haulage up-river. Groups of four or five lighters pulled by horses were a common sight on the Ouse and its tributaries. Bury St Edmunds got most of its coal from Lynn via the Ouse and Lark, known to locals as 'the coal river'. Winter ice and summer drought hampered the progress of the lighters, and wagons carried coal inland from Lynn if river traffic was obstructed, but coal prices at Cambridge doubled as a consequence.

Coal was cheaper at Lynn than at other East Anglian ports, and the extensive inland waterways allowed it to be distributed as far south as Haverhill in Essex and as far east as East Harling in Norfolk. The abolition of local coal taxes in 1831 also boosted trade. In 1845 over 250,000 tons were landed at Lynn. Lynn imported more coal from the North-East than any other provincial port from Jacobean times until the railways robbed its merchants of most of this lucrative coastal trade. The trade's significance can be appreciated from their references to Newcastle and the North-East as the 'Black Indies' as early as Elizabeth's reign, while no fewer than 18 of the 24-strong Company of Porters who weighed and measured the valuable bulk commodities passing through the port were assigned to coal.

Taxes on trade

A theme running through Lynn's long commercial history is the taxation of home and foreign trade by national and local governments.

12. Lynn harbour in 1841 from the new bridge over the Eau Brink Cut. The port's first steam tug can be seen on the horizon. Shipbuilding on the River Nar is shown on the right.

Bribery and corruption in H.M. Customs were rife in Elizabethan times. Francis Shaxton of Lynn were one of England's greatest smugglers, abetted by local customs officials remote from central control, and he escaped punishment. John Wallis, leading merchant of Jacobean Lynn, seems to have avoided paying customs duties and export licences, apparently with the blessing of the Privy Council. In an effort to impose tighter controls on them, from 1565 provincial customs officials were obliged to keep port books.

Smuggling was inevitably encouraged by parliament's raising of duties on merchandise passing through England's ports. In 1711 duties were added on hides, coffee, tea, drugs, gilt, silver, wine and cocoa, and Lynn's customs officers were urged to be more vigilant. At this time they often seized brandy, wine, rum, paper, cloth and East Indian silks and spices. In 1716 the Board of Commissioners in London warned 'of ships hovering on the coast waiting for the opportunity to run their cargoes of brandy' and other goods and 'to carry off wool', implying local officials were conniving in it.

Battles between smugglers and customs officials were frequent. The seizure of brandy in a Lynn house in 1718 led to a riot, the leaders of which were whipped round the town. In 1815 the revenue cutter attached to the Custom House captured a vessel off Hunstanton carrying 840 tons of geneva, and escorted it to the Purfleet. The smugglers were taken to the town gaol, from where they escaped through an open window into the night. In 1838 customs officers were more successful in discovering the smuggling of tobacco by carriers from Fakenham and Wisbech, who met at Lynn's *Maid's Head*. As free trade was gradually introduced by parliament from the 1830s and duties on imports and exports were reduced, smuggling became less profitable, but customs officials remained wary of licensing Lynn fishing boats if their owners were suspected of smuggling 'runs'.

The trade of the port was also milked by the corporation, although freemen of the borough escaped more lightly than other merchants. After 1545, 4d. a chaldron was charged on coal unloaded from vessels not registered at Lynn, for the support of the town's paupers. Ships entering the harbour and using its facilities were obliged to pay various dues, of which beaconage, moorage and wharfage were the most profitable. Tolls were calculated on merchandise passing in and out of the port, though the income from exports was modest apart from lastage on Lynn's staple export, corn. Far more valuable were the up-river tolls on coal, salt, corn and other cargoes. These local dues and tolls were largely directed towards the maintenance and improvement of the port: its channels, banks, quays and cranes. No public works affected Lynn's welfare more.

Lynn's two great trades in wine and corn are represented by these figure heads on
the Custom House.

Chapter Three

Town Industries

Shipping

Between 1565 and 1587 the number of Lynn-owned ships registered in the port books trebled from 17 to 60, while the tonnage quadrupled. During the following two centuries English trade and shipping grew apace. R. Davis's figures of tonnage belonging to the largest ports in 1582 place Lynn tenth, behind London, Bristol, Newcastle, Hull, Ipswich and Yarmouth. By 1788 Sunderland and the smaller collier-owning ports of Whitehaven, Scarborough and Whitby boasted more tonnage, while Lynn's 17,100 tons of shipping could not match Liverpool's 76,000 tons. The number of vessels registered at Lynn continued to increase, from 85 in 1776 to 116 in 1831 and to 180 by 1850, but the total tonnage at that date was only 19,800, merely 3,000 more than in 1788.

Although most of the ships using Lynn were owned elsewhere, the town was home for at least 800 sailors in 1850, and more than 100 master mariners. The latter had always been involved in the ownership as well as the sailing of vessels, other eighths or sixteenths of the boats being owned by tradesmen, farmers and professional families. The bulk of the town's shipping was controlled by the merchant dynasties, however. Brewing, transport and property interests generated the wealth to buy ships, and, in turn, the profits from coastal and foreign trade were ploughed back into business empires.

Most of the buying and selling of vessels involved smaller capitalists, often at auction at the *Duke's Head*. In 1786 William and Thomas Bagge sold the *Prudence* for £770 to Jeremiah Bouch, a master mariner, who borrowed £600 from the Bagges to pay for it! Financial problems may explain why Bouch sold shares in the ship to two other master mariners. Soon after, on 18 September 1791, she was lost off the coast of Holland, and Bouch collected insurance of £350. The circumstances of this are somewhat suspicious because Bouch was to pay the Bagges £300, with interest, by 13 September 1791.

The hazards did not deter Bouch or others. Earlier, in 1785, he and Alexander Smith paid Simon Temple £853 for a half share in the *Alexander*, a vessel of 200 tons Temple had built at South Shields. They sold an eighth share in the vessel to John Pickering, a publican, for £200. Pickering left his share to his widow Mary, who sold a sixteenth of the ship to Edwin Kerry, a farmer near Lynn, for £100. In 1788 the whole ship was sold to the Bagges for £1,333. The Pickerings had dabbled in shipping before: in 1774 they bought full or part ownership in three newly built lighters, borrowing money from the Bagges to do so. In 1797 all three were sold to the Bagges for £200!

Lynn's seaborne commerce inevitably encouraged its merchants to invest in shipbuilding. About 1390, Queen Margaret of Sweden pleaded with Richard II to allow her to hire three Lynn ships to fight Baltic pirates. A little earlier Edward III had taken 19 ships from Lynn, 17 from Newcastle, 16 from Hull and 12 from Ipswich to equip an expedition against France. It is almost certain that some of these Lynn vessels had been built locally, like *Le Philipe*, constructed for Edward in three months for £66. Lynn had plentiful supplies of timber, pitch, tar and hemp, mostly imported from the Baltic. Shipbuilding was consolidated here in the 15th century when the English began to make bigger and better ocean-going vessels, copying German designs. Ships with a single mast and a square sail gave way to vessels of two or three masts, with three-cornered sails, and castles at stem and stern. One such was carved on a pew end at St Nicholas' Chapel about 1420.

13. A drawing by Henry Baines (1823-94) of shipbuilding on the River Nar.

Tudor monarchs attempted to boost the building of large ships in England by paying a bounty of over 5s. a ton — big merchant ships could quickly be converted into warships. Shipbuilding in Lynn was probably a flourishing enterprise influenced most by local demand. Ships were built for outsiders, however, such as the *St Paul* of London, launched 1629. Perhaps this vessel was built by Thomas Smyleton, a 'shipcarpenter' who in 1628 leased land at St Ann's Yard from the corporation so that he could store timber 'to buyld shippes and other vessels'. When Lynn petitioned Oliver Cromwell against the construction of the Denver Sluice in 1654, reference was made to the 'constant build of ships' in the town, sufficient to maintain its stock of 'above' 80 vessels.

In the 18th century frequent references to launchings occur in the town calendars. Yards were located at North End, near St Ann's Fort, and on the Nar, in South Lynn. Vessels were often towed to the Purfleet for finishing. The wreck in the Wash of a vessel belonging to Samuel Browne homeward bound with Norwegian timber in 1717 reveals solid evidence of the industry. The badly damaged ship, which had been built in Sweden for £440, was towed to a dry dock at Lynn and rebuilt by George Wilkinson, after which she was declared to be 'English'. Crisp Molineux told his West Indian planter friends in 1768 how cheap English ships were compared with others, saying: 'I think I can build one at Lynn cheaper and full as good as in any port of England'.

Relations between the Bagges and George Walker were almost certainly typical of those between merchant and shipbuilder, the latter having rented a Nar yard and warehouses from the family in 1773 and received a string of orders thereafter. Here the *Prudence* was built in 1777. She was a vessel of 100 tons, with one deck and two masts, described as 'a square-stemmed brigantine with neither a galley nor figure', about sixty feet long and twenty broad, with a hold 11 feet deep. Walker was paid £430 in 10 instalments coinciding with completion of stages in construction, such as laying the decks. The Bagges also paid the 18 craftsmen who finished the ship: Robert Haycocks was paid £93 for ironwork, for example. Ropes, sails, masts, rigs, casks and anchors were all contributed by individual tradesmen. When she was launched into the Nar in August 1777 she had cost £893, and the Bagges also paid the bill for the ale drunk then and a celebration supper for 33 people.

Most of the ships built in 18th-century Lynn seem to have been brigs of between 100 and 200 tons, typical of most English yards. It is impossible to say how many shipbuilders were working for Lynn's merchants at any one time, maybe no more than five or six. Hugh Moseley, who rented a yard on the Nar from Samuel Browne for £24 a year and built for several local shipowners, was perhaps fairly typical. In 1763 he lengthened the *Suzanna* for the Bagges and built a sloop of 80 tons for the 'ropemaker' Hugh Crawforth in 1766. The *Auspicious*, at 600 tons said to be the largest ship ever built at Lynn, was launched at St Ann's in 1796. William Armes remembered that in his younger days there was 'always' a large ship under construction for the East Indian or other trade routes at Mr. Bottomley's Nar yard, to which Armes' own factory in St Nicholas Street (built on the site of a shipyard) supplied tons of rope. Crowds turned out for the early-morning spring tides to watch the launchings. Once a vessel slipped into the Nar a tidal wave of displaced water forced back the 'gaping' and 'terrified' spectators. Directories record only two Lynn shipbuilders in 1845 and 1854, and by 1864 none remained. The industry was killed by the inability of the Wash port to take larger vessels and the demise of the wooden sailing ship. Newcastle and Glasgow built the new iron steamships.

Shipping and shipbuilding generated employment in various ancillary industries, of which the manufacture of rope and sails was the most important. Hemp is required to make rope. In the 17th century demand became too much for English growers and imports became vital, although the draining of the Fens encouraged the cultivation and preparation of large amounts in local villages. In 1663 Samuel Pepys visited his relatives near Wisbech finding his uncle and aunt Perkins with their daughters 'in a sad, poor thatched cottage', like a poor barn or stable 'peeling of hemp' in which 'I did give myself good content to see their manner of peeling hemp'. By 1700 the corporation was letting long pieces of land near the town walls and at the old monastic sites to manufacturers for laying out and twisting ropes. Armes recalled as a boy 'peeping' over the wall of the corporation ropewalk, near the present railway station, seeing men 'spinning long yarns' the entire length of it.

In the early 18th century parliament encouraged the manufacture of sailcloth in England to reduce dependence on imported naval stores. In 1740 the corporation employed 'poor persons' in a sailcloth 'factory' near the East Gate. Poor Law rate books reveal a cluster of 'sail chambers' or workshops close to the Ouse and Millfleet. There were eight sailmakers recorded in the 1845 directory besides at least two 'mast and block' makers.

Salt making, fishing and whaling

It was stressed in Chapter One that salt making was almost certainly the mainspring of Lynn's early development. The industry seems already to have been declining by 1100, although it long persisted. As late as 1586 Thomas Wilkes bought a crown patent to manufacture and sell white salt at Lynn, Boston and Hull. How much longer salterns operated around the Wash is impossible to know. Salt was produced much more cheaply in the warmer climate of southern Europe, where seawater could be evaporated naturally.

Rock salt from the newly discovered mines in Cheshire was being shipped to Lynn via Liverpool from the early 18th century. At the same time 'white salt', made by evaporating seawater using coal as fuel, was being imported from the North-East. One ship bringing 50 tons of it from South Shields to Lynn in 1754 lost most of her cargo 'by violent, stormy weather'.

Great quantities of cod and herring were imported by Europeans from the teaming fisheries of the Baltic and Norway. Barrels of salted fish were a feature of Lynn's medieval fairs. In 1325 King Street was known as Stockfish Row, suggesting that this quarter was the hub of the town's fish market. About 1600 the corporation leased to merchants special fish houses for storage on the nearby Common Staithe. To the immediate north of the Tuesday Market Place, at the mouth of the River Gaywood, was the harbour of Lynn's fishing fleet. Space for washing and drying the catch seems to have been mostly found in South Lynn, at the mouth of the Nar. The corporation directed the spreading of shingle on which the fish were dried.

In 1528 Lynn's Icelandic fishing fleet was no more than 10 ships, while Yarmouth's was 30-strong and another 30 sailed from the Norfolk ports of Cley, Cromer and Blakeney. Lynn's North Sea fleet of four vessels was also much smaller than Yarmouth's fleet of 20, although the Wash port sent six ships to fish in Scottish waters and Yarmouth eight. In the later 17th century Lynn's fishermen seem to have abandoned voyages into northern seas, concentrating on the waters closer to home. Fish was so plentiful at Lynn in the 18th century that the corporation was persuaded to relax the time it was on sale solely to townspeople. In 1752 the fishermen told the town hall that higglers and pedlars needed fresh fish to take to 'distant' markets 'for which purpose they often ride all night'. By-laws to protect the fish and shellfish stocks of the Wash from over-exploitation were difficult to enforce, and the requirement that all fishermen apply for a licence failed to stop interlopers, despite heavy fines.

Parliament promoted England's whaling fleet by legislation; an Act of Parliament of 1771 was 'for the better support and establishing of the Greenland Whale Fishery'. The crown paid bounties of 40s. a ton on whale imports, and the ships escaped customs duties. Lynn's whaling industry was almost certainly given a fillip by the 1771 act. In 1774 the Bagges purchased a ship for £1,550, which was renamed the *Experiment*. Lynn's 'Greenland Company', of about twelve merchants, contributed equal shares to the enormous cost, £4,630, of refitting her. Whaling was an expensive but rewarding business. De la Rochefoucauld is a useful eye witness of the character of Lynn's whaling fleet in 1784:

> I noticed that one of the ships was built in a peculiar way and asked what was the purpose of it. I was told that it was fitted out for whaling. Lynn sends out five of these vessels. They each have forty-five men on board and carry six small rowing boats on the bridge; these are very lightly built for quick launching into the sea. Their voyages last for eight or nine months, in which they get one, two, or three whales. It is well known that the owners earn the whole freight of their vessel in a single voyage and sometimes the cost of construction.

Lynn's five whaling ships in fact sailed for Greenland every March and returned in July. When the whales were sighted in the North Atlantic the small boats were lowered, from which the sailors hurled harpoons. Once the 'fish' had given up the fight it was pulled to the ship and cut up on the way back to the Wash. This was dangerous work. In 1788 the *Archangel* arrived at Lynn from Greenland with two whales, its surgeon having shot a polar bear to save the captain. In 1797 the *Experiment* and the *Fountain* sailed home to Norfolk with the rich prizes of, respectively, 10 and 12 'fish'. In May 1808 the Bagges' half share of the outfitting of the *Experiment* cost £1,014, but they still made a profit. The 160 tons of oil extracted from the 11 'fish' brought to the Nar by the *Experiment* in 1818 sold for £6,000. Other whalers owned by individual merchants though fitted out by the 'Greenland Company' were the *Bedford, Belona, Fountain* and *Archangel*.

In 1812 William Richards called Lynn's whaling industry 'no ungainful concern'. The homecoming of the whaling ships to the River Nar was a major event in South Lynn every summer. The huge vessels filled the narrow river. No description can better that of William Armes:

> The town bells were rung, the citizens and troops of school boys lined the banks of the Nar, and the huge ships, with (in natural phrase) 'royal yards aloft' entered that important river. They had flags of all kinds waving in the wind, and garlands made in Greenland suspended between the masts; and, then, upon the decks around the masts and in the lower rigging, were standing erect huge pieces of black whalebone and jaw-bones of enomous size; and oh! how the good citizens stared and how the boys wondered, and almost wept, as they looked at those huge jaw-bones and thought of poor Jonah. . . . And then there were the horses with tow lines on the north, and lots of hardy sailors, harpooners, etc., with lines upon the stream, and then the surface of the water was covered with long and trim whale boats, and there was shouting and cheering and but for the absence of ice it was in fact another Greenland *pro tem.*

The stink of boiling the blubber for its oil in huge coppers afflicted South Lynn for several weeks, though the locals believed the vapour to be fortifying! Coopers made barrels for the oil nearby, and it was used for lighting St Margaret's church and other public places in the town. Bone was carved into cutlery and umbrella ribs.

Crushed animal bones were used as an agricultural fertiliser from the 18th century, and *White's Directory* (1836) records a mill at the mouth of the Nar operated by 'John Masters and Company'. There was another mill at Narborough about ten miles up this same river. Until the 1820s both mills were supplied with whalebone from the two blubber houses on the Nar at South Lynn. Bones were also collected from farmers and slaughterhouses, and imported from Europe. The bones were boiled to remove the fat (used as grease for carts and wagons), then chopped and milled. The meal was shipped up-river from Lynn's Boal Quay.

England's whaling fleet reached 164 ships in 1815, about a third being based in Hull. Lynn's fleet declined fast because of the competition of Hull, London and Grimsby. One of the blubber houses was demolished before 1900; the other was, unfortunately, pulled down about 1950. Giant whalebones set up as decoration in the gardens of Lynn's master mariners have disappeared, too.

Brewing and the drink trade

Brewing was a nationwide and vital activity in the Middle Ages because of the generally poor quality of drinking water; ale was a staple part of the diet of all social classes. When the plague struck Lynn in 1557 its brewers were castigated by the corporation for deserting their houses and depriving the inhabitants of drink. Although brewing took place throughout urban and rural England, rather than being concentrated in large towns, because of the high cost of transporting something so bulky, Lynn's brewing industry was certainly serving more than local requirements by 1300, its merchants exporting more corn and ale than any other provincial port.

In the 1520s Lincoln had 4,000 citizens and the number of its alehouses grew from 20 in 1515 to 30 in 1553; in Lynn, with the same population, the statistics were similar. As elsewhere in the country, in the 15th and 16th centuries the corporation tried to enforce licensing restrictions, ordering brewers not to sell to houses without a sign, for example, but in spite of penalties such as forfeiture of the ale for distribution to the poor and friars, the Hall Books indicate that this task was extremely difficult. Inns, clustered in and near the market-places, were for the upper-class traveller, offering stabling and luxury accommodation beyond the pockets of the clientele of the alehouses. Taverns were something of a cross between the two, selling wine more than ale. Places selling wine and stabling horses were classified as inns by the corporation in 1743. Public houses seem to have multiplied in the 16th century as Lynn's commercial activity quickened. Alderman John Spence, who owned the *Bull* in Cooks Row (High Street North) observed in 1610:

> The towne of Lynn is a lardge and populous towne and there is a greate resorte of people there both by sea and by land and therefore it is filt that there should be many victualers to geve enterteynment to travellers and seafaringe men.

About 1550 a special water pipe was laid for brewers from the Kettlemills outside the East Gate to King Street. Almost all the merchant complexes facing King Street had malt-houses and breweries: with the Ouse and its ships immediately to the west and the town's alehouses within easy reach this was the ideal location.

Tied houses were obviously normal in Lynn before Benjamin Holley obliged his tenant, Thomas Denham, to buy his beer in 1669. When Michael Revett died in 1636 he owned several public houses, including the *Maid's Head*, and the *Red Lyon* in Boston. Did he send beer by boat across the Wash? Beer was certainly sent up the Ouse. Jacobean Lynn's largest brewers were probably the Atkins, who exported large amounts of ale to Scotland and supplied town houses from their Greenland Fishery headquarters. Part of this timber-framed building of 1605 was, apparently, a tavern.

In the 1660s a dynamic family settled in King Street, next to their brewery; through several generations the Bagges were apprenticed son to father, like Thomas was to William in 1755. These two bought out a spendthrift cousin in 1767 and built the King Street brewery into a thriving concern. The Bagges needed beer to provision their growing merchant fleet, and some was exported to Europe, but the development of their brewing

14. Thomas Philip Bagge (1773-1829) established his family as country squires and developed its shipping and brewery interests in Lynn. The façade of the King Street Brewery still exists.

empire was dependent on the acquisition of a chain of town houses.

The growth of Lynn in the 18th century involved the building of new taverns as well as the conversion of shops or workshops: the *Lattice House* of 1714 is an example of the latter. The Bagges' account books testify to heavy investment in improving their public houses.

The *Ship Inn* in Boal Street was let for 40s. a year to Mary Spicer (living apart from her husband) in 1775 after she had signed a bond to take beer only from the Bagges and found friends to stand surety for losses — standard terms. Unfortunate or incompetent tenants were sued by the Bagges for big debts and ejected, like Robert Large in 1776. Inventories survive for a number of their establishments. The *Unicorn* in Norfolk Street, for example, in 1785 contained 10 rooms. Bedrooms, parlours, bars and dining rooms were all furnished with walnut or mahogany tables, desks, dressers and chairs, as well as carpets, looking glasses and window blinds. There were tea, coffee and chocolate pots, while decanters show wine was served as well as beer.

Three of the four 'capital inns' of the town were located in the Tuesday Market Place, all built or rebuilt about 1700. The *Angel* was rented from the corporation by the Bagges, and was the most popular until its demolition in 1830. Enjoying the most prestige and dominating the market-place from the east was the *Duke's Head*, bought by Samuel Browne in 1731. In 1773 an agreement was drawn up by which Browne let the inn to Samuel Horncastle of London for 10 years. The annual rent was to be £60. Horncastle was to borrow £1,200 from four men of Thetford and Downham to buy horses, carriages, hay, drink and 'other necessaries', while Browne was to spend £400 on repairs. Horncastle was to buy his wine from Browne at 'customary prices' and not to brew on the premises except for sale there.

Maxey Allen, who owned 16 houses in 1775, served by the brewery behind his mansion in St Ann's Street, was probably the town's largest brewer at the time. Of these establishments only the *Mayden's Head* and the *Crown and Mitre* remain today. In 1800 he leased land from the corporation at the South Gate and rebuilt the *Crown* there to tap the trade of the road hauliers. A stocktake of the St Ann's brewery followed his death in 1804. Malt, spirits, beers, hops, casks and coal were valued at over £7,200, after £1,492 duty owing on malt and beer had been deducted.

In 1743 there were 11 public houses brewing on site for retail, but most drinking establishments were tied to breweries, in particular to those of three merchant families, the Allens, Bagges and Everards, who were acquiring new outlets and taking over rivals. In 1774, for example, this trio shared the assets of Thomas Hendry, whose business had been substantial. Smaller brewers were often driven to supplying unlicensed alehousekeepers, as John Sparke did when selling 20 barrels of beer to an 'illegal' publican and carpenter, William Thompson, in 1754. By 1806 the big brewers controlled 64 of the town's 68 taverns, and obstructed newcomers to the trade: Blackburne and Yates Bonner were refused a publican's licence that year by magistrates subject to their 'great influence'.

Lynn's population doubled from 10,000 to 20,000 in the first half of the 19th century, creating new opportunities for brewers. Between 1804 and 1845 the number of public houses leapt from 68 to a hundred and forty-five. Many of these new outlets were the infamous pothouses or 'Tom and Jerries' allowed by the Beer Act of 1830 on payment of a £2 licensing fee. Tories accused Liberal magistrates of granting licences in order to erode the monopoly of the Bagges and Everards, but the Beer Act also reflected the desire of landowners for higher malt consumption. Most beerhouses were temporary and dingy affairs run by wives and widows to supplement family incomes. Their number fell from 63 in 1836 to 24 in 1854 as some collapsed and others became 'real' pubs. Many were on the riverside, serving the hordes of sailors, bargees and porters. Thew describes these taverns 'reaping a rich harvest', allowing landlords, like Mr. Boulding of the *Duke of Wellington* in Nelson Street, to make small fortunes.

In 1845 Lynn's drink trade was supplied by at least six small brewers, described in the directories as 'retailers', and nine big or 'common' brewers. The Bagges and Everards were still adding to their chains of public houses. Allen's brewery, in St Ann's Street, had been taken over by the Hogges, who rebuilt it at Setch, just to the south of Lynn. The most significant of the newcomers was Elijah Eyre (1800-63). Born in Derbyshire, Eyre migrated to Lynn to make his fortune in the 1820s, and established a small business in Broad Street. In 1834 he acquired a mortgage on a property in Bridge Street by the Millfleet, the Ladybridge brewery, which he and a succession of partners expanded. He also bought public houses in and around Lynn. About 1860 he considerably increased his share of Lynn's drink trade by renting Everards' brewery in Baker Lane. Business interests and 'large establishments' in London and Derby turned Eyre into a classic Victorian entrepreneur. His reputation as a fair-dealing employer and citizen transformed his funeral into a local day of mourning, when shops closed. He left a personal fortune of over £70,000.

Water, corn milling and farming

The Austin friars and Greyfriars had conduits channelling water from springs in Wootton and Middleton, respectively, but the rest of Lynn was dependent on fresh water from the River Gaywood by the 1420s, when a canal was cut to the Kettlemills outside the East Gate. The Kettlemills was a big timber wheel hung with metal containers, or 'kettles', worked by horses. The water it raised was brought to town by wooden pipes, although even in the 16th century the system did not extend to all the main streets. Moreover, piped water was the privilege of the wealthy; poorer people had to fetch water from the pools in the two market-places, or the friaries.

The system, with refinements, was maintained into the 19th century. Tree trunks bored hollow on the spot to serve as water pipes fascinated the young William Armes in 1810. Four giant water tanks or reservoirs were constructed in the 16th century as a precaution against drought. In 1679 Richard Jolles was instrumental in the erection of a windmill at the Kettlemills to raise water to a wooden tank in a tower on the town wall. A waterfall was constructed to drive another 'water engine'. In 1738 Mackerell observed:

> Kettle-mill, is an engine which works by wind, water and horses at the East end of the town, to supply it with fresh water, there being a Main of Wooden Trees bored hollow, or leaden pipes, which convey the water to the furthermost End of the Town, and the Inhabitants supplied with it as very moderate rents.

In 1761 the corporation's visiting committee found the windmill for 'throwing water' into the town in a state of decay. The dam to stop the tides swelling up the River Gaywood and contaminating the mills was found to be defective in 1762. About 1780 the corporation installed a new water engine, powered by the fall of the River Gaywood, with three times the capacity of the old, leaving the horse engine for emergencies. Both engines were discarded in favour of a Newcomen engine, but it proved so hungry for coal and unreliable that it was abandoned for another water engine. In 1812 Richards poured scorn on corporation bungling because the new water engine performed worse than the old, forcing many inhabitants to rely on the fleets at low tide. Population growth made the Kettlemills more inadequate, but not until 1829 was the new Kettlemills built. It had a 'Stephenson' steam engine to raise water into a tower holding 4,000 gallons. By 1852 there were two engines, and iron pipes were laid throughout the town.

In the Middle Ages Lynn's bakers were served by two tidal mills. One was built by the bishop of Norwich on the River Gaywood for the inhabitants of the Newland; the other had been erected somewhat earlier on the Millfleet by the lords of South Lynn. There was also a horsemill owned by the bishops at the southern end of Broad Street, close to 'Baxter's Row' (Tower Street). There is no record of a windmill, but is the miller riding home to his windmill caricatured on the 14th-century brass of Walsoken in St Margaret's church a local man? Millstones discovered in the 1960s in Stonegate may have belonged to the tidal

15. The Kettle Mills, or Lynn waterworks, in the early 19th century.

16. This engraving shows the Greyfriars Tower and the adjacent windmill for pressing oil from linseed. All Saints' church at South Lynn is visible in the distance; its tower fell in 1763.

corn mill further up the Millfleet, while small lava querns found in Baker Lane and Broad Street suggest domestic milling.

In 1448 the Holy Trinity Gild acquired the tidal Millfleet mill for the townspeople. It is unclear how and when the other two public mills managed by the bishops ceased operations, though they both probably disappeared about 1500. The corporation leased out the Millfleet mill: in 1519 Robert Feltwell of Marham was allowed 'the common mills' to farm for five years at £37 a year, to serve the bakers of the town 'afore the people of the country'. Raistrick's map of 1725 suggests that the mill was a single-storey stone building.

Private corn milling was forbidden by the town authorities. One motive was perhaps to stop milling becoming a monopoly of a clique of bakers, as high bread prices would trigger unrest, but preservation of the revenue springing from the town mills was another consideration. Enforcement of the public monopoly proved extremely difficult, however, and millers were fined for grinding at their own mills and mills outside Lynn. Private (horse?) mills serving the borough's bakeries were obviously proliferating by 1550 when the corporation threatened to remove their spindles. Restrictions of this kind encouraged the building of mills in the immediate hinterland.

Even more galling to the corporation was the lack of water power at the Millfleet. In 1598 a windmill was at last erected on the millhill at South Lynn by John Ferne, for £38, but it was dismantled in 1652. The corporation found wind no more reliable than water-power, and the sole corn mill shown on Henry Bell's 'groundplat' of Lynn about 1661 is that astride the Millfleet. During the 18th century this watermill fell into decay because of the expense of clearing the channels to work it, and when Richards wrote in 1812 every vestige had 'long ago' disappeared.

The millhill at South Lynn was the mound on the line of the defences between the 'old' and 'little' Guannock Gates. A windmill had certainly been rebuilt here by 1680, when the Hall Book records a decision to remove it because it threatened the profits of a new tenant at the Millfleet. Was it removed? A corn windmill operating here in 1741 was blown down by the great gale of September, but quickly reconstructed. In 1753 Richard Simpson, the proprietor of this mill, complained that the corporation's new 'plantation' had blocked access to it, and was given permission to dismantle it and re-erect it at Gaywood. Richards tells us that windmills supplied a good proportion of the flour and meal required by the town in 1812. In 1836 *White's Directory* recorded eight millers in Lynn, including five who operated windmills at Gaywood.

Though the town must always have required food 'imports' from the surrounding country-side, some degree of self-sufficiency was possible for centuries, the fields within and outside the gates inviting cultivation. Meadows yielded abundant crops of hay. In 1729 Alderman Allen's haystack near the East Gate was struck by lightning and ignited. The Lynn Improvement Act of 1803 ordered all haystacks to be at least 50 yards from houses to reduce fire risks.

Merchants, like Michael Revett in 1636, left their wives gardens adjacent to their houses and warehouses 'to bleach and dry clothes, to take herbs, and to recreate herself'. Other tradesmen depended on gardens or orchards for a living. The deliberate destruction of 'the orchards' belonging to Thomas Lundford by Gaywood labourers in 1753 shows the extent of town market gardening. Cucumbers, cauliflowers, radishes, carrots, lettuces, onions, savoys, cabbage and celery were all so badly damaged that poor Lundford was ruined. In the 19th century house-building deprived the inhabitants of their garden city. Armes talks about the sudden disappearance of most of these open spaces.

Cattle feature on many old prints of the town. Meadows at West Lynn and outside the town walls to the east were as important to farmers as the fields inside the defences. Lynn butchers like Robert Manning and Clement Anger bought sheep in west Norfolk for fattening locally as early as the 1480s. In 1555 two butchers were heavily fined for breaking the town's conduit to water their own pastures first. In 1836 there were at least 24 cowkeepers living in Lynn, six being designated 'farmers in South Lynn parish', much of which was still arable and meadow. The development of the town seems not to have squeezed out the keeping of cows and pigs. In 1852 Joseph Hodgkinson lived in the newly built Wood Street, where cowsheds abounded and 'when the cows are removed in summer, the places are generally stocked with pigs'.

Miscellaneous manufactures

Documentary and archaeological evidence confirm that medieval Lynn was the home of a woollen cloth industry. Webster Row (Broad Street), Fullers Row (St James Street) and Spinner Lane (Paradise Lane) appear to indicate the traditional locations of these workers, together with the less obvious Listergate (Chapel Street), the street of the dyers. According to local historians a stream called Colville Fleet ran down the middle of Broad Street and was used by weavers to wash cloth. The Newland Survey of c.1270 strongly suggests that Lynn's woollen cloth industry was concentrated near the East Gate. A fulling mill was built on the River Gaywood here in 1393 to replace the fulling pits nearby. The open spaces near the river were also ideal for the tenters on which fullers and dyers stretched their cloth. Whether these tradesmen served other than local markets is doubtful, although there were enough bedcover, or coverlet, weavers for there to have been a surplus for export.

During the 17th century the manufacture of worsteds seems to have revived at Lynn, despite the legislation favouring Norwich. Some Dutch and Flemish 'strangers' had settled in the town before 1600, weaving their own brand of woollen cloth — the so-called 'New Draperies'. Acts of Parliament to regulate Norfolk's worsted industry confirm the presence of a weaving community here, and in 1673 Robert Hayward was elected by 16 master weavers to enforce them, although his appointment was disallowed on a technicality by the mayor of Norwich. The calendar of Lynn's freemen records a good sprinkling of clothworkers in the 17th century and a new dyehouse was built near the East Gate by a Norwich dyer in the 1670s.

By the 17th century large amounts of flax were being grown in the Fens for the making of linen. Several linenweavers became Lynn freemen. In 1635-6 one of them, William Johnson, petitioned Norfolk Quarter Sessions complaining of his treatment by officials at Swaffham market. He must have used a horse and cart to peddle his wares in Norfolk and Cambridgeshire markets. The sale of coarse linen by Lynn men was long established: in 1560 the corporation banned the bleaching and drying of linen in the Tuesday Market Place because of water shortages. Starch for stiffening linen was also made in Lynn. 'The West Prospect of King's Lynn', of about 1725, shows a starch windmill somewhere near St Ann's Fort. There was another factory in South Lynn on the 'premises' of Thomas Buckingham (d.1704).

The calendar of borough freemen lists skinners and tanners. Ox, cow and goat hides were tanned by immersion in a decoction of oak bark, after treatment with lime to remove the hair. Plentiful supplies of water would have been required by the tanners, who were probably concentrated near the East Gate, by the River Gaywood. A 'tan yard' and a lime kiln were both recorded in this district in 1736. Other tanners used the Purfleet. Skinner Row (St James' Street) is not far from here. A Lynn fellmonger who died in 1692 had a shop and warehouses as well as an alum house and tan-yard adjoining his domestic quarters.

Oil was needed for lubrication, lighting and soap making. One source was the whaling industry, another was crushing coleseed or rapeseed. Large quantities of rape were grown in the Fens by the 17th century. Bell's 'Groundplat of Lynn', of 1661, shows an 'oyle mill' on the Greyfriars field by the Millfleet. It is clearly visible on a western prospect of the

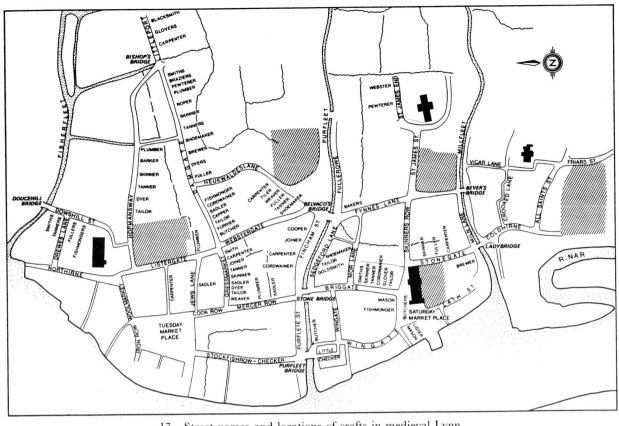

17.   Street names and locations of crafts in medieval Lynn.

18.   Aickman's Iron Foundry in King Street was fronted by medieval buildings before this demolition, in 1827.

town in 1780, and in 1928 the *Lynn Advertiser* featured a photograph of an oil mill at the same spot, claiming that it was the earliest of its type in England. Another was built at South Lynn by Roger Sotheby in 1651 on corporation land, but destroyed by fire in 1737.

The sprinkling of 'sopeboylers' in the calendar of borough freemen shows that soap was made in Lynn in the 17th century in spite of a monopoly bought from Charles I by the London 'Society of Soapmakers'. Plentiful supplies of rapeseed oil and coal for the furnaces must have encouraged the industry. The ashes required were obtained by burning fern and other plants from nearby woodlands. The heavy excise duty imposed on soap in the 18th century failed to stifle the growth of the market for what was becoming a normal household product. In 1762 a soap-making partnership was agreed between Thomas Goddard of Lynn and William Rawson of Sutton in the Isle of Ely. Did the latter grow rape? Goddard had been a soapboiler for some time before 1762 and was able to contribute £400 to the £600 'capital stock' to launch the partnership. They may have sold their factory to Edward Cook, whose soap businesses at Norwich and Lynn were of some size about 1800. He specialised in high-quality products made from edible fats and ashes of plants gathered from the Mediterranean coast. Cook experimented with the discovery of the French chemist, Leblanc, who turned salt to soda ash as a raw material for soap-making, breaking the dependence on plants. Cook expanded his works at Lynn in the first two decades of the 19th century before moving to London.

Large-scale imports of tobacco from the Americas and Europe began in the early 17th century, and the habit of pipe smoking fell within the grasp of labouring people, to the disgust of parliament. The first reference to tobacco entering Norfolk is of imports to Lynn from Holland in 1612. Lynn merchants were importing large quantities by 1700. Smoking stimulated the manufacture of pipes, with clay shipped to Lynn from the south coast, and they were imported and exported. Surprisingly, only a handful of tobacco-pipe makers are recorded in the directories for 1822, 1836 and 1845, although two tobacco 'factories' are mentioned. According to Thew, the owner of the factory in St Ann's Street left Lynn after having difficulties with the excise authorities.

No physical remains of a glasshouse or factory have been found at Lynn, but pictorial and documentary evidence leaves no doubt about the manufacture of glass in the town. When James I sold Sir Robert Mansell a monopoly of English glassmaking in 1618, at least one of his 20 factories was at Lynn, using local sand and Newcastle coal. The Lynn glasshouse was closed in 1690 following heavy taxation on glass bottles, but it reopened when petitions for a reduction of the tax were successful. Just before these events Bell's 'Groundplat' showed a glasshouse in Pilot Street, by the River Gaywood, well sited for sand and coal boats. Bell's prospect of Lynn from the west about 1710 includes a second glass factory, with a domed roof, almost certainly that built in 1678 at Spinner Lane. It is also visible on Raistrick's map of 1725, when it had been converted into a Presbyterian chapel. There is no sign of the Pilot Street works on this map. The Lynn glass industry had probably been killed by competition from London and Newcastle.

Bellfounding in Lynn is recorded as early as anywhere, the name '*Magister Johannes Riston*', who was casting before 1300, appearing on a bell at Bexwell in Norfolk. Riston's foundry may have been taken over by John Goding, whose name is cast on a bell at Workington in Suffolk: '*Johannes Godynge de Lenne me fecit*' (John Goding of Lynn made me). This bell would have been transported up the Ouse and Lark. Other bellfounders were working in Lynn during the 14th century, notably the Bellyeteres, who continued making bells there until the 1440s. The craft was re-established in Lynn by Charles Newman of Norwich in the 1680s. At least 30 of the bells made by Newman survive in Norfolk.

White's Directory for 1845 describes Lynn thus: 'In the town are several large malthouses and breweries, two extensive cork-cutting establishments, a sacking manufactory, several rope and twine makers, a tobacco manufactory, three iron foundries, several millwrights, agricultural machine makers, etc.'. Burnett's *A Handbook of King's Lynn* of 1846 is less full, asking readers to be amazed by the 'fact' that the town's 'only manufactory' was the sack and matting establishment of Armes and Marsters. Burnett's rash generalisation about the absence of manufacturing industry does not detract from an important point, namely that the expansion of Lynn in the first half of the 19th century had been along traditional lines, corn and coal still remaining its staples. Building, brewing and marine enterprises had been promoted by this growth, but the town had failed to develop strong manufacturing industries despite its huge fuel imports, local raw materials and a hinterland as broad as that of any English port.

Medieval doorway in St Nicholas' Street.

Chapter Four

An English Market Town

Markets

That there were already weekly markets in the vicinity of the Saturday and Tuesday market-places by the early 12th century seems beyond doubt. Their growth must have been rapid: markets allowed farmers to feed an expanding urban society, which in turn encouraged them to produce more food for profit and to purchase manufactured goods. In 1289 there was a dispute involving the bishop of Norwich about a market held every day of the week 'except Tuesday' in the Saturday Market Place 'at Crosmarket near the Church of St Margaret'. On Tuesdays all trading was in the Tuesday Market Place, when 'strangers', or the farmers and merchants from outside Lynn, visited the town. The Saturday Market Place was likewise open to all on Saturdays. Commodities traded at the markets included wine, salt, fish, corn, cloth, household goods and livestock of all kinds.

The East Gate seems to have been the busiest gate, which may explain why the Tuesday Market Place was the location of the town's market cross by the later Middle Ages, rather than the smaller Saturday Market Place. In 1601 the corporation was talking about the need for a 'new market house' for 'the market folk' to be built around 'the conduit pool'. A new market cross was erected, the space inside being occupied by butchers, who used its shutters as stalls. The rebuilding of the western side of the Tuesday Market Place in 1620 was accompanied by the construction of new shambles for the butchers. Some booths built for butchers to the east of St Margaret's church in 1587 had been converted into permanent shops by the 1620s. Many other traders laid their goods out on the ground. In 1691 the corporation resolved 'to encourage all persons resorting to town to sell provision of victuals in public markets' and 'to prevent unjust exactions' by ordering market officials not to levy tolls for groundage if traders did without stalls, trestles, benches or seats.

The Saturday and Tuesday markets developed apace in the 18th century. Bell's elegant market cross of 1710 was a symbol of commercial prosperity. In 1738 Lynn's weekly markets were amongst the largest and most impressive in East Anglia if Mackerell is to be believed:

> The markets are very plentiful, having large supplies of fleshmeats, variety of fresh water and sea fish, poultry and wild-fowls of all sorts, which are brought here at reasonable rates, and those not only to supply the town, but all the country round about, who for the most part resort hither for what they want.

In 1752 the corporation was worried by the poor condition of the Tuesday Market Place and its lack of lighting since 'a great weekly concourse' of merchants and farmers 'transacting' all kinds of business used it.

The corporation's control of the East and South Gates reflected a desire to tax road traffic as much as concern over defence. Townspeople engaged in overland trade found this tax-gathering extremely irksome. In 1720 a petition from 'a great number' of Lynn's inhabitants complained against the tolls, arguing 'it was a great prejudice and discouragement to the trade thereof'. The corporation abolished the tolls soon after.

There was no bridge across the Ouse at Lynn until 1821, but this did not stop the farmers of West Lynn and Marshland bringing their produce across the river. In 1752 the corporation investigated complaints that Andrew Pigge, the ferryboat owner, was not providing a good service to the Marshland people bringing produce to market.

Improved road and river communications directed farmers and merchants to Lynn's markets to the detriment of its rivals. In 1771 Arthur Young found the smaller markets of Norfolk 'very inferior' to the big weekly events at Lynn, Yarmouth and Norwich. The rounded corners so characteristic of the lanes running from the town's riverside streets to the warehouses and yards by the Ouse are a legacy of the traffic in coal, timber, manure and corn. In 1830 Lynn was the destination for at least 55 carriers' carts and wagons every Tuesday and Saturday, full of women armed with big baskets of produce, bargain hunters and parcels for delivery and collection. Taverns were the busy stations for this carrier network, the *Maid's Head* and the *Angel* in the Tuesday Market Place being the most popular. The latter was demolished with Bell's market cross in 1830 to make way for Lynn's new market house, which had 42 shops for butchers alone.

Horses, cattle, sheep and pigs were all traded in Lynn's markets until 1806, when a beast market was opened just outside the South Gate. People complained that this site was too small, and a petition to the corporation from farmers and citizens asking for a stock market close to the town's corn market was accompanied by a subscription of over £1,300. A new cattle market on Paradise Field, near the Tuesday Market Place, was opened in November 1826. Expert observers reported four times the number of beasts sold there than at the old market. Every Tuesday thousands of cattle were driven to market through the town's narrow streets, already chock-a-block with carts and shoppers. The introduction of steamships encouraged the farmers of west Norfolk to send fatstock from Lynn to London.

Weekly markets were the mechanisms by which English urban populations were supplied with foodstuffs, so town governments were acutely aware of the need to draw farmers from the surrounding countryside to market. They were equally sensitive to the problems associated with making sure that supplies were openly and fairly distributed. Market-places were designed to do this. Buying and selling of food and other necessities at fixed times and regulated prices restricted the exploitation of the community for private profit. Forestalling, the purchasing of commodities before they were offered at the market, only to sell them at higher than normal prices there, was considered a betrayal of public trust, as bad as regrating, the buying up of food in the market for resale there.

Problems with the management of Lynn's markets litter the Hall Books of the corporation, always frustrated by the difficulties of this, its most critical task. In the 16th century brewers and farmers coming into the town on market days had their 'secret dealings' to raise prices suppressed by the mayor. He was a frequent visitor to the Common Staithe by the Ouse to fix the price of coal sold to the poor. Persons allowing livestock to wander about the Tuesday Market Place between 5 a.m. and 9 p.m. were fined 12d. Butchers and other trade groups were obliged to appoint wardens to inspect the stalls of their counterparts from 'the country' for quality.

The Court Leet, composed of richer householders, met every year to elect the constables and headboroughs who were the mayor's lieutenants on market days. Each of the town's 10 wards was represented by two headboroughs and a constable. Of the various public duties of the town's 20 headboroughs, the most dramatic was checking the weights and measures of shops, taverns and market people. Clashes with tradesmen were not infrequent. In 1656, for example, Francis Pratt obtained a verdict against the headborough Francis Whalley, whom he had sued for damages, but the corporation compensated its official. Headboroughs continued well into the 19th century. Thew talks about how they would 'pounce down' on old women selling butter in the markets to destroy false weights and confiscate stock.

Just as difficult was the collection of market tolls, an important source of borough revenue. In 1782 William Rollett was given an assistant to gather these dues because of 'the extraordinary trouble' the market traders were apparently causing. Rollett, the corporation's sergeant-at-mace, was also employed to ring the bell for the start and finish of market hours, for which he was paid £1 a year. Timekeeping was vital to the corporation's control of the markets. In 1623 two bells were bought to be set up in the market-places 'for the better orderinge of the same'. New bells were made for both market-places in 1657 to warn all 'hucksters' and 'higglers' against trading contrary to the 'publique good' by buying and reselling before and during markets before the bell was rung.

The greatest challenge to the town authorities was the tendency of traders to avoid the market-places altogether. In 1665 fruiterers were warned to sell in the market and not in the streets. In 1704 butchers and other traders 'resorting and coming' to Lynn on market days with corn, poultry, pigs, fish, butter, cheese, eggs, bacon and all other 'such like victuals' were told to expose their goods in 'open market' for sale, and not to be found 'hawking about the streets or in private houses', or be fined 1s. for each offence. The market officials were instructed to discover and prosecute anyone that 'buy up any such provisions' to sell again before the ringing of the market bell. Offenders were often tried by the mayor and magistrates at the Quarter Sessions in the Town Hall. In 1758 a waterman from Ely called Samuel Starkey was arrested for he did 'unjustly ingross' by buying up four score smelts from a Lynn fisherman, William Bouch, to sell up-river. Bouch was also in trouble for not bringing his catch to market. Thomas Cadman was a pigman who was convicted of regrating pork in the 'publick' Saturday Market Place and sentenced to two months' imprisonment.

Butchers were the greatest trouble-makers. In the 15th century they were frequently criticised for selling in the streets and private houses on Saturdays, and ordered to trade near St Margaret's church. Despite the provision of shambles the butchers were loath to make use of them. In 1661 there were 22 booths in the Saturday Market Place and 30 in the Tuesday. To avoid paying extra for renting these shambles most butchers followed the example of other traders and set up their own stalls, though in 1677 this was forbidden unless the shambles were full. In 1690 the butchers were forcefully reminded by the corporation that they should sell meat in the stalls and shambles provided on market days, not in private houses and on the streets 'contrary to the ancient custom and government of the said burgh', besides being accused of having sold 'unwholesome and bad meat'. They were fined 5s. for each offence. In 1702 the market officials were ordered to execute Lynn's by-laws against butchers more strictly. When the new shambles opened in the Saturday

19. The Tuesday Market Place about 1800, with Henry Bell's Market Cross and the butchers' shambles on either side of it. The second building from the left is the *Angel Inn*, much frequented by market folk.

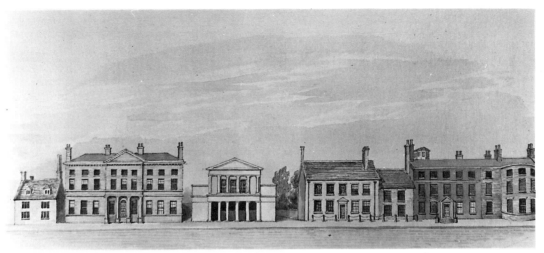

20. This drawing by W. Taylor in 1842 features the Market House of 1830 on the west side of the Tuesday Market Place. The house with the look-out for watching ships (far right) was the Lynn mansion of the Bagges. George Hogge erected the other mansion (left) in 1768 after the destruction by fire of Charles Turner's house. Its façade was rebuilt in the 1950s and Barclay's Bank occupies it today.

Market Place in 1779 for 35 butchers (21 from Lynn and 14 from 'the country') most were reluctant to enter the building.

Fishermen granted licences were expected to feed the townspeople as cheaply and quickly as possible every day of the working week. This meant going to market. In the 16th century Lynn fishermen were often accused of colluding with Dutchmen and other 'strangers' to regrate and forestall herring and salmon. Seals were also eaten. In 1650 the mariners of Lynn petitioned the corporation against 'strangers' landing seals and selling at exorbitant prices to local dealers. They wanted the mayor to fix the prices. In 1666 the fishermen were instructed to use the stalls to the north of the market cross. In 1735 the corporation reminded fishmongers to sell first in the Tuesday Market Place for four hours, Monday to Friday. In 1752 fishermen were admonished for not exposing oysters at market for one hour before selling them on the streets 'as hath been accustomed'.

Fairs
In 1204 King John's charter made no mention of fairs because these had already been granted to the lord of the town, Bishop de Grey of Norwich. To him the monarch had confirmed the rights to two annual fairs of 15 days each. One was held six days each side of the feast of St Margaret (20 July) in the Saturday Market Place. The fair in Damgate, or Norfolk Street, near the Tuesday Market Place, began on the feast of St Nicholas (20 August) and partly belonged to the Earls of Arundel. The dates of both fairs were changed. In the reign of Henry IV the fair in the Saturday Market Place was moved from 20 July to 1 August, to avoid competition with the big fair at Boston in Lincolnshire. Damgate's fair was changed from August to February in the reign of Edward IV for similar reasons.

Fairs were vital links in medieval England's economic chain. Those held in or near large towns and accessible by sea or river transport, cheaper and sometimes faster and safer than road travel, particularly attracted traders. St Bartholomew's in London, Sturbridge near Cambridge, Ely, St Ives, Boston and Lynn all hosted thriving fairs because of being near

21. An aerial view of the Saturday Market Place, the scene of one of Lynn's fairs in the Middle Ages. The quadrangular complexes of Hampton Court (top left), Hanseatic Warehouse (adjacent) and Thoresby College (top middle right) are clear. The long, large building immediately below Thoresby College is the Trinity Gildhall, much extended by the Assembly Rooms built in 1767. St Margaret's

sea or inland ports serving England's rich eastern counties. English and European merchants mingled with the great lay and ecclesiastical landowners of the Fens. In the 15th century the senior nuns of St Radegund's convent, near Cambridge, and their retainers made boat trips to Lynn every year to stock up with household goods. Salt, fish, wine, spices, furs, wool, cloth, armour, jewels, pitch, timber, millstones and horses were bought and sold by barter as well as with money.

Fairs provided merchants with the opportunity to collect or pay debts accrued over previous years. Fenland sheep farmers received payment for their wool from Flemish and English cloth manufacturers at Lynn. Lynn's traders sailed up-river to fairs like St Ives and Sturbridge, where Cambridge men turned awkward in 1510 over the tolls paid by 'strangers' for mooring their boats. Rivalries were sharp, yet men from Cambridge and elsewhere in the eastern counties owned properties at Lynn because of the advantages of a foothold in the Wash port. During the town's fairs 'foreign' merchants, i.e. those not free of the borough, could trade without the restrictions imposed on them by the town's rulers at other times.

When a chronicler of current events called William de Newburgh described Lynn about 1190 as '*urbs commeatu et commerciis noblis*' its two fairs may have loomed large in his mind. Something of the significance of the town's medieval fairs can be appreciated from the fact that the king sent agents there to buy falcons, furs and wines. Fairs must have given Lynn's economy a tremendous boost as shops and taverns benefited from the thousands of visitors. To settle the disputes which were bound to arise at fairs the Court of Piepowder was established to administer summary justice, for visitors could not wait weeks for legal proceedings to finish ('piepowder' is an English corruption of the French term '*pieds poudreux*', referring to the dusty feet of travellers). At Lynn the piepowder court was in the hands of the bishops of Norwich before the 1520s, whose stewards proclaimed the opening and closing of the fairs.

When the lordship of the town was transferred from the bishops to the corporation by Act of Parliament in 1537, the fairs were not forgotten. The corporation was given the right to hold a fair on 3 February, the day after the feast of the 'Purification of the Blessed Virgin', and on 16 August, the day after the feast of the 'Assumption of the Blessed Virgin', together with tolls and other profits, including management of the piepowder court. All shops not hired by traders were to be closed during the six days of activity at each fair.

Neither of Lynn's fairs was held in 1540 because of plague. Worse followed: in 1541 an Act of Parliament inspired by the merchants of Cambridge and Ely suppressed both the town's fairs on the grounds that others in the eastern counties had been harmed. Too much 'saltfish' and herring was bought up by Lynn men. Despite the corporation's decision not 'to sue' the crown for the return of its fairs, because of their unprofitability, the loss was a dent to civic and commercial pride. An act of 1559 restored the February fair after the corporation petitioned the crown to repeal the act of 1541. From this time, if not before, it became normal at Lynn to talk of 'the mart' rather than 'the fair'.

By the 1560s the whole length of Norfolk Street from the Tuesday Market Place to the East Gate was taken by traders who rented shops, booths and stalls. In his *Description of England* of 1577, Harrison compares 'Lin Mart' with St Bart's in London and Sturbridge, near Cambridge, both amongst Europe's greatest fairs. Naturally, criminals found the mart irresistible. In January 1565 the sheriff of Norfolk was informed of 'the sundry suspicious and lewde disposed persons' who 'be cutte purses and notable thieves' planning 'to meete at Lynne Mart'. To counter these gangs the corporation employed 12 male residents of local almshouses to patrol the mart, dressed in scarlet coats blazoned with the town arms and carrying heavy staves. Other safeguards besides this aged police force were needed, and during the 1640s the corporation posted armed men at East and South Gates, and in the riverside lanes, to keep out 'rogues' and 'vagabonds' trying to enter Lynn at mart time.

The corporation milked the mart. In 1609 stalls were let to 'strangers' at 12d. a foot and to borough freemen at 6d., while unfree locals paid 8d. Butchers and fishmongers who rented shambles in the Tuesday Market Place were obliged to vacate them for the use of others. Collecting the tolls from the holders of all these booths was a perennial headache. Hall Books for the 17th century are peppered with complaints against traders who had failed or refused to pay tolls during the mart. Booths were refused to men in arrears. In 1650 the chamberlain was ordered 'to pull up' the stalls of men who had not paid tolls, and to let the space to others. Occupiers of shops in the Tuesday Market Place were also supposed to pay the corporation 3s. 4d. in the pound from rents received in February. Not surprisingly, town officials experienced difficulty collecting the money, and in 1653 and 1672 the Town Hall determined to build stalls against these shops if tolls were refused.

Rent books provide good insights into the character of the mart. Three examples span a vital period: 1659, 1719 and 1788. Drapers, clothiers, mercers, glovers and nailers were easily the best represented in the Tuesday Market Place over these 130 years. Chapmen and goldsmiths were mentioned in 1659, and chairmakers, cutlers, potters, weavers, haberdashers, upholsterers, ironmongers, spicers and tobacco sellers were among the other traders present. In 1670 the linen-drapers were ordered to sell their linen and cloths 'wholesail' on the Common Staithe, to the west of the market-place; a similar directive had been issued in 1605 and the corporation was considering moving the whole mart there, though the shopkeepers would doubtless have objected. This riverside location was used only in 1681.

How much did the mart tolls bring the corporation? It collected about £70 in 1659 and 1719, £5 going to pay the 12 aged redcoats (only seven were recorded in 1659). In 1788, however, the corporation collected only £45, the rental of 29 booths accounting for almost all of it. Stalls and tables numbered a mere 35 this year, and only seven shops were let. Improvements in road and river travel made annual fairs less important as trading bonanzas. Only Sturbridge Fair, outside Cambridge, was something of an exception. Daniel Defoe visited it in the 1720s and described it as not only the greatest in 'the whole nation' but in 'the world'. Lynn benefited as much of the merchandise was transported by water through the port, enormous amounts of cheese passing up-river, as disputes over tolls tell, and huge quantities of hops and wool sent downstream. Lynn merchants were amongst the traders: Samuel Browne, for example, was elected mayor of Lynn on 29 August 1741, only to die on business at 'Stirbich' on 16 September.

In 1750 the corporation decided to reduce the mart from its traditional 12 days to six. It was not finished as a commercial event, Jonas Phillips of Norwich with his 'show booth' of glass products, for example, was a regular visitor in the 1750s, yet the spotlight in the regional press on mart entertainments was significant. Typically, in 1757 the public was alerted to the forthcoming appearance of James Hilton of Bedford, with 150 tricks of 'dexterity of hands', using rings, jewels and cards. In 1795 the *Norfolk Journal* reported that the mart was 'much resorted to by the genteel company' of the county, but the tradesmen who came to the fair were 'not half so numerous as they were 30 years since'. The economic role of the mart declined in the lifetime of William Richards, who described it in 1812 as 'but a shadow of what it was formerly'. William Armes, however, credits it with more commercial clout. He claimed that the merchandise available there 'far exceeded' anything in the High Street shops. Booths run by Nottingham traders were 'thronged' by country girls wanting new shoes. Linen, cloth, furs and hats were other popular buys. The February mart launched the new spring fashions. Armes records other interesting facts such as the four squat Jews clad in cloaks and turbans who patrolled the entrances to the Tuesday

Market Place selling stationery. The 12 mart guards were still to be found in the Market Cross, sipping hot purl or porter from the nearby *Angel Inn*.

The Lynn mart declined sharply in the 1820s. *The General History of the County of Norfolk* (1829) carried this comment:

> Like most establishments of this nature, it is no longer attended for the purpose it was first granted, business having yielded to pleasure and amusement. Formerly Lynn Mart and Sturbridge (Sturbitch) fair, were the only places where small traders in this, and in the adjoining counties, supplied themselves with their respective goods. No transactions of this nature now take place, and the only remains to be perceived are the 'mart prices', still used by grocers. Here the thrifty housewives for twenty miles around, laid in their annual store of soap, starch, etc. and the booth of 'Green' from Limehouse, was for three generations the emporium of such articles, but these no longer attend.

All the East Anglian fairs were rapidly losing their commercial *raison d'être* by the 1840s. The Norwich newspapers reported the transformation of Lynn mart from one of England's great trading fairs to a 'pleasure fair', bazaars replacing booths. Show-folk and the entertainment on offer each February were the subject of articles in the new *Lynn Advertiser*.

Another fair, the Cheese Fair, was held in October to supply town and country folk with winter stocks of cheese, butter, potatoes, onions, apples and fish. King Street and the Purfleet quay accommodated the stalls. Special dinners, with roast pork and apple sauce on the menu, were taken at noon in local taverns to celebrate the fair's opening. In 1812 Richards judged the fair to be 'insignificant', but Norwich newspapers for 1830 described trade as 'brisk'. Not until later did Lynn's papers campaign for its abolition because of its lurid sideshows and roundabouts. In 1878 the *Lynn Advertiser* reported that the fair had 'gone at last', 'the substantial piles' of Leicestershire cheese of 'yesteryear' having long been displaced by stewed peas, boiled peas, mussels, whelks and similar food.

The growing number of beasts passing through Lynn in the 1830s and 1840s was the mainspring for two new cattle fairs held at the Broad Street market in April and November. Increasing numbers of cattle were being driven into East Anglia from the north for fattening and sale in the bigger urban markets, Lynn being the 'gateway' to the region.

Shops

Shops of all kinds could be found on the streets of medieval Lynn. High Street from the Purfleet to the Tuesday Market Place was the home of tradesmen selling luxury goods, as the label 'Mercer Row' tells. 'Cook Row' was the name given to the northern end. Here was a concentration of caterers kept busy on market days. 'Grassmarket' ran from the south-east corner of the market-place to Broad Street, or 'Webster Row', before continuing as 'Damgate' to the East Gate. Tailors, drapers and haberdashers had shops along this long street. The nibbling away of the southern and eastern sides of the Tuesday Market Place was probably through temporary booths becoming permanent shops. Other shops appear to have been purpose-built for retailers, without any connection to houses, but with solars, or rooms, above each for storage. The Red Register in 1349 mentions 11 shops with solars in High Street.

Bad food and merchandise were as damaging to the community as forestalling and regrating. Entries in the Hall Books of the 15th and 16th centuries strongly suggest that trade groups were incapable or unwilling to exercise quality controls. Lynn's merchant rulers attempted, therefore, to impose by-laws on craftsmen whose sense of public responsibility was perceived as inadequate or subordinate to self-interest. All master craftsmen were instructed to present their new apprentices to the common council sitting at the Trinity Gildhall, to enrol their indentures there, and to return seven years later to swear them in as freemen of the borough. Wage rates, hours of work and retail prices were of equal concern as this training period. After the passing of the Statute of Artificers in 1563 the wages, working hours and length of apprenticeship of craftsmen were all fixed by the borough magistrates on behalf of the crown. The Tudor state itself had stepped in.

The recovery of Lynn's economy after 1560 is revealed by the number of immigrant craftsmen of inferior skill setting up business without permission in, for example, tailoring, blacksmithing and locksmithing. The corporation took action. The carpenters were instructed to elect two wardens or headsmen to inspect the work of colleagues and see that each had sufficient 'cunning and ability'. Shoemaking in particular attracted unlicensed men. In 1565 'the whole company' (i.e. the trade gild) of shoemakers was told to assemble every November to elect two wardens or headsmen to be sworn before the mayor and report to him on the state of the trade. 'Foreigners' or 'strangers' were sometimes allowed to become shoemakers: Jewish, Scottish and Dutch cordwainers are all recorded.

Parker has shown how the merchants of Tudor and Stuart Lynn abandoned the retail trade to others, becoming wholesalers first and foremost. Their new houses were without shops. This process was gradual, however. Thomas Sandell kept a shop at his St Nicholas' Street mansion when Sir Walter Raleigh visited him in 1589, and his neighbours did likewise. Retailing was important to the Revetts and other merchant families in the Tuesday Market Place in the early 17th century. Merchants were still building shops if not running them in 1650, when an alderman was given permission by his peers to let the shop recently erected at the west end of his house.

Efforts by the corporation to separate the activities of various tradesmen are indicative of the process of economic specialisation at work. As early as the 1560s neither chandlers nor fishmongers were allowed to operate as grocers, mercers or haberdashers, who were forbidden to sell 'the things which appertain' to chandlers or fishmongers. For each month any shopkeeper disobeyed he was liable to a £5 fine.

In the 17th century the corporation was anxious about the number of shopkeepers and artisans who were not burgesses, because of the loss of revenue as much as a determination to control quality. Tradesmen who failed to become freemen were subject to tours of inspection by aldermen. Their shops were ordered to be shut up in 1612, 1683, 1702, 1709 and 1714. The local and national statutes designed to regulate the life and labour of artisans were increasingly ignored in the course of the 18th century, however. Urban commercial activity was slowly abandoned to market forces.

The corporation did not merely police Lynn's tradesmen. The Hall Books contain many examples of loans and gifts to shopkeepers in difficulties from the charitable funds it held. In 1727, for example, 25s. was lent free of interest to a Lynn shoemaker who was given security by a Downham currier and a Wormegay tanner. A corporation shop at Ladybridge, over the Millfleet, was let free to another shoemaker if the bridge and common privy there were kept clean. In 1739 Benjamin Tilson, barber and peruke maker, was paid £5 by the chamberlain to furnish materials for a shop as soon as one was hired. Alderman Browne was to supervise the 'laying out' of the shop and the purchase of the 'proper materials'.

In the 18th century large and fashionable shops were rebuilt in the High Street by a wide range of tradesmen, and patronised by merchants and gentry. Big barrel-shaped windows of many panes fronted spacious interiors full of merchandise. Superior shopkeepers used the Norfolk newspapers to advertise their wares, like the upholsterer in 1752 who had acquired a new stock of wallpaper. Warehouses, or emporiums, were also opened by Norwich and London merchants, whose expensive linens, carpets, glass, teas, coffees, chocolates and hats attracted the town's rich. In 1765 a grocer called Thomas Sommersby was cajoled by a certain Elizabeth Brown into making up a spurious order of sugar, currants, raisins, tea, soap, starch, blueing, nutmegs, coffee and green tea. Other cases in the Quarter Session books tell of the temptation of shop-lifting. At the other end of the scale were hawkers and pedlars, 'cart-shopkeepers' free of local tax and rent burdens who could sell at 'knock down' prices, injuring the trade of the shopkeepers. In 1772 the borough's two M.P.s were requested to vote for the 'total suppression' of hawkers and pedlars because they were damaging 'to the country in general and to this town in particular'.

William Armes reminisced in 1864 on the retailing reformation that had unfolded in Lynn over half a century:

> I stay not, therefore, to remark upon the old tradesmen — the 'Rodwells', 'Gales', 'Andrews' etc. — of the former time; or upon the quaint old shop fronts of these venerable men, now displaced by sheet upon sheet of plate glass along the High Street; nor upon the manner in which, because of the competition of the Mart, they published 'Mart Prices', as they were called, some 15 per cent below the ordinary rate, nor how the foolish public were gammoned by these venerable tradesmen, not seeing that reduction in February meant imposition all the year beside. But, I suppose neither shopmen or public much troubled then about 'Adam Smith' or 'Political Economy'. The old shopkeepers were, indeed, a right jolly lot. They read from the old text — that 'who so maketh haste to be rich shall hardly be innocent'; *and they were in no hurry.* They measured time in a philosophical way, and 'took no anxious thought for the morrow'. No bustle or hurry then; and possibly, if some of our fizzing, fussing, steaming modern men had to go now and then and take a turn amongst the customers in one of those old shops, they would come out wiser, at all events, *more patient men.*

Most successful retailers tended to retire from trade after having amassed small fortunes, though others took shops in larger towns, hoping for still greater pickings. Commercial premises in Lynn's main shopping streets were soon sold. Thew observed in 1891 that he had seen every shop in the High Street change hands save his own property on the corner of the Saturday Market Place, the home of the *Lynn Advertiser*, started by his father in 1841. The larger shopkeepers eagerly bought advertising space in newspapers to tell the public about 'entire' new fronts and interiors to their premises. The spread of plate glass and ugly upper storeys in Lynn's main shopping streets appalled members of the 'Conversazione and Society of Arts'. Nevertheless traditional interests were still exercised by the larger shopkeepers, who employed several assistants and apprentices. Butchers often slaughtered their own meat. Bakers made confectionery and sold flour as well as bread. Blending, weighing and labelling teas and coffees, besides candlemaking and curing bacon, were amongst the daily tasks of the grocer. These substantial tradesmen, who supplied small shopkeepers wholesale, prided themselves on their various skills or 'trades', which were given separate entries in commercial directories — the same grocer is often listed under 'tea dealers', 'cheesemongers' and 'tallow chandlers'. Makers of clothes, hats, shoes, jewellery, clocks, furniture, baskets, brushes, saddles, guns, umbrellas, ironmongery and medicines still feature in the directories of the 1830s and 1840s. Of the 3,035 families living in Lynn in 1831, over half were classified by the census as being in trade, handicraft and manufacture, emphasising how towns were largely still self-sufficient.

The larger tradesmen (they did not like the term 'shopkeeper') depended on the custom of the urban and rural gentry, rather than the lower classes, who went to the markets or neighbourhood shops. Sidelines helped to attract more custom. James Burch sold tickets for the London stage coaches from his High Street tailoring shop, attracting farmers and tradesmen to his business, and he was manager of the Lynn Savings Bank, too. Quality as much as price was a key factor. Coulton's memories throw light on the shopping habits of the middle class in the 19th century. Sugar and most other daily items were purchased 'literally next door' to his family's house in St James' Street. Candles and kitchen soap were bought at another grocer's in the same street, whose weekly tallow boilings 'infected the whole town with their odour'. The young Coulton and his mother then turned sharply at St Margaret's church into the High Street to visit 'the principal' grocer of the town. His window was 'a grand show' full of cheeses and bacons, raisins and citron peel and boxes of crackers at Christmas. Two or three 'great cheeses' were tasted by the Coultons. Summertime trips to the fruiterers were considered a treat by the boy because of 'as rich a show as any in England', made possible by the Fenland soil.

When Queen Victoria came to the throne in 1837, however, most of Lynn's retail outlets were small affairs, almost all located in the minor streets of the town. *White's Directory* for 1845 records over 50 'shopkeepers', who sold 'grocery' and other necessities. Poor people needing provisions were given credit in times of distress to retain their custom when times improved, yet economic slumps killed off small shops. Of the 46 'shopkeepers' registered in *White's Directory* in 1836, only 13 of the names recur in the directory for 1845. The terrible winter and unemployment of 1841-2 must have taken a heavy toll. High Street tradesmen serving the rich enjoyed a much better survival rate.

Banks

English kings in the Middle Ages used native and foreign merchants as bankers. Vast sums were borrowed to finance war and administration in return for the farm of the wool and other customs. Lynn capitalists were involved in this financial system, as we have seen in the case of the Melchbourne brothers and John Weasenham, leading bankers to Edward III (*see* Chapter Two). Such men must have advanced credit to those who bought wholesale from them. Lynn's 'Great Gild' of the Holy Trinity appears to have made loans to members requiring commercial support. Others procured loans from goldsmiths, who often acted as bankers. Precious metals and plate were 'bought' by the lenders from the borrowers below cost price and retained as pledges to be redeemed at the true value, thus 'avoiding' the illicit payment of interest, or usury. Richards wrote in 1812:

> A considerable body of Jews also had settled here, and must have been among the most active and useful part of the population; which further corroborates the report of its [Lynn] being in those days a place of no small commercial note and consequence, for those people were not likely to settle in any great numbers, except in places of that description.

Unfortunately we know little about the activities of these Lynn Jews, although probably most were pawnbrokers, free from the Christian prohibition against usury to lend money on the security of corn, wool, cloth, wine, leather, jewellery, armour or other property. Churchmen felt no guilt about borrowing from the Jews. Of the debts legally accruing to the crown after the death of a Lynn Jew in the '*incendo de Lenna*' of 1190, a pogrom, one was unsuccessfully demanded from the prior of St Margaret's.

Banking did not change its character overmuch between 1500 and 1800; wealthy merchants and lawyers lent money to all who could afford their rates of interest. Lynn corporation also used its various charitable funds to support local tradesmen with small, but vital, short-term loans. It was itself forced into borrowing far more, however, on the security of its income from tolls and taxes. To fund turnpike and other building projects, the corporation often advertised in London newspapers, offering annuities for loans. Money was also advanced by the merchants of Lynn to cover the corporation's urgent bills, such as the wages of workmen engaged on civic building. In 1769 the 'Society of Shipmasters' in Lynn loaned the corporation £300 at four-and-a-half per cent interest.

The flow of credit from Lynn merchants to smaller capitalists and customers to fuel business life in town and country was important. When Samuel Browne's commercial empire was being managed by his trustees in the late 1780s, banking affairs were a high priority. Over £18,400 was owed to Browne by borrowers at his death in 1784. Of this total £6,600 was owed by William and Thomas Bagge, and £2,300 by his brother Scarlet. Another £2,000 was due from Joseph Hart of Cambridge, who wrote to Philip Case, Browne's father-in-law, in 1789 to suggest that the five per cent interest on the loan was too much in view of his 'long connection in trade' with Browne, and to ask for 'a little consideration' to be shown under 'the circumstances' by reduction of the rate to four and a half per cent. Most

22. The Lynn Bank was opened in 1782 in this fine house on King Staithe Square. The counting house built in 1789 is to the right.

23. The door of 27 King Street, a house remodelled in the 1730s. Bagge and Bacon sold their bank here to Everard and Blencowe in 1826.

of Browne's debtors were small businessmen. Between March 1785 and January 1789 the interest on the loans made by Samuel amounted to £6,530.

The absence of formal banking facilities at Lynn was obviously a bottleneck in its commercial development, and the Gurneys of Norwich joined in partnership with John Birkbeck of Yorkshire to break it. They started a bank in a fine house on King Staithe Square in 1782. It was saved from a panic or 'run' in 1809 by the Bagges, who stood behind the counter with Daniel Gurney until Mr. Cresswell returned from London by post-chaise with gold. There were branches at Swaffham and Fakenham, which branch alone issued £70,000 in £5 and £10 notes in 1815. How the bank worked in the early decades of the 19th century is best appreciated from what its official historian wrote:

> In those days the clearing between the various banks was a matter of considerable difficulty and expense. There were few cheques, and business transactions were generally settled by means of local notes. The clearing for Norwich, Lynn, Swaffham and Fakenham took place once a week at Houghton, a small village near the seat of the Walpoles, as being the most convenient centre, where the messengers arrived on horseback. The old saddlebags used on these occasions were for a long time preserved at the Lynn Bank, and tales were handed down of the adventures of these 'clearing clerks' of bygone days. One, it was said, took an involuntary part in a fox hunt; another dropped his bridle in opening a gate, and had a chase of another kind across country; while alarms of highwaymen entered much into these recitals.

Swaffham was later chosen as the place for 'the clearing', clerks making the journey by stage coach rather than horseback.

Other Lynn merchants extended their interests into banking. In 1814 William and Thomas Bagge took over the bank founded by Audley and Fydell in 1796. Bagge and Bacon's Bank traded from 27 King Street. In 1826 John Prescott Blencowe and five members of the Everard family raised £6,057 to buy it. The partners agreed to make the provision of credit dependent on the approval of all, to keep their wine business completely separate from the bank, and to employ their sons in the counting house as apprentices. In 1845 'Gurney' and 'Everards' faced competition from two more banks, operating from the Tuesday Market Place: 'The East of England' and 'Massey and Jarvis'.

Market woman, 1818, with poultry
basket.

Chapter Five

The Merchants of Lynn

Merchants and gildsmen

Who were the first merchants of Lynn? Probably the men of Gaywood and other West Norfolk townships trading with the merchants who sailed into 'the Lin'. The locative names of 12th-century migrants show arrivals from all those eastern counties served by waterways emptying into the Wash. Maritime connections were also important, however. 'William of Yarmouth' was settled at Lynn by 1150. Traders from Southwold, Bury, Yaxley, Wisbech, Ely, Cambridge and even London established bases in Lynn to share its salt, wool and corn traffic, and Lynn's expansion attracted European merchants, such as John Lestris, from the Baltic, who lived in the town about 1150. Scandinavian names were common enough before 1200 to suggest immigration. Ports in Friesland and at the mouth of the Rhine not only traded with Lynn, but sent settlers, while merchants from Beauvais and other northern French towns were among Lynn's cosmopolitan upper class in medieval times, and John de Ispania was mayor in 1280 and 1282.

Lynn's commercial élite remained fluid throughout the Middle Ages. Between 1342 and 1392, for example, under half the merchants obtaining the freedom of the borough did so by paternity rather than apprenticeship or gift. Lynn merchants also migrated up-river, to develop enterprises in market centres like Yaxley, Ely and Cambridge. London exerted the strongest pull; in the period 1310-1427 at least 16 Lynn merchants finished careers as lord mayor of that city. Others found it advantageous to become almost permanent residents in other European ports. One of Margery Kempe's sons, for example, appears to have settled in Danzig, and Bergen had a small colony of Lynn merchants heavily involved in the fish trade.

The survival of the Red Register, in particular, has permitted the social history of Lynn's medieval merchants to be studied. Dr. Beauroy has thoroughly researched 125 local wills recorded for the years 1276-1429, of which 12 belonged to mayors of the town. The Black Death seems to have accounted for the deaths of 18 of these people. Most of the testators were married men. Their families were closely knit and small, with an average of 2.4 children recorded. Sons were their fathers' favourites — Peter Melchbourne was probably not alone in asking God's help for a male heir! Wives received custody of their sons only as long as they remained unmarried; if a widow remarried they were to become wards of others. Clerics were often chosen to serve as executors with a member of the family circle. Most real estate was bequeathed to wives and sons. In 1307, for example, John Ode left everything to his three sons and four daughters after their mother's death, but the girls were excluded from houses, shops and land, having to make do with annual rents of 20 or 25s. Sons also received their father's armour and swords. Those who opted out of the counting house and became friars still received support: in 1312 John Lambert's will provided for his Dominican son Nicholas to be paid an annual rent of 20s. for clothing. Other legatees were grandchildren, nephews, nieces and what may be poorer relatives, while servants were also beneficiaries. In 1348, for example, Helen Attadurss transferred to her son the property her master had left her.

The nuclear family was typical of merchant households in Lynn rather than the extended one including parents, aunts and other relatives. Did female partners enjoy equal status? How many marriages were love matches? Husbands bequeathed wives their most cherished

24. Walter Coney's house, in the Saturday Market Place, was built about 1450 and demolished in 1816.

possessions, the silver Griffin's egg on an stand left by Peter Melchbourne being one of the most remarkable. Money was also allocated for the education of children, often giving elder brothers and sisters a supervisory role. There is no mention of *who* the educators were, but perhaps they were friars. The wills are also fruitful sources for those interested in reconstructing the merchants' lifestyle. Jewels, silver, furs, silks, robes and fine furniture like feather beds bequeathed to relatives and servants testify to its luxury. It depended, of course, on the import and export trade of one of England's leading seaports, revealed in the wills by references to warehouses, tenements, quays and shops, although they are strangely silent about ships.

More Flemish brasses illustrating the fame and riches of departed merchants would help us flesh out the documentary evidence. St Margaret's church was once full of them, but most have been destroyed by Puritans and others like the sexton who, in about 1808, sold brasses to a brazier and on discovery hanged himself in the belfry. Only two brasses remain. One shows Robert Braunche (d. 1364) and his two wives seated at a feast where peacock, 'the food of lovers and the meat of lords', is being served to a royal guest. The other brass portrays Adam Walsoken (d. 1349) and his wife Margaret amidst a vintage harvest. It symbolises the great wealth generated for the merchants of Lynn by the wine trade between the Wash and France. Its extent influenced Walter Rye to represent Geoffrey Chaucer as a Lynn man. The poet's father was one of the king's butlers and closely connected with the Lynn vintner John Weasenham.

The public lives of the merchants were, before 1550, channelled through their gilds. Richards, writing in 1812 with access to records now lost, is an essential guide to these all-pervasive corporations. He identified five 'merchant' gilds in Lynn. The gild of St William brought together those trading with Scandinavia, and in particular Bergen. Others belonged to the gild of St Giles and St Julian, closely attached to St James' chapel. The Corpus Christi and St George's gilds both built halls in King Street, not far from St Nicholas' chapel. The oldest and most important was the Holy Trinity or 'Great Gild', which was the gild merchant of Lynn. Its fine hall of the 1420s in the Saturday Market Place remains the civic centre of the borough.

The Great Gild was already in existence in 1204, when its part in town government was confirmed by King John and Bishop de Grey. Merchants could enrol only by paying a 100s. entry fee, but sons of gildsmen claiming right of entry by paternity paid a mere 4s. Others joined this band of privileged citizens by completing an apprenticeship of seven years. Women were allowed associate membership. The famous Margery Kempe joined it in 1420.

New members were expected to parade before the gildsmen in their finest clothes, topped by a gold or silver circlet. The assembly elected officers annually. The alderman was chosen first. He picked four colleagues to elect eight others to form a jury or governing body of 12 men. They appointed assistants, of whom the four bailiffs were most important, followed by the dean, or activities manager. A clerk kept records. Disciplinary matters loomed large in the life of the gild, as the number of written rules for regulating conduct tell. Members in hall could be fined for a variety of offences, including the disclosure of secrets, foul language, being late, improper dress and drunkenness. They suggest that the standards of behaviour of Lynn's upper crust left a lot to be desired.

The Great Gild was a Christian body whose members felt a heavy obligation towards the town's poor. Its charitable plans were discussed at a morwespech, or meeting, in the first week of Lent, and about £30 was spent each year. The blind, disabled, lepers, mendicant friars and 'poor' clerks running schools were all given aid. Shoes, bread and money were distributed among the poor whenever there was a funeral of a gildsman. The gild may have maintained almshouses for the aged poor; the gild of St Giles and St Julian provided two almshouses near St James' chapel, one for men and one for women. Richards contrasted this kind of philanthropy with the parsimony of the merchants of Lynn in 1812.

Lynn's merchants also made substantial contributions to the fabric of St Margaret's church and its two chapels of St James and St Nicholas. The Great Gild supported 13 chaplains to pray for the souls of departed brethren in these places, a most serious business, for neglect of duty warranted the dismissal of the priest. The gild also supplied most of the costly wax candles required to light the buildings. The death of a gildsman was attended with an elaborate torch-lit funeral, all members being in the cortège. Their chaplains were obliged to say 30 masses for the deceased brother. In 1391 the bells of St Margaret's were silenced because of the unsafe condition of the north-west tower — save for the funerals of gildsmen! Every Trinity Sunday a requiem mass was sung for the ancestors of the king and all past aldermen, members and benefactors of the gild.

Tudor and Stuart merchants

Battley has examined the character and activities of an important English urban élite by studying 67 men who held mayoral office at Lynn between 1500 and 1603. She emphasises how the throwing off of the yoke of the bishops of Norwich and the acquisition of local monastic lands in the 1530s strengthened their position, largely thanks to the state policy of Henry VIII: 'The history of Lynn's civic élite is essentially a history of appropriation'. Its membership was clarified by a by-law in 1547 when a sharp distinction was made between 'merchants', who 'adventured' overseas by ship and traded wholesale, and mere shopkeepers and middlemen.

Most of the 67 mayors studied by Battley died (at an average age of 55) before their wives, who were allowed to enjoy their former comforts and security as long as they remained unmarried. Thus in 1549 Edward Baker bequeathed his wife a house, two gardens, a tenement, a warehouse, household goods, shares in three ships, £100 in cash and permission to use a stable stall 'for her friends when they come to her'. The bulk of a father's property, however, passed to his son and heir rather than to wives or other children. There was one critical break with the medieval past: public bequests were secular in character. Before the Reformation the churches and monasteries of Lynn and West Norfolk received substantial gifts of land, plate, vestments and money. Chantries were endowed. But after Henry VIII had stripped the Church of its wealth and social role the merchants of Lynn directed bigger bequests towards charitable schemes for the upkeep of the poor.

Metters' investigation of 123 merchants and rulers of Lynn between 1591 and 1640 shows that nearly all were migrants to the Wash port. Widows, sisters and daughters of fellow traders were their marriage partners. Rapid rises in town-hall political life, from freeman to councillor to alderman, often followed by elections to the mayoralty and to parliament, run through the most impressive biographies. Some families acquired professional status by becoming collectors of customs for the crown or lawyers, profiting from the growing volume of paperwork in private and public affairs. Education for sons was consequently of great importance. Money was also invested in country estates in the search for gentlemanly status. Because brewing and property were as fruitful sources of income as trade for many men, the label 'merchant' should be treated with caution. Yet Metters shows that the most dynamic families were almost always traders and shipowners who grew fat on imports and exports of corn, coal, wine and luxury goods.

These Lynn merchants were fleeting figures. Families 'disappeared' almost as soon as they reached the top of the urban tree. Those who benefited from the Dissolution of the Monasteries and full independence from the bishops, the Ampfles, Guytons, Millers, Peppers and Waters, must have been among the richest of English townsmen in the 1530s, but by the 1580s another oligarchy was installed, of whom the most outstanding were the Atkins, Bakers, Snellings, and Slaneys. John Wallis was the most notable Jacobean merchant of Lynn. Probably a Cambridge man apprenticed to a Lynn merchant called John Nelson in 1591, he was apparently launched on his dazzling career by marriage to his master's daughter. Wallis was mayor four times and twice M.P. for Lynn. Skills as a trader at home and abroad must account for his accumulation of wealth and power, while securing warrants from the Lord Treasurer to allow him to ship goods duty free tells of connections in high places. His family did not last as merchants in Lynn, however. Sir Henry Spelman, in his *History and Fate of Sacrilege* (1632), had no doubt that the failure of Lynn's merchants to produce heirs was God's penalty for their part in the spoilation of the monasteries:

> For other matters, I will only note what I have observed touching them in the general — when I was young, they flourished extraordinarily with shipping, trading, plenty of merchandise, native and foreign; some men of very great worth, as Killingree, Grave, Clayburne, Vilet, Lendall; many of good note, as Grant, Overend, Hoe, Baker, Waters and many more of later time — but all of them, with their male posterity, are in effect extinct and gone; and as at this day they have little shipping or trade otherwise than to the Black Indies, as they call it (that is Newcastle, for coal), so there is not a man amongst them of any estimation for his wealth, or of any note (that I can hear of), descended from any that was an alderman there in the beginning of Queen Elizabeth.

High infant mortality rates were partly responsible for the difficulty in sustaining the male line, however; male heirs were as precious as in the Middle Ages. Wharton Gervase's son

25. William Atkin, son of John Atkin who built the Greenland Fishery, was mayor in 1619. This is the earliest portrait of a Lynn mayor.

26. St Nicholas' chapel has many memorials to Lynn's merchant families. This one commemorates Thomas Greene (d. 1675) and his wife, who had nine children.

had 10 children by his first wife and eight by his second. No fewer than 11 died young. Lynn's Tudor and Stuart upper class was constantly renewed through migration.

This should not lead us to believe that there were no successful dynasties in Lynn, at least for two or three generations. The Revett family is a good example. Michael Revett adopted the title 'notary public' rather than 'merchant' or 'gentleman', for he was a lawyer, and his three sons followed their father as councillors, aldermen and lawyers. They were executors or witnesses of so many Lynn merchants' wills that their family prestige and professional status is beyond question. Just as often they witnessed merchants signing bonds, bills and writings. They were appointed trouble-shooters by men desperate to settle disputes over property and ships. The corporation entrusted them with keeping the accounts of the coal and millstone stocks on the Common Staithe. One of the Revetts served as town clerk from 1614 until his death in 1633, often 'abroade employed about the Towne's busines'. The Revetts were hard-headed businessmen, however, whose professional pursuits were probably less lucrative than their interests in land, houses, breweries and shops.

Other families were adept at using wealth generated by trade to promote new or secondary professional careers. John Lead's profits from overseas trade and shipping allowed him to branch into banking as well as property. Matthew Clarke was sent by his father (unusually for Lynn merchants) to take a Cambridge degree before following him as alderman, mayor and searcher for the port. The Revetts, Leads and Clarkes are examples of urban gentlemen whose gradual detachment from overseas trade was reinforced by their ownership of landed property in west Norfolk. Nevertheless they did not desert the town for the life of country gentlemen, they were too dependent on it.

Glimpses of the private lives of merchant families are, again, provided by their wills. Forty of the 67 mayors investigated by Battley died before their wives, who often remarried two or three times. Former colleagues and apprentices of their husbands were eager suitors. Household servants were numerous. Privacy in the mansions of the riverside streets was almost impossible, although some merchants, like Matthew Clarke, had fine libraries to escape into. Servants might even sleep in the same room as masters and mistresses. Frequent disputes over legacies show that families were sometimes split by rivalry, jealousy and greed.

Sexual habits are only hinted at in the cases brought before the most local of church tribunals in the diocese, the archdeacon's court at St Nicholas' chapel. In 1551 Alderman John MacKanter was summoned to answer charges of sexual incontinence with several women, only for the case to be dismissed. The ruling group was too powerful to be pilloried in public for bad behaviour. The only case of sexual deviance to become open scandal in this period was to do with a practice the corporation could not stomach. According to witnesses, Thomas Baker was an irrepressible homosexual. When he was mayor a draper claimed that Baker refused his request for citizenship unless he would 'untress his points and put down his breeches that he [Baker] might clasp his naked breech'. Baker was also accused of buggery with Dutch sailors and apparently asked various shipmasters to whip him. In 1608 he was expelled from aldermanic office for committing 'diverse misdemeanors and evil behaviour to the great disgrace of the government of this Burgh' and 'to the scandal of this society', but was restored after taking the corporation to the court of King's Bench and, still defiant, died an alderman in 1626.

Later Lynn merchants

Some of those sons of gentry, professionals and traders from the eastern counties who migrated to Lynn in the late 17th century to become merchants succeeded in founding families of several generations. More sons seem to have survived infancy. That the eldest son of so many of them was christened after his father and inherited his commercial empire reflects the desire of families for continuity: Samuel for the Brownes, Edward for the Everards, George for the Hogges, John for the Turners. More positive attitudes to trade on the part of the landed classes raised the status of merchants, too. Of the merchant families discussed below, only the Turners were pulled away from the town to the country. Urban civilisation was coming of age. Lynn's 'high caste folk' not only strengthened their solidarity by intermarriage, but found little trouble in taking partners from the gentry or mixing with some of the greatest aristocrats of England. The Cokes of Holkham, the Townshends of Raynham and the Walpoles of Houghton rubbed shoulders with the merchants of Lynn. Sir Robert Walpole always treated these urban grandees 'royally' at Houghton, and the favour was sumptuously returned at the Town Hall. Defoe observed in 1722 that there were more gentry in Lynn than in Yarmouth or even Norwich and 'consequently more gaiety', 'the place abounding in good company'.

The Turners occupy a central place in the social and political history of Lynn for over a century. The family provided 14 mayors between 1678 and 1768, some of them being elected more than once. John Turner (1632-1712), the son of a lawyer of North Elmham, was apprenticed to a Cambridge merchant before seeking his fortune at Lynn, and married the widow of a rich vintner. He and Simon Tayler represented the town in parliament in 1684, when both were knighted for their loyalty. John's brother Charles (1648-1711) was Lynn's most distinguished lawyer. Their younger brother remained at North Elmham, but his three sons profited from the trail blazed by their uncles. Charles Turner II was Lynn's M.P. for 43 years until his death in 1738. He married Robert Walpole's sister and purchased the Turner estate at Warham in north Norfolk about 1709. His brothers William and John are less noteworthy. John Turner III (1712-80) was the son of the latter and inherited the baronetcy conferred on his uncle Charles. He studied law at Cambridge and London, married the daughter of a Warwickshire squire and spent much of his annual income of £1,210 developing Warham. Friends were invited there for Christmas parties which Turner liked to be 'tolerably jolly according to ancient custom'. Bad management of men and property led to his downfall and, with it, the Turners. The Warham estate had to be sold and the house was demolished. At least one other member of the family had a similar record. John Turner, son of Charles I, was forced to flee Lynn because of debt in 1731.

A contemporary of the first Turners was Henry Bell. Born in 1647 into a merchant household, he attended the local grammar school and Cambridge University, returning to Lynn and the family business. He was a part-time architect for the Turners and other patrons in Lynn and Northampton. His monuments are the Custom House and other buildings of Lynn's architectural renaissance, which he designed and recorded in prospects, groundplates and writings. His significance is more than local: 'Here in the flesh is the true bourgeois gentilhomme, the self-assured townsman and tradesman with the education, the values and the interests of the cultivated aristocrat'. Nor is Bell the only son of Lynn merchants to make an impact on the national stage in this role. Perhaps the best known other is Sir Benjamin Keene (1697-1758), who was Britain's ambassador in Spain and Portugal at a critical time in European history. He attended the universites of Cambridge and Leiden, in Holland, to study law before attracting the patronage of Walpole. His younger brother Edmund became Bishop of Ely.

The Bagges were the most successful of the merchants of Lynn if this is measured in terms of staying power, of the longest line. John Bagge sprang from an old Norfolk landed family. He came to Lynn to take a brewery in King Street. Both his marriages were to the daughters of local merchants. Of his sons, William (1700-62) was the most enterprising. William's two sons enjoyed a flourishing partnership in brewing and shipping. Thomas Bagge (1740-1807) married the daughter of Philip Case in 1768 and lived in Nelson Street, close to the Town Hall, where he was made mayor four times. That he was an urban magnate of some

27. Sir John Turner (1632-1712).

28. This fine classical mansion was erected for Charles Turner on the west side of the Tuesday Market Place about 1703. Henry Bell was almost certainly the architect. It was destroyed by fire in March 1768.

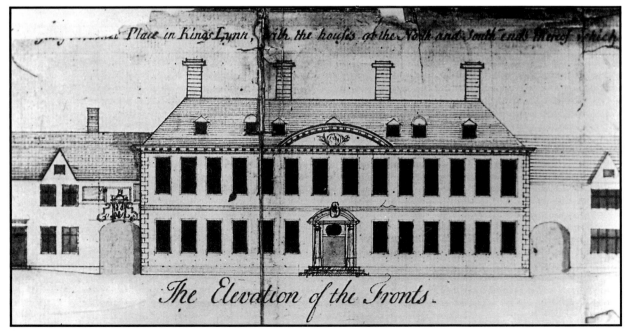

The Elevation of the Fronts.

substance is indicated by the offer, in 1796, of a peerage from the Prime Minister, William Pitt. His eldest son was Thomas Philip Bagge, who died in 1829, four years after his brother William. William was the father of the twins William (1810-80) and Richard (1810-90). These brothers developed the family estates in west Norfolk. By 1871 William had 3,770 acres at Stradsett, with a gross annual rental of £6,258, while Richard owned 2,890 acres at Gaywood, with a rental of £6,978. The Bagges had come full circle from land to trade and back in less than 200 years, though business interests in Lynn were maintained and the family continued to play a part in borough politics. Between 1711 and 1901 the Bagges provided the town with 18 mayors.

The Stradsett and Gaywood estates passed to the Bagges through the marriage of Thomas to Pleasance Case, the eldest daughter of a man not a trader, but who is central to this account. Philip Case (1712-92) was a Norfolk lawyer whose county connections launched a glittering career. Viscount Townshend appointed him Clerk of the Peace for the county and comptroller of the customs for Lynn, Wisbech and Wells. The merchants of Lynn employed him to transact their property deals and other business in Norfolk and London for several decades. Two of his three daughters married Lynn merchants after attending boarding school in Norwich. Case was 'without doubt' a man of the highest integrity and reputation and for half a century he 'virtually controlled' the public and social life of Lynn. He was mayor four times. Only a handful of other professionals could expect to be treated on equal terms by the corporation families. Sir William Browne (1692-1774) acquired an impressive reputation for his works on medical science, but he had considerable contempt for his urban lords, and left for London and the Presidency of the Fellows of the Royal College of Preceptors.

Professional jobs for educated men were available at the Custom House. It seems likely that the famous Vancouver family had Dutch origins, but John Vancouver was a fully-fledged Englishman in 1748, when he was made deputy of the Custom House by Charles Turner, the Collector. His appointment by the corporation as the Collector of the town dues, or local taxes on shipping, supplemented his income. John's eldest son succeeded his father at the Custom House. Of the other five children of John and Bridget Vancouver, by far the most significant was George (1757-98), sent into the Royal Navy and sailing in 1772 on Captain Cook's ship *Resolution*. George made two exploratory voyages with Cook. In 1790 he was appointed commander of the *Discovery*, with orders to survey the west coast of North America. Five Lynn men sailed with him on this voyage.

Society and culture

We should regard the merchants of Lynn as urban lords as much as traders, men involved in the running of a 'city state' as much as counting houses. Daily business affairs were increasingly directed by able and trusted lieutenants, whose own careers were thereby promoted. J. P. Blencowe, who lived opposite St Margaret's church, was 'the leading light' in the merchant house of Everard. Aldermen Dillingham (who still wore an old-fashioned pigtail about 1800) and Greene were 'the presiding genii' of, respectively, Messrs. Hogge and Bagge. Just as important to Lynn's merchants were their shipmasters. In 1741 Samuel Browne's executors were instructed to buy all his former shipmasters and their wives scarves, gloves and hatbands for his funeral. John Mountain was to have a new ship. Browne's son bequeathed all his shipmasters five guineas each in 1785, although £50 went to his cooper, Robert Frays.

Three of the largest households belonging to the merchants of Lynn were in Nelson Street, close to the Town Hall: those of the Brownes, Selfs and Bagges, in houses numbered today, respectively, 15, 11 and 9. In 1785 Samuel Browne's furniture alone was worth £815, while the mansion was sold in 1789 for £4,000. Lionel Self's home was also luxurious, as

29. The classical doorway of the Browne family mansion in Nelson Street.

the sale catalogue of 1843 reveals. The weighing machines, granary utensils and other items show that domestic and commercial life still co-existed. An inventory survives of Thomas Bagge's house in 1827, listing bed, dressing, breakfast, dining and drawing rooms as well as kitchens, cellars and a coach house. Mahogany furniture of all kinds abounded, as did rugs, clocks, pictures and books. The auctioneers valued the house contents at £1,045. To maintain large properties was expensive, involving frequent employment of bricklayers, carpenters and decorators. Taxes imposed by the government on land, houses, windows and carriages had to be paid at the Town Hall, while there were church and poor rates due to local officials. From April 1785 to March 1789 Samuel Browne's executors paid out £960 in taxation and insurance due from him.

Family ties were paramount for Lynn's merchants. Successful careers in trade were less for the glory of town or country than for 'the benefit' of the family, as Samuel Browne IV (1703-41) said in his will. He expected his eldest, 'dutiful' son to concur. Young Samuel Browne V (1729-84) inherited all his father's properties, but was urged to take his brothers into partnership once they were of age. They were to be allowed money for a ship or an apprenticeship, but Samuel IV believed that they could be as well taught in his own counting house as 'at any other place', and recommended they be 'under the care' of his worthy friend Mr. Hackett, who had promised 'to take care of them'. All six younger brothers and sisters were also to be paid £1,500 when they attained 21 years of age. Samuel IV even gave Samuel V all the household goods except a little picture set in gold bequeathed to his 'dutiful' daughter Elizabeth. Since the boy was only 12 years old, however, and his mother and four other siblings were already buried in St Nicholas', Samuel IV made his own sister and three close friends trustees. He wanted only relations and 'some very few intimate friends' to be present at his funeral, as had been the case at that of his wife. Family privacy was becoming more important.

Second marriages were frequent as many husbands died early. That between Edmund Rolfe and Sarah, the widow of John Bagge, was unhappy, and she left him for six months in 1763. She returned, however, and promised to behave 'as a wife ought to a husband who most dearly loved her'. Most marriages seem to have been love matches. Charles Burney was accused of interloping and fortune-hunting when he married the widow of a rich merchant, Mrs. Allen, but his critics were silenced when she lost her money but not the good doctor. The marriage of Thomas Bagge and Pleasance Case in 1768 was almost certainly that of two young lovers also, her father disapproving because of his son-in-law's inferior wealth and status. Fanny Burney viewed the wedding from a garden opposite St Margaret's church, appalled by 'the prodigious mob' which had gathered to watch. She disliked such a private affair becoming so public, and 'trembled' for the bride.

Family or domestic worlds were kept turning by the work of the servants 'below stairs' responsible for fires, cooking and washing. This was female labour, often controlled by a woman. The plan of Thomas Bagge's house in the Tuesday Market Place in 1801 shows the housekeeper's sitting room above the kitchen, to which it was linked by stairs. Men were employed, too. In 1842 Richard Bagge had two gardeners and a gamekeeper at Gaywood besides a groom, butler and footman at his Lynn house. Male servants were used by the ladies of Lynn to carry lanterns during evening walking, serving also as bodyguards. Coachmen and footmen could be reassuring escorts when constables were few. Travelling between his Lynn mansion and Gaywood or Islington family homes on his strong cob, William Bagge was always closely followed by his 'old servant', Bell. Affection for servants was often real and lasting. In 1741 Samuel Browne wished for his 'old' servants to be continued at Nelson Street unless they proved to be 'incapable' or 'commited any faults for which they deserve to be discharged'.

The riverside mansions were centres of entertainment for Lynn's high society during the winter. Two houses on the Tuesday Market Place had good reputations for merrymaking. Poorer citizens would stand outside and stare through the windows. The spectacle at the Hogges' mansion in January 1785 was marred by a dreadful accident: boys swinging on a chain fixed to a stone obelisk outside the door dislodged a lamp which fell onto two women, killing one of them. In 1812 William Bagge gave such a splendid supper and ball to his friends that 'the market place was illuminated by the brilliancy of the light within'. A week later the families of the corporation staged a ball and supper at the Town Hall for 170 people, including gentry from 20 miles around Lynn. About two hundred and seventy ladies and gentlemen attended a Town Hall banquet in 1804. The crowds watching the arrivals would have gasped at the menu. Duck, turkey, chicken, ham, beef, mutton, venison, lobsters, sturgeon, partridge, pigeons, stewed peas, mince pies, clear jellies, orange pudding and other delicacies weighted the tables.

Dinner parties and musical soirées were a regular feature of the social calendars of Lynn's top families. The desire of parents for their daughters to make good marriages led them to press their daughters to become musically proficient. Charles Burney was tempted to Lynn in 1750 by a special subscription to provide him with a salary as organist of St Margaret's, but his sponsors saw him also as a perfect tutor who could expect 'the most respectable pupils' from all 'the best families in the town and neighbourhood'. Dancing masters were brought to Lynn to instruct children at home and to direct balls for young people at the Town Hall. Wall du Val, from London, taught fencing as well as dancing at Lynn in 1774, accompanied by a teacher of French called François Vernon.

The culture-hungry merchants of Lynn also regarded as status symbols good libraries and copies of the works of the European masters such as Claude, Reubens, Rembrandt and Van Dyck. The latter fashion was stimulated by 'the real things' at the aristocratic houses of Norfolk. Walpole's collection of pictures at Houghton was the most celebrated in England, but his grandson, the third Earl of Orford, sold most of it to Catherine the Great of Russia for £40,550 in 1779. These masterpieces were carted from Houghton to Lynn for shipping to St Petersburg. The Custom House account books show Lynn merchants importing Dutch paintings by 1700. Henry Bell was an important collector of Netherlands art.

He left his son 12 of his paintings, attributed to Heemskerck, Schalcken, Holbein and Rembrandt (the two last somewhat dubiously).

Road improvements and fast stage coaches allowed the corporation families to take regular leisure and business trips. Some bought or rented houses in London. Mrs. Allen left the cold Norfolk borough for the metropolis for the winter before she married Burney.

His house in Poland Street was a favourite haunt of temporary Lynn exiles like the Turners. Annual spring excursions to Bath were made by Philip Case, Edward Everard, Reverend Charles Bagge and the ambitious Crisp Molineux: 'I have been with some of the principal gentlemen of that town to Bath' (1769). Balls, gambling and salon life were more attractive than the bathing. Wives and daughters seem sometimes to have taken long journeys alone. In May 1839, for example, Pleasance Bagge passed through Burton, Liverpool, Lancaster and Harrogate. The shorter journeys to the races and concerts in Swaffham and Fakenham attended by the Norfolk gentry were also popular.

Rural sports were also enjoyed in the early 19th century. Some corporation families began to spend as much time at their country houses as at Lynn. Thomas Allen kept a pack of beagles or harriers at his house near Shouldham, driving to Lynn with his coach and four, the vehicle he was fond of 'tooling' along the road. The Bagges kennelled hounds opposite their Nelson Street house. Hunting, shooting and fishing were now part of their

30. Fanny Burney (1752-1840) heads the roll of female novelists who influenced English literature in the late 18th century. She was born in Lynn. Her journals contain astute observations on its character during her frequent visits.

lives. The Holkham game books of this period record regular deliveries of pheasants, partridges and hares to Lynn's élite. Did it help to shoot them? Membership of the Norfolk County Cricket Club was bringing merchants and squires closer together by the 1820s, too.

Interesting insights into Lynn's high society in the 18th century can be gleaned from the observations of 'outsiders'. Fanny Burney is the most illuminating. She spent summers in Lynn after her family had returned to London. Fanny rose early for walks in the fields around the town because nobody was about then; it was impossible for her to do likewise when she was in London 'for fear of robbers — but here everybody is known, and one has nothing to apprehend'. Yet she loathed the social life of Lynn's upper class families:

Such a set of tittle tattle, prittle prattle visitants! Oh fear! I am sick of the ceremony and fuss of these dull people! So much dressing — chit chat — complimentary nonsense. In short, a country town is my detestation — all the conversation is scandal, all the attention, dress, and almost all the heart, folly, envy and censoriousness. A city or a small village are the only places which, I think, can be comfortable, for a country town, I think, has all the bad qualities, without one of the good ones, of both.

Fanny's stepsister, Maria Allen, shared these sentiments, despite being a native of the borough. She found Town Hall balls 'horribly stupid', drinking tea and 'rebuffing old Turner', though she danced minuets and cotillions with some of the town's 'stupid wretches'.

Charles Burney's initial dislike of Lynn was compounded by the appalling state of St Margaret's organ and the ignorance of music amongst his patrons: 'Even Sir J [John Turner] who is the oracle of Apollo in this country is extremely shallow'. Horace Walpole was irritated by the nice conversation in Lynn salons and listening to daughters playing the harpsichord or seeing 'an alderman's copies of Reubens and Carlo Marat'. He acknowledged the commonsensical virtues of his stuffy supporters and how their language had become more polished since 'I lived amongst them'. Walpole ascribed this cultural change to the facility of travel to London by stage coach.

The West Indian planter Crisp Molineux tempted merchants of Lynn to parties at his Norfolk seat in Garboldisham. This dull, but amicable, colonial was created a freeman of the borough in 1770, receiving an honour 'which they hold at so high a rate'. Molineux described Lynn's merchants as 'very opulent men', which is solid testimony from a man who was himself very rich. A rather more humble temporary resident was a young man who became a famous writer on agriculture. Arthur Young was apprenticed by his clergyman father to a Lynn merchant about 1760. He ignored hints that 'mere merchant clerks did not attend Town Hall balls' and danced happily with 'the principal belles'. His charm won over Fanny Burney.

World's End

It was an unhappy coincidence for the merchants of Lynn in 1847 that the harbour branch of the railway stopped at 'World's End', the spot at the confluence of the Nar and Ouse where the corporation of 1610 had encouraged John Spence to build a strong bank against flooding. Armes was an eye witness of the initial shock that the coming of the railway had on the town:

> On the introduction of the new system of railways and free trade, the corn merchants of Lynn became naturally alarmed. They said that their occupation was gone, and they, in some cases, evidenced their sincerity by entirely abandoning their premises and retiring from the conflict. The whole aspect along the river was changed — 'TO BE LET', was posted upon several extensive warehouses, which but a very short time previously many enterprising men would have been anxious to hire.

What more dramatic event for closing the story of the merchants of Lynn than the sudden introduction of a transport system that took away their command of inland commerce? The seaports serving the coalfields and industrial hinterlands of northern Britain had been outgrowing Lynn for several decades, as Armes had seen:

> I shall never forget the impression made upon me when I first left home, and saw, upon the quays, and upon the rivers, the busy commerce of the North of England. I had been tutored in the old school, and taught to believe, that the town in which I lived stood distinguished, as amongst the wealthy and mercantile towns of England. And so, indeed, in some respects, it did. Its principal merchants were men of large wealth, and the many carriages, at that time, settling down company at the frequent and splendid assemblies at the Old Town Hall, fully indicated the style of the grandees at Lynn. The mayors' feasts, and other occasional splendid banquets, were got up in a style of which the present rising generation can form but an inadequate conception, and, perhaps, so complete is the transition, that the best index, in this respect, to the habits of olden time, is to be found in the manifold and extensive culinary apparatus still to be seen in the spacious kitchens under the Town Hall.

By 1900 many of the mansions once belonging to town merchants had fallen into decay and were being stripped of the best parts of their interiors. Thew sadly observed how some of these houses remained 'to shew on what a palatial scale our merchant princes lived', but 'others have been sadly cut up and deprived of their ancient dignity'. Beloe was furious with the treatment of Allen's house in St Ann's Street by 'a stranger' who cared nothing about sweeping away 'one of the palaces of our merchants' for the sake of a few pounds. The disappearance of the staircases and fireplaces of these magnificent houses to the halls of the landed gentry was, at least, consistent with the direction taken by most of the families formerly occupying them. This migration to the countryside was underway before 1850: the Allens to Shouldham, the Everards to Congham, the Hogges to Bilney and the Bagges to Gaywood, Islington and Stradsett. Pratt is another good witness of this change in the social character of the town as its old merchant families moved out:

> The Tuesday Market Place has changed from a residential part of the town to a purely business district, private houses were inhabited by Mrs. Hogge [now Barclay's Bank], the Smeethams, Hardings, Taylors, Sir Lewis Jarvis and the brothers Cook. . . . The brothers Robert and Henry Cook [grandfather and great-uncle, respectively, of the present Leake family] were typical early-Victorian merchants. Always dressed in black broadcloth with silk hats, they might be seen every day pacing up and down the pavement in front of their houses on the north side of the market place like captains walking the quarter deck. They were the first Lynn merchants to employ steam ships.

Window on the south side of the Gildhall of St George.

Chapter Six

Townspeople

Numbers and poverty

Of the estimated 9,000 inhabitants of Lynn on the Eve of the Black Death in 1349, most were labouring people. Many were victims of the 'Great Pestilence'. A calculation based on the poll tax of 1377 suggests that the population was then about five thousand five hundred, a total increasing only slightly before 1565, but faster afterwards. For a long period the town's population was temporarily reduced each summer as townspeople went to help with the harvest.

Lynn always depended upon a steady flow of migrants from the countryside to sustain its numbers. Burials in the town exceeded baptisms by 5,728 between 1659 and 1760, for example, despite the disappearance of bubonic plague. Immigration from abroad was not heavy, however, in spite of the evidence discussed in the previous chapter. We know that 20 Dutch families had arrived in Lynn in 1566, and that there were 266 aliens in the town in 1571, the majority by far from Holland. The mayor told the Privy Council: 'The said strangers are for the greatest part pore, of good behaviour . . .'.

Study of English urban populations in the 1660s is facilitated by the records of the hearth tax, granted to the crown as a perpetual revenue by parliament in 1662. It was abolished in 1689 because of the hostility to it of the middle classes. The tax was of a shilling for every hearth in the occupation of each citizen whose house was worth more than 20s. a year, and liable for poor and church rates. It was payable twice a year in September and March. According to the returns for Norfolk at Michaelmas 1664, the borough of Lynn had at least 950 householders, who paid for 2,918 hearths. The records do not allow us to discover the number of households in Lynn exempt from paying the tax then because of their poverty, but comparison with other towns suggests 40 per cent or more. This figure implies a total of 1,330 households in the town. To translate it into a population total requires a multiplier of at least 4.5 to take account of household size, indicating a population of 5,985 or more; the number of servants and paupers compensates for those families with fewer than four or five people. The uncertainties inherent in these calculations should not cloud the fact that a large proportion of Lynn's population was probably living in dire poverty. It was, no doubt, concentrated in quarters like the North End.

Lynn was almost certainly afflicted by a greater degree of poverty in the 1660s than most other important English towns, such as York or Bristol. It was similar to Hull and Newcastle in being exposed to coastal as well as overland migration of the poor. The port of Lynn was also too dependent for employment on the seasonal corn and coal trades, rather than manufacturing industries. Many families, moreover, then and later, had only low incomes because fathers and sons were absent at sea for long periods. Of the 400 sailors belonging to Lynn in 1757, over 250 had been pressed by the Royal Navy; the rest were away from the town on merchant vessels. Estimates suggest a population of over 10,000 at this time, following several decades of modest growth, but a slight decline after the 1750s; Poor Law officials counted just under 10,000 inhabitants in 1789. There were 10,096 people enumerated at Lynn in the 1801 census.

When Defoe visited Lynn in 1722 he was struck by the good location and well-built character of this rich and populous 'thriving port-town'. He failed to note the labouring classes. The contrasts of rich and poor in the crowded streets of Georgian Lynn must have

31. A timber-framed house of about 1600, with brick infilling, in St Ann's Street.

32. John Cross was one of the great characters of early 19th-century Lynn, as his appearance on several engravings of the period confirms. In this drawing by W. White the Old Pilot Office can be seen.

been as stark as in today's seaports of Africa and Asia. In 1812 William Richards introduced his readers to the evidence of 'ancient people' who remembered the times when Lynn was 'notorious' amongst country folk for its chronic poverty. Was this the 1730s and 1740s? Lord Orford visited Lynn in 1738 to talk of local worries over 'the decay of trade' and maladministration of the workhouse, 'for here you are pestered by beggars to a great degree'. Poverty had not disappeared by 1812: Richards claims that over 1,000 of the town's 11,000 inhabitants required weekly allowances through the Poor Law because of a slump in the coal and corn trades.

In the half century after 1800 Lynn doubled its population (from 10,000 to 20,000), largely by the migration of East Anglians tired of labouring in the countryside for little reward. In 1850 the town's lower classes were still engaged in maritime and traditional pursuits. Of the 833 male labourers listed as 'not agricultural' at Lynn in 1831, at least half supplied the muscle power required for loading and unloading ships, lighters and wagons. In 1845 the port was also home for over 750 seamen (though most were often away).

Ten per cent of Lynn's 20,000 inhabitants in 1850 were to be found in the fishing quarter of North End. Of the 788 servants identified by the census returns of 1831 no less than 666 were young women, almost all aged between 14 and 26, and mostly migrants from Lynn's rural hinterland.

It is testimony to the poverty of town and country in Norfolk that its labourers were often keen to escape. When offered free voyages to British colonies by the Poor Law Commission in the 1830s, many were tempted by the prospect of farming their own land. Between 1835 and 1837 Norfolk sent out the astonishing total of 3,354 such emigrants. Others emigrated with help from parish authorities. In 1836 over 800 Norfolk people sailed from Lynn and 3,000 from Yarmouth; in 1837 over 1,500 departed from Lynn and 600 from Yarmouth — almost all these emigrants went to Canada. At Lynn, in May 1832, at least 84 'respectable labourers' who could not find work in Norfolk left England watched by a crowd. In January 1839 emigrant ships of 'principally paupers' were too overcrowded and too much 'in haste' for the liking of Lynn's customs officers, who believed each vessel required a surgeon.

Disasters

Lynn's river has always posed a threat of floods whenever high winds and high tides coincide. Medieval sea banks were inadequate to contain them on every occasion. In 1301 a great flood is supposed to have inundated the town, washing away quays and damaging many of Lynn's timber dwellings. Lynn was said to have been badly hit and impoverished by floods in 1337-8. We have local information from a Franciscan friar compiling a chronicle of current events. From the Greyfriars tower he would have had a bird's eye view of the disasters he recorded. The winters of 1364 and 1374 were both times of great storms and floods in and about Lynn. Ships were driven ashore. Houses were submerged. In 1363 and 1374 there were also bad frosts from December to March, apparently causing water shortages, and so a rise in its price.

Fires periodically ravaged medieval towns, vulnerable because of the timber and thatch buildings. Sometimes they assumed terrible dimensions, as at Boston in 1287 and Norwich in 1414 and 1507. Lynn's 'great fire' was in 1331. Buildings were pulled down in an attempt to halt its progress. Smaller fires occurred in 1277, 1282 and 1421, when Margery Kempe prayed for it to go out, but the Trinity Gildhall was destroyed before snow dampened the flames. Her amanuensis recorded: 'On a tyme per happyd to be a gret fyer in Lynn Biscop fyer brent up pe Gylde-halle of pe Trinite'. There must have been many smaller fires for which no evidence survives. Thanks to the Greyfriar mentioned above we know about two in 1363, at the Carmelite house and the tolbooth.

Great storms often inflicted crushing blows on the harvest, leading to food shortages or even famine. Drought and war had similar consequences. Crisis years of this kind in medieval England were catalogued at Lynn by Capgrave. In 1259 there was 'a great hungir' and 'men and bestis died for default of mete'. In July 1288 rain, thunder and lightning destroyed the cornfields, forcing up the price of a bushel of wheat from 3d. to 2s. 1314 saw heavy rains destroy the harvest and bakers resorting to drying corn in their ovens so it could be ground. Provisions were extremely scarce, and Capgrave reports death from starvation ('summe deied for hungir') as well as an increase in robbery and rising food prices. From June until Christmas 1348 almost constant rain destroyed crops. Corn imports were needed to feed the nation after the grass and corn had dried up in a drought from March to July 1353. In 1407 the weather was so bad during the winter that birds were frozen alive. Capgrave also mentions a hurricane blowing down houses in 1362 and a great earthquake in June 1381.

Lynn's calendars of 'notable events' tell of the dangers and hardships endured by townspeople in the post-medieval centuries. There were 'great earthquakes' in 1563 and 1602. Floods were common. The storm of April 1607 brought such 'an extraordinary tide' that river banks were broken and 'muich hurt' done in Lynn and marshland villages. Water lapped at the market cross. Lynn seems to have escaped the worst of that national calamity of November 1703 known as 'the great storm' (the west coast of England was hardest hit), though six local ships and 30 sailors were lost, and damage to buildings in the town was extensive. Storms in 1713 and 1714 did 'prodigious' damage to town houses, too. The most dramatic storm to engulf Lynn in modern times was that of September 1741, when the spires of St Nicholas' and St Margaret's were blown down. Shipping belonging to the town was lost and houses wrecked; Lynn suffered 'insupportable losses' and the inhabitants great 'privations'. In 1779, on New Year's Day, yet another strong gale whipped up an 'extraordinary high tide', the highest in living memory, so that river banks broke and 'vast damage' was done 'in and about this town'. In February 1816 an 'exceeding high tide' at Lynn was several feet above the normal spring tides, flooding houses to three feet or more and causing much 'distress' and 'trouble'.

Water had always claimed the lives of those who worked or played by the banks of the Ouse and its fleets. Boys swimming were vulnerable, like the three drowned in the Fisher Fleet in July 1727. Harvest men from Yorkshire bathing here in August 1818 lost one of their gang. Even the ferry could be dangerous. One of the worst accidents happened in February 1796, when the overloaded boat, carrying more than 30 people, was upset by collision with a clay barge. Of the 11 lives lost, two were those of a young couple about to be married, later found 'clasped in each other's arms'.

Ships at anchor in the Ouse could also be a threat to the town. Fires were not only used in repairs but by crews attempting to dry holds. These activities were often too close to warehouses and dwellings and the corporation warned owners against them, in 1752 ordering holds to be dried with sedge or straw. Perhaps the most dramatic recorded incident of a fire on board ship endangering the town was in 1717. A vessel at the end of St Margaret's Lane caught light, at 250 tons becoming an inferno of major proportions. In December the mayor organised a collection to reward those who had assisted in extinguishing 'the late dreadful fire' by 'playing the engine and the horses'. Two fire engines were acquired by the town in 1770, one donated by the 'insurers of the Sun Fire Office', the other at 'the expense' of the parishioners.

Epidemics and disease

Leprosy was endemic in early-medieval society, and there were at least six lazar houses in and about Lynn in 1348, provided by the rich for the disease's victims. Sufferers warned others of their approach by a bell. In 1389 a town committee was appointed to investigate the problem. Margery Kempe met lepers in Lynn's streets and kissed the women, besides visiting the lazar houses, habits which made citizens all the more wary of her. In 1430 a suspected leper was ordered to leave the town within two weeks on pain of a 40s. fine.

No disaster in medieval England compares with the Black Death, or the 'Great Pestilence' as it was called by contemporaries, which arrived in England in the spring of 1348. This bubonic plague degenerated into a still more deadly pneumonic form in the colder weather of north-west Europe. Perhaps 40 per cent of England's 5,000,000 inhabitants perished in the terrible outbreak of 1348-9. Because the plague killed so many young people who would have become parents, the recovery of numbers was slow. Moreover, the disease returned in 1361-2, 1368-9, 1375, 1390-1 and 1439, if in less devastating epidemics. Famine and starvation were associated with the Black Death because of the disruption of economic life. Can we imagine the catastrophic effects of this epidemic as comparable to a nuclear war?

East Anglia was the hardest hit of the English regions, affected as badly as Scandinavia and Italy. Norfolk and Suffolk were caught in a pincer movement as the plague advanced north from London and west from the ports. Between May and September 1349 about half of the region's population was victim to this terrifying disease. Fever and vomiting were followed by internal bleeding and the growth of suppurating black buboes. The Great Pestilence peaked in the summer, before the rat fleas which transmitted it died of cold. The poor suffered most because their thatched cottages attracted nesting rats, but all social classes were vulnerable. Of the 799 parish priests in Norfolk on the eve of the Black Death, only 272 remained after its passage. Bishop Bateman of Norwich used his horse to keep ahead of the plague, and survived to found Trinity Hall, Cambridge, to train men to fill the gaps in the clerical ranks. The towns suffered heavy casualties because of their high population densities. Norwich was the second city of England, with approximately twenty thousand people in 1348, of whom 50 per cent succumbed. Yarmouth's 10,000 inhabitants fell by half within a few months, while Bury St Edmunds lost at least 3,500 of its 7,000 citizens, including 40 monks. Lynn's experience must have been similar. The Gild of Corpus Christi reported to the king in 1389 that *the majority* of townspeople perished in 1349, though this was surely an exaggeration. Urban populations must have been reduced also by flight into the countryside, as severe outbreaks of plague in East Anglia generated in the 1430s, 1460s and 1470s.

Plague continued to be a problem. Between 1570 and 1670 the English population increased from three to five million, despite the fact that over 650,000 died of the disease. All towns of any size were devastated by epidemics of it, and Lynn, as a port, was particularly open to attack. Plague struck the town in 1516, 1540, 1555, 1574, 1584, 1589, 1593, 1597, 1602, 1610, 1622, 1625, 1630, 1636, 1645 and 1665 — sometimes for several months at a time. No accurate statistics of deaths exist, but a tenth of the townspeople may have perished in 1597-8 if the sources are reliable.

In 1584-5 aldermen were requested to report to the mayor the needs of plague victims, and a tax was levied for their relief, including the fees of a surgeon. The corporation's main counters to the epidemics were to turn away road and river traffic, to isolate victims within the walls and to bury the dead as soon as possible. 'Pesthouses' made of timber were erected at the Blackfriars and other open spaces. In 1665-6 timber shelters were built outside the town walls. The relatives and friends of those in the pesthouses were warned to stay away because of the 'great danger' of spreading the disease, and Moses Hurst was appointed to stand guard with a musket to deter visitors.

Plague devastated English towns for the last time in 1666. Some historians claim that the application of a more effective quarantine policy at British ports was the most important reason for this. Because plague was imported from Eurasia, the only sensible course of action was to isolate Britain from Europe in danger periods. Quarantine before 1666 had not been strict enough: in 1644-5 ships from Sunderland suspected of carrying plague were simply directed into the River Nar on arriving at Lynn. The tightening of these measures, under instructions from the government, may help to explain the disappearance of the disease. In July 1712, for example, plague broke out in northern Germany, and a 40-day quarantine was imposed at Lynn on ships from the Baltic, Elbe and Weser, with watchmen posted to prevent sailors leaving the vessels. In August 1720 ships from the Mediterranean were ordered to be quarantined and 'paupers' on board were only to be touched with 'sticks'. By September quarantine was extended to ships from France, and it was applied to vessels from the Mediterranean until September 1721. Renewed plague was still a nightmare in 1743, when the Town Hall was alarmed by the approach of a Dutch ship believed to be carrying victims of the plague, of which the 'inseparable companions' were 'famine and desolation'.

Smallpox was another kind of plague, of which far more were ill than died. Epidemics of it ravaged Lynn in the hot summers of 1719, 1738 and 1754, when the graveyard of St Margaret's was finally closed for burials. St Nicholas' accommodated most of the victims.

The corporation responded to the smallpox threat in 1758 by raising £75 for the innoculation of 'such poor people, inhabitants, of this borough as shall chuse to accept that benefit'. On the return of the disease in 1762 the Poor Law authorities rented houses as hospitals for soldiers who had smallpox, or would be 'afflicted with it'. They were fiercely attacked by 34 of the 'principal' shopkeepers of Lynn for inoculating the poor 'by which means the smallpox here will probably be continued amongst us' to 'further' damage trade. They believed that inoculation endangered the lives of those 'who never had that distemper', while shoppers avoided the town. The Poor Law authorities concurred, but smallpox persisted at Lynn, and there were particularly bad epidemics in 1816, 1839 and 1845.

Lynn was also the home of typhus and typhoid, or 'the fever'. When William Richards arrived there from London in September 1783 he found 'it had been for some time a very sickly and mortal season'. Especially notable epidemics of 'fever' occurred in 1779, 1780, 1823 and 1826. Dr. Hamilton, who practised at Lynn from 1749 to 1793, was a student of this 'remitting fever', which was 'the great epidemical or rather endemical disease' of the town for centuries. Primitive sanitary conditions promoted forms of typhus and typhoid at Lynn into the 20th century.

In 1831 a new and dreadful epidemic came to England from Europe — 'King Cholera'. By October the corporation had set up a Board of Health composed of local doctors, following the directions of an Act of Parliament, speedily passed by frantic politicians. Notices were posted urging the inhabitants to clean up homes. Pigsties were banned from the vicinities of cottages. Walls and ceilings of living rooms were to be whitewashed. Drunkenness was to be avoided because the intemperate were, supposedly, more 'liable' to cholera. Reverend Hankinson preached at St Margaret's about the dangers of cholera in densely-populated towns like Lynn. Ships from Sunderland believed to be carrying cholera victims were quarantined.

The epidemic struck in the summer of 1832. On 4 August *The Norfolk Chronicle* reported 35 deaths at Lynn in 17 weeks; at least seven others occurred before the disease petered out in September. Over 120 people were infected. Cases in the villages near Lynn were blamed on the filthy conditions among the labourers, but not all the 42 deaths in the town itself were of poor people: the wife of a merchant was among the casualties. In September 1834 there was panic at reports of a revival of the disease, but cholera did not return until 1848, when the crews of ships from Sunderland were the first victims, though only two deaths were recorded. In 1854 a third epidemic claimed nine victims at Lynn.

The environment

By 1400 the mayor and community of Lynn were responsible for official measures to tackle the environmental problems generated by a large seaport and market town. Animals were always wandering the streets. Keeping open the fleets for navigation and drainage was another uphill task, and repairs to conduits bringing fresh water, and to roads and bridges, were essential. There was always rubbish to be removed from the streets to muckhills, best located beside the fleets or river to allow high tides or barges to remove them. Special covered carts modelled on those used in London were provided for the carriage of 'animal entrails'. The authorities were never able to deal with these problems successfully in the Middle Ages, however, and their successors fared little better.

The corporation in the 16th and 17th centuries did show increasing concern about the state of the town, stimulated by the complaints of 'foreign' merchants about the filth obstructing fleets and roads. Fear of the plague also triggered action. The constant repetition by the Town Hall of its orders and warnings to citizens, however, indicates their failure to take effect. As discussed in Chapter Three, one sphere of corporation action was the provision of a piped water supply, which needed constant maintenance. Another was the provision of

33.   The Purfleet, or 'great drain' of Lynn, was an open sewer most offensive at low tide.

34.   North Place was one of the many heavily populated yards in the fishing quarter of Lynn.

public toilets. In 1653 the slaughtering of animals in 'publick places' was banned. The weekly street sweepings ordered by the corporation from as early as 1516 were still performed only half-heartedly in the late 17th century, while the scavengers with carts appointed in 1644 to collect refuse daily from streets and houses were to be accompanied by a constable.

There was traffic congestion and problems with the streets also. In 1656 the corporation ordered all inhabitants not 'to suffer' carts, timber and other lumber 'to lye in the streets', to use carts with shod wheels, nor to 'suffer moveable stalls or blocks to stand in the streets and markets'. Increasing road traffic churned up streets and pavements, but not until 1750 did the corporation appoint John Bowes as 'pavior' to mend and repair them. Special attention was given to the market-places. In 1769 boys from the workhouse were employed to pull up grass in the Tuesday Market Place, which had recently been paved. Aldermen living here were encouraged to plant trees.

By the 17th century the corporation was pressing citizens to deposit refuse at muckhills outside the East and South Gates rather than in the haven, the traditional dustbin of the town, now becoming dangerously silted. Boats were finding it difficult to reach the watergates of merchant houses to load and deliver cargoes. In 1658 all the lanes leading to the medieval muckhills by the Ouse were fenced off to stop dumping. In 1693 and 1706 further orders were issued against dumping in the river and fleets; the headboroughs were to impose 10s. fines for each cart-load tipped.

Keeping the fleets open demanded frequent civic action. Because it was 'the great and principal drain of the country', the Purfleet gave the greatest cause for concern to the merchants, also anxious over navigation. Silt, straw and rubbish clogged it, property owners on its banks being blamed. In 1721 Edmund Rolfe was commissioned by his colleagues to dig out the Purfleet and stop the offences 'dayly comited' by careless citizens. In 1765 the corporation indicted three boatmen who had been paid to clear the fleet, only to deposit the rubbish in the main harbour. In 1768 it was decided to renew the Purfleet quays and bricklayers were invited to tender for the job. The fleets were again full of filth in 1779.

Not until the Paving Acts of 1803 and 1806 did the corporation take strong action to improve the health of the town. Paving, cleaning, lighting and policing were all part of the new laws to be implemented by a commission consisting of big property owners. Refuse disposal was contracted out. Streets were widened and straightened to take increased traffic. These reforms of the urban environment, however, revealed little official concern for the health of the labouring classes crammed into the yards described in Chapter One, behind the façades of the main streets.

The horror of these is depicted in the report prepared by William Lee, of the government's Board of Health, in 1852. Doctors described the filth and disease to be found in them. Families were denied health, comfort and privacy:

> King Street — Nurse's Yard. A long, narrow court, bad pavement, and bad drainage. Yard about 6 feet wide, and a high wall in front of the houses. Twelve families, one privy, and one tap. Rent for two rooms £1. 6s. clear of rates. In the centre of the best street in the town. The drain through the yard belongs to the Paving Commissioners. One of the tenants says she would leave, but she cannot, because she is backward in her rent; several of the others are also in the same state. Another says she pays 2s. 1d. for one room. At one time there were 54 children in this yard.

Neighbours who complained to landlords were 'abused' and often too much in arrears with rent to be defiant. Complaints to local doctors were frequent. In Law's Yard there were only three taps 'on' from seven to nine in the morning for more than 200 persons: 'We should wish very much that the place should be altered, and made more clean'.

Good drainage had been impossible in Lynn before 1821, when the digging of the Eau Brink Cut lowered the river bed. The Estuary Cut of 1852 had a similar effect. The boon to health now allowed by sewers freely draining into the Ouse was denied to most of the yard dwellers, however, since they did not fall within the jurisdiction of the Paving Commissioners.

Overcrowding in damp and filthy yards bred disease. In Linay's Yard the wife of Thomas Wigginton told Lee that the family had lived there for just over a year and had 'lost two children since we came'. John Griffiths, in Watson's Yard, where every house had been divided, had a bad fever. In Saddington's Yard Nathaniel Barker called Lee into his house to complain of two privies close to his window, being 'very offensive and injurious'. He had always been in a bad state of health: 'Have diseased heart ,and lungs; am dropsical, and all decaying inside'. He was 40 years of age. His wife had good health, 'but she is not much at home as she has to hawk about for a living'.

The Board of Health's enquiry had been called as a result of a petition from Lynn's doctors to the board, claiming that the town's death rate was over 'the legal limit' of 23 per thousand, higher than in other East Anglian towns and an indicator of appalling standards of living. They hoped to jog the borough into adopting the Public Health Act of 1848. Nevertheless, despite the evidence discovered by Lee, Lynn's parsimonious ratepayers would not do so. Some of these doctors were remarkable men, such as Dr. Hunter, the son of a tailor who returned to Lynn after training at Edinburgh University and lived amongst the poor at North End. Coulton remembered him as typical of his profession, dressed in long coat and tall silk hat, carrying a knobbed cane.

The origins of the Lynn Dispensary, opened in January 1813, can be found in the mounting pressure from doctors employed by the Poor Law authorities to treat the sick. Similar schemes were already operating in other places, and that at Norwich no doubt gave Lynn's enthusiasts their model. Subscriptions raised enough for a house to be purchased in St James' Street for £450, where an apothecary could liaise with the surgeon at the workhouse. About two thousand people a year received medical aid on the recommendations of members of its management committee. Whooping cough, scarlet fever, measles, smallpox and typhoid were more dramatic, but no more fatal, than that quiet and widespread killer, tuberculosis, bred by bad housing.

The dispensary's existence was effectively ended by the New Poor Law of 1834, which obliged local officials to curb expenditure on labouring families outside the workhouse. Parochial contributions to the dispensary were stopped by the Board of Guardians elected to manage the Poor Law union of Lynn's four parishes. Disgruntled subscribers turned to another project designed to safeguard the public health of the town, the Lynn and West Norfolk Hospital. This new institution was opened in 1835 following a campaign instigated by local landed gentry and the town's doctors; in 1833 Sir William Folkes of Hillington had chaired the exclusive meeting at which the fund raising began. After the cholera scare of 1831-2, which panicked all social classes, a building to isolate the victims of epidemics seemed a sensible idea.

Poverty and survival

After the Reformation and dissolution of the monasteries and religious gilds, bequests by individual Lynn merchants to provide the poor with money, food or coal in the winter became vital to them. More than 66 per cent of Lynn merchants dying in the 16th century gave money for the use of the poor, often entrusting charitable funds to the corporation, and Battley has correctly talked of the 'laicization of charity' in that period. Some men left as much as £100, as Thomas Sandell did in 1614; Samuel Browne bequeathed £100 in 1784 to be invested by the corporation for the supply of coals each winter to the poor of Sedgeford ward. Aged poor townsfolk lucky enough to catch the eye of aldermen were placed in almshouses and maintained by various bequests. Tradesmen would accept poor children

35.   The Lynn and West Norfolk Hospital, built in 1835 and demolished in 1988.

as apprentices if £10 or £20 went with the deal, like the £20 premium paid from Sparrow's charity to the bookbinder, Richard Marshall, for taking Thomas Hunt in 1788.

Richards seems unwarranted in accusing the merchants of Lynn in 1812 of a lack of benevolence or charity. In 1822 *Pigot's Directory* could only admire the number of Lynn's charities: 'the young, the aged and the infirm are alike protected from the evils of poverty'. This was over-optimistic, however. During bad winters and difficult times it was only *spontaneous* and *temporary* charitable effort by the rich of the town which saved the poor from starvation.

So grave did the need to support the poor sometimes become that the corporation was forced to take charitable initiatives itself. To counter sudden shortages of fuel and food, the Tudor and Stuart corporation bought coal and rye for storage in public warehouses by the Ouse, ready for distribution to the poor at prices they could afford, or free, at moments of crisis. In 1650 Alderman Green was told to purchase 100 chalders of 'good coles' for the poor of the town as soon as ships arrived. Rye was bought in Amsterdam the same year for sale to labouring people at low prices. In 1643 peas were given to poor seamen and others.

The year 1757 was a testing time. In January and February a frozen river stopped trade and fostered unemployment, whilst falling temperatures and high food prices accumulated human misery. Coal was distributed free of charge. In June bread prices were still going up, so George Hogge lent the corporation £1,000 at four per cent interest to allow

Mr. Alderson and Stephen Allen to sail to Hull for wheat. The common crier advertised distribution of this grain amongst the inhabitants 'at large' at the rate of £28 a last, samples being available for inspection at the mayor's house. Three lasts were sold to three of the town's bakers at £25 a last. Some £204 raised by subscription was used to sell flour to the poor at half price. By September Mr. Hogge had been repaid £839, but money was still due from some bakers, such as Mr. Crevy of Downham, who owed £8.

Lynn's merchants were inclined to support legislation to curb the free market and protect the poor against high prices. In 1757 they petitioned the king for an Act of Parliament to stop wheat and barley being distilled for spirits in 'these times of scarcity'. Parliament finally obliged in 1759, and Lynn's merchants welcomed the act as good for 'morale' and the 'constitution' of the labouring classes as well as allowing more corn to be exported. In 1766 the corporation even petitioned for an act to stop the export of wheat and flour because of the hardships being experienced by the poor. In November a subscription was opened to buy flour for the relief of the town's 'industrious' poor, to be sold each Friday under the direction of those who gave five guineas.

1795 was another bad year. In February the corporation opened two subscriptions of £100 with £50 donations to enable the poor to buy bread at reduced prices. By July prices were even higher, and it was decided:

> Whereas bread is now at an unusual High Price; Resolved and Ordered that two thousand quartern loaves of household, or standard wheaten, Bread be distributed, at the expense of this Corporation, among the Poor of this Borough, weekly, from the present time, until the First Day of September next ensuing, at the reduced price of six pence a loaf; And that the Aldermen of the several Wards of this Borough, and their respective Deputies, and the Guardians of the Poor be, and they are hereby, requested to make a distribution of such bread, according to their Discretion.

This generosity brought the corporation a debt of £1,300 for wheat and flour by 23 October, the September deadline proving optimistic.

Poverty, hunger and sickness were endemic in years of bad trade and weather, like 1826. 'The Society for visiting and relieving the sick and Indigent Poor' in their own homes attracted 200 subscribers, the most active of whom were the wives and daughters of rich families. No relief was given in money. Poor people were assigned quantities of food, fuel and clothing on tickets, to be exchanged at the society's depot. The corporation regarded the society as a turning-point in charitable endeavour at Lynn. By personal and frequent 'inspection' of the homes of the poor, the most 'deserving' cases could be identified. Only those adjudged to be honest, sober and religious could expect a 'a helping hand' when poverty-stricken or ill. Men and women classified as responsible for their own plight ('the idle, the dissolute and the deceitful') were to be ostracised rather than aided. In 1831, when 'sickness and distress' were as severe as in 1826, the society collected £386 for its operations.

The sea was cruel, taking numerous victims from the port, which encouraged more permanent charitable effort amongst those most closely connected with shipping. The Lynn 'Seaman's and Orphan's Society' had its annual general meeting at the *Duke's Head* attended by shipowners and politicians, always entertained by 'nautical recitations from a hearty tar'. In 1825 the meeting raised £702. The 'Shipwrecked Seaman's, Fisherman's and Mariner's Benevolent Society' was founded in 1839 to give relief to widows and orphans, of whom 19 were helped in 1840. A fisherman was also given £5 to buy a boat. Of the 418 sailors and relatives enrolled in the society by 1842, at least 213 had received aid. Maritime disasters rocked Lynn. The storm of August 1833 destroyed three ships and crews, leaving unsupported 10 widows, a mother, 32 children, an orphan and a fatherless unborn child. Church congregations and individuals subscribed £444 for the relief of these unfortunates.

The Poor Law

Charity was never enough, and the corporation was forced to develop official and permanent measures to support the poor. Even before the Reformation the corporation was concerned about the 'masterless' poor, and in 1520 all unemployed artisans and labourers were ordered to the Tuesday Market Place every day to wait an hour to be hired, or run the risk of being punished as vagabonds. Badges of lead were issued to aged and impotent persons to allow them to beg in the streets, but the able-bodied poor were expected to work for their upkeep. Job creation schemes were introduced, notably attempts to convert the remains of St James' chapel to a cloth factory, but they failed.

In 1601 parishes were charged with the administration of a Poor Law whereby the able-bodied unemployed were to be set to work and the impotent maintained by a levy on property owners. Lynn's merchant rulers struggled to find an effective system. In 1638 the town's able-bodied paupers were obliged to attend St Margaret's church every Friday to be allocated jobs and 'doles' by the corporation's aldermen. In 1651 the corporation instructed the overseers 'to buy wooll to set the poor to work' and 'to send the poor people to the Yorkshire men brought hither to set them on work accordingly'. Shirts made at the factory were sold by the overseers and wages paid to the workers. Further experiments in the 1650s suggest that the factory was short-lived, however. Susan Clarke was then given £100 to teach the poor to spin and knit for the stocking trade in a warehouse on King's Staithe Square. Wages were not to be paid in 'commodities' rather than money 'without the poor people's good liking'.

The Elizabethan Poor Law had not given the parish of St Margaret's the power it wanted to tackle the poverty in its streets. The corporation asked Sir Robert Walpole to pilot a local act through parliament in 1701, which established 'the Court of Guardians of the Borough of King's Lynn'. This body included the key members of the corporation and 18 other guardians elected by ratepayers. They set out to make a new Poor Law regime, focused on the workhouse of St James. The court elected a governor, deputy governor and treasurer annually. The daily management of the system was handled by paid officials, the master of the workhouse and his wife receiving full board, £20 a year salary and a share of any earnings made by the inmates. Each year a doctor was elected to visit the sick poor, who were sometimes sent to London hospitals for surgery. Teachers were appointed to inculcate literacy into workhouse children, who were also taught spinning, weaving and sewing. These teachers were often dedicated people, such as Mary Browne, a teacher at the workhouse from 1708 to 1722, earning 10s. a month. Personal assistant to the Governor was the beadle, whose policing role included the performance of public whippings on paupers who misbehaved. Important also were the unpaid overseers elected by the magistrats to assess and collect the poor rate. Without efficiency and determination on their part the system was starved of funds. They were frequently criticised by the Court of Guardians for failing to squeeze enough money from the ratepayers and the corporation was forced to make loans to St James' during bad winters or other times of unusual expenditure.

Paupers could discharge themselves at any time and expect to be helped to make a fresh start outside. One family leaving the workhouse in September 1766 was given five guineas to buy furniture. The Court tried to turn those remaining into a healthy and disciplined workforce, while the labelling of the inmates as a 'family' indicates a moral purpose also. The building was improved. Chimneys were inserted into the chapel, nursery and common lodging room, where a 'german stove' was installed in 1751. In 1763 several rooms were divided to separate old and young, sick and healthy, and male and female. Expenditure stretched to 12 straw hats and two dozen gloves for the boys and girls in 1745. Gruel, broth, porridge, bread, cheese, meat and ale were provided. Schemes for spinning yarn for profit in the workhouse were discussed with contractors, but never implemented. The main

36. St James' Workhouse included the transepts of the medieval chapel of the same name.

problem was the character of the workforce: of the roughly hundred and fifty inmates in summertime and the two hundred in winter, many were women and children or unruly young people taking refuge for short periods. There were also some vagrants.

Despite the efforts of the Court of Guardians to regenerate 'the family' at St James', a hard core of adult inmates resisted. In 1727 Charles Wingfield was whipped after being 'convicted' of card playing and leaving St James' without 'permission'. William Cooper was charged with carnal knowledge of a female inmate, who had been made pregnant, and publicly whipped. In 1751 Elizabeth Wright was given seven lashes for being 'idle', 'disorderly' and 'incorrigible'. Swearing, spoiling wool, lying in bed late and laziness appear to have been endemic in the workhouse. In 1751 the Court had all offences and punishments written on parchment and framed. The master was to read them to all inmates on the first Sunday of each month; if any pauper was absent, he or she was to be refused dinner that day. Twelve months hard labour in St James' grounds was the ultimate punishment for persistent offenders.

The most important aspect of the Poor Law in 18th-century Lynn was the relief of applicants 'outdoors', or in their own homes. This was far more economical and less troublesome than keeping people 'indoors' at St James', and the workhouse could not have contained all applicants for relief, particularly in bad winters when work was scarce and food prices high. The winters of 1766-7 and 1767-8 were both disastrous, and twice the workhouse master was given gratuities for his 'extra trouble' in providing and delivering food to over 600 people every day, while others were obliged to journey to St James' for meals. The order that all applicants should bear the stigma of pauperism by wearing a badge was obviously intended to deter. Hundreds of people required regular payments. In August 1770 there were 131 families, 280 people, 'on weekly establishment', costing the treasurer £11.

Occasional payments, as gifts or loans, to individuals and families in need were more numerous. Big families often required income supplements, such as the 5s. a week for four weeks allowed to Martin Bonnington, his wife and seven children in 1739. Robert Boardman's pregnant wife was lent £3 on receipt of a promise to repay from her husband. Relief was often in the form of clothing or other items, avoiding the risk of money being misappropriated, although in 1758 the widow Trickett was given 20s. for 'cloathing herself and Ann Lawes', a poor child kept 'from being a charge to this parish'.

More urgent than clothes to many applicants for poor relief was money to pay the rent on their cottages. Most requests were granted because the consequences of mass evictions were too dreadful to contemplate. So heavy was the demand for rent allowances or loans that both were frozen in 1736, 1746 and 1763, although exceptions were made for the wives of servicemen. In 1755 the wives of 12 impressed seamen were lent £1 each for rent, to be repaid by their husbands. If sailors died on active service a messenger was sent to London to collect their wages so that debts could be honoured. In 1755 the workhouse master returned from the Admiralty with wages amounting to over £30 owing to nine Lynn war dead.

Poor men were sometimes allowed subsidies to keep them out of the workhouse. In 1733 John Winkley was given an ass and baskets 'to carry fish into the country' and other things needed by a pedlar. Carpenters, shoemakers and fishermen were provided with similar aid if they promised to repay it as soon as possible. Disability allowances were also paid, like the 12d. a week to Sarah Loveday, she having 'an impediment' in her speech and being 'unfit for service'. Blind, lame, disabled and insane poor people were helped through payments to their relatives or friends. Money was made available for burials, including 2s. and 'no more' allowed in 1736 for beer after the funerals. In 1731 the widow Hammond's burial cost 19s. 10d., of which 1s. had been spent on a gallon of beer and 7s. on the coffin. In 1739 coffins for paupers were forbidden and the dead buried without ceremony in the ground around St James'.

Lynn's 1701 Poor Law operated with some degree of humanity and flexibility. The bad harvests and economic dislocation of the French Wars (1793-1815), however, imposed an almost intolerable burden on ratepayers, tradesmen above all, who attacked the big merchants for avoiding their share of taxation. Several rowdy meetings between these parties took place in the Town Hall, leading to an amendment of the 1701 act by parliament in 1808. This did not assuage all discontent. William Richards, for example, believed that the town's paupers were being cossetted, extravagant sums being used to buy meat, cheese, butter, milk, potatoes, peas and coal, while the poor rates were too heavy for 'the inhabitants'. The Baptist minister approved of the new economy drive at 'the playhouse' of St James in 1810, although most of the thousand people on relief were being helped at home, a man and wife with five children being allowed only 12½d. a week.

Rising poor rates all over England south of the Trent resulted in the Poor Law Amendment Act of 1834, which attempted to combine cuts in public spending with the moral reform of the labourer. Parishes were grouped into unions where single workhouses would house paupers. Conditions in them were to be harsher, or 'less eligible', than those of labourers outside, so only genuine cases among the able-bodied poor would endure the strict regime. Others would migrate to underpopulated industrial towns. Outdoor relief would still be given to the old and sick. The ideological simplicity of this 'solution' to the pauper problem was flawed by the huge sums required to build workhouses large enough to accommodate all who needed relief.

St James' workhouse was enlarged and altered to take 200 inmates for £750. The building had deteriorated because of the parsimony of the Poor Law authorities, however, and the work undertaken in 1835 failed to correct its faulty structure. On 20 August 1854 its central tower collapsed as the clock was being repaired by Mr. Andrews, who had intrepidly climbed up. He and a pauper named Cana, whose head was 'squeezed perfectly flat' by a sheet of lead, were killed, and the workhouse master and another man were buried alive in the debris. That there were only two casualties was thanks to the inmates being at church or out walking on that fine Sunday morning. An official enquiry absolved Lynn's Board of Guardians from blame, but it had to build a new and much larger workhouse about half a mile from the old, nicely away from public view. It was opened in 1856 at a cost of £14,000, having accommodation for 468 inmates, classified according to sex, age and physical state.

Door at Thoresby College in Queen Street (1510).

Chapter Seven

Religion and Society

The medieval Church

St Margaret's was a priory church, with a monastery on its southern flank where the Benedictine monks were sheltered from the cold north winds. This community, which dressed in black and white habits, was never large. Most of their time was taken up with praying, studying, writing, teaching and visiting the sick. The prior was always a man of 'no small consequence' amongst the religious community at Lynn, and 'esteemed by the principal persons of that place'. He was rector of the parish of St Margaret's and therefore entitled to the tithes, burial and other fees and offerings. He nominated a parish priest for the cure of souls. Once the church was founded the bishop of Norwich had no direct concern with it except as head of the diocese, but he did sometimes preach there.

St Margaret's was really two churches in one. The chancel was under the control of the prior and the nave under that of the townspeople. In 1438 the prior tried to open a blocked doorway in the cross aisle and was fiercely opposed by the parishioners as intruding into 'that part of the church for which the churchwardens answered to the mayor. Every Easter the churchwardens presented accounts to the mayor and the alderman of the Great Gild. The building and repair of the nave of the mother church and its two chapels of ease depended on the efforts of the parishioners. Between 1433 and 1437 the whole town was rated to raise money to rebuild the belltower of St Margaret's. The parishioners also supplied St Margaret's, St Nicholas' and St James' with bread and wine; orders about the mode of rating for holy bread are recorded in the Hall Books.

The large congregation of St Nicholas' campaigned for full parochial independence from the mother church of St Margaret. Why should the sacraments of baptism and marriage not be celebrated there? Representatives of the congregation petitioned Rome for parish status in 1378 and were successful, but the prior, who stood to lose influence and income, supported by the Great Gild, organised a counter petition and the *status quo ante* was restored. A second petition sent by the congregation of St Nicholas' in 1426, following the rebuilding of the chapel, met the same opposition and lack of success. The figures for attendance at Easter communion at Lynn in 1426, compiled to advance the pleas for independence of the two chapels of ease, show impressive congregations: St Margaret's, 1,600; St Nicholas', 1,400; and St James', nine hundred. Not until 1627 did St Nicholas' chapel obtain baptismal rights.

In the late 14th and early 15th centuries the Church was attacked by radical priests for being too remote and worldly to satisfy the needs of its flock. These men, followers of John Wyclif (1324-84), nicknamed Lollards after their habit of lullabying, or singing low, included William Sawtre, a parochial chaplain at St Margaret's. It seems unlikely that many of the urban poor at Lynn and elsewhere attended church services. The separation of priest and congregation by a screen between chancel and nave, and the use of Latin, 'mystified' Christianity. The Lollards wanted an English Bible so that the people could more directly learn Christian teachings, but these could be interpreted against the interests of the ruling classes, as the Peasants' Revolt of 1381, with its slogan 'When Adam delved and Eve span, who was then a gentleman?', demonstrated.

Sawtre was the hero of William Richards, who proudly presented him in his *History of Lynn* (1812) as 'probably' a native of the town and the first Englishman to be burnt for his religion. The cleric condemned lazy clergy as not deserving the tithes supporting them, and declared pilgrimages were a waste of money better spent on the poor. Even more radically, and heretically, he denied that during the consecration the bread and wine were 'transubstantiated' into the body and blood of Christ. After interrogation and torture at the episcopal palace in 1399, Sawtre recanted. He was forced to disclaim his heretical opinions publicly before Bishop Despencer and the townspeople in the churchyard of St James', and again the following day at the church of the Hospital of St John, in Norfolk Street. He then went to London where he became chaplain of St Osith and found support among the strong Lollard community of the city. There he taught that communion with God did not need the Church — any man could be a priest! He was ordered to appear before Archbishop Arundel and the Provincial Council in the Chapter House of St Paul's in February 1401. This time .Sawtre defended himself and the consequence was his execution at Smithfield by burning.

The four great orders of friars — Dominicans (Black), Carmelites (White), Franciscans (Grey) and Augustinians (Black) — were all established at Lynn by 1300. The Franciscans were linked to the Friars of the Sack, who had disappeared from Lynn by 1314. Friars, at least in the early days of the orders, were learned and pious

37. This gateway is the sole surviving piece of the Augustinian friary at Lynn.

men, many of whom had rejected comfortable bourgeois households to follow the most spartan of existences. The Carmelites at South Lynn are said to have slept in their coffins. Norfolk gentry and Lynn merchants granted them land and money, making possible the development of churches, libraries, infirmaries, mills and chapter houses. Many of the merchants left instructions to be buried in their cemeteries, to the chagrin of the prior of St Margaret's, who lost burial fees as a result. A compromise was reached in 1360 whereby the prior was given a quarter of all offerings made at funerals in the friary churches.

There were 40 Carmelites at Lynn in 1377 and 46 Augustinians there in 1446. The other two orders may have boasted similar numbers in the town. These friars were not only social workers, but many were highly educated men, who wrote religious and historical books (in English and Latin). Some ranked among the most distinguished scholars of medieval England. Most adventurous and famous was the Franciscan Nicholas of Lynn (d. 1369), who made six voyages into the North Atlantic and may have reached America 130 years before Columbus. Nicholas described his expeditions in *Inventio Fortunata*, which he presented to Edward III and which was used by successive monarchs. This friar was referred to by Chaucer as 'that reverend clerke'. He had an observatory at the top of the Greyfriars tower.

Only the gateway remains of the Augustinian friary where lived John Capgrave (1393-1464), a Lynn man ('my countre is northfolk of the town of Lynne'). He studied at Oxford and London and visited Rome. Capgrave was Provincial of his order, with responsibility for 41 friaries throughout Britain, for several years. His best known works are *The Chronicles of England to 1417* and the *Illustrious Henries*. His interests were not surprising. He received Henry VI at the friary in 1446 when the monarch was 'in the course of the solemn pilgrimage' to holy places. In 1498 Henry VII also lodged at the Augustinian friary on his way to Walsingham. More pilgrims headed for this north Norfolk shrine than to any place save Canterbury.

Jews arrived in English towns before the friars. Despised for their role in the history of Christianity, their success in trade brought increased hatred. Anti-semitism led to massacres in 1189-90. A pogrom started in London after altercations between Jews and enthusiasts for Richard I's crusade. The inhabitants of other large towns followed the Londoners' example; Lynn's massacre is supposed to have arisen from the threat to a Jew who had been converted to Christianity. His fellows chased him through the streets and into St Margaret's church. Townspeople intervened to save the convert, and foreign sailors seized the opportunity to pillage the Jews (Jew's Lane was off the Tuesday Market Place). Another account substitutes a band of crusaders on the point of departure for the Holy Land for the sailors. The story is suspect, however, since Jews would have been unlikely to provoke bloody reaction by persecuting a convert to Christianity. It is more likely that townspeople in debt to Jews encouraged all and sundry to attack them, to be rid of their creditors. On the day after the massacre a celebrated Jewish physician returned home to Lynn to condemn the guilty; he, too, was murdered.

Margery Kempe

This survey of religious life in Lynn would be incomplete without an account of the extraordinary Margery Kempe (1373-1440?), the female mystic whose life, dictated to an amanuensis, stands as the first autobiography in English. She herself was illiterate. *The Book of Margery Kempe* is not just a record of a series of amazing religious experiences and pilgrimages in England and Europe, but a social history of unique interest.

Margery rebelled against the weak character of a husband who displayed little sexual restraint while she endured 14 pregnancies. He desisted only when she helped to pay his debts. Margery began to wear cloaks of many colours and fine headgear to shock the patriarchs of bourgeois Lynn, provoking one man to throw a bowl of water over her head in the street. The conversion of this 'creature', as Margery labels herself, to Christ, in the self-appointed twin roles of holy bride and saviour of a sinful populace, broke the tolerance of many. Her terrible outbursts of shrieking in church, implicitly claiming a special relationship with God, challenged the authority of the Church, while wearing white and living apart from her husband to emphasise her religious mission antagonised laymen and cleric alike. The prior of St Margaret's allowed Margery into the Benedictine cloisters to stop her going into church! A Carmelite friar called Alan of Lynn befriended her as a woman whose religious experiences deserved to be taken seriously. Alan may have introduced her to the *Revelations of St Bridget of Sweden* (1303-72), who forsook a comfortable family life for Christ. Her example greatly influenced Margery.

Easter was the period of greatest intensity for Margery. On Palm Sunday there was a procession in the churchyard of St Margaret's, led by the priest. He smote the doors with his staff and entered, followed by the townspeople, to witness the crucifix revealed from behind its lenten curtain. During the mass Margery sobbed 'most abundantly' and cried when she saw Jesus as much with her 'spiritual eye' as the crucifix with her 'bodily eye'. A Doctor of Divinity preaching on a Palm Sunday found the congregation cursing her as she responded to his sermon with loud shrieks. One Holy Thursday Margery went in procession with the townspeople, but fell down 'in the field' as she 'saw in her soul' Our Lady, St Mary Magdalene and the 12 Apostles taking leave of Jesus, and wept 'as though she would have burst'. Good Friday was the day Lynn priests and merchants knelt with burning torches before the Easter Sepulchre in St Margaret's, representing the death and burial of Jesus. Margery wept for five or six hours for the townspeople, the poor, the Jews, the Saracens and heretics, so that God might break their 'blindness'.

She could not resist the temptation to exhibit her religious zeal before some of the best-known friars in England. One accepted her outbursts when he preached a sermon in the churchyard of St James'. The following occasion, however, he decided that the wailing woman was not sent by Christ to purify the town, as she claimed, but was possessed by the devil, and should not hear him; she was only to be admitted to his sermons if she promised to be quiet. Margery said that this encouraged her enemies to denounce her, but all attempts by her friends to persuade 'the good friar' to receive her were fruitless. One year, on St James' Day (25 July), he preached against her in St James' churchyard before a big crowd, many from outside the town, despite the protests of those who 'trusted and loved her very much'. Margery claimed that even her friends deserted her.

When the chapter of the Dominicans held conference at Lynn, one of their number, Thomas Constance, confirmed her weeping and wailing to be a special gift of God. His support appears to have turned the tide. One Lent an Augustinian friar preached 'in his own house' at Lynn before a large congregation, including Margery. She was overwhelmed by visions of Christ's Passion, but he defended her when people objected to the crying. Other learned preachers did likewise, and Bishop Wakering put up 'meekly' with her violent seizures of emotion on another occasion at St Margaret's. Yet Margery's friend and mentor, Alan, was forbidden by the Provincial Prior of the Carmelites to see her, on the grounds that she was a heretic. This was a terrible blow to her. Only the anchorite at the Dominican house remained her loyal confessor throughout her troubles.

She and her companions visited Boston, Leicester, Lincoln, Canterbury and London. She had keen disputations with various mayors and bishops who suspected her of being a Lollard, perhaps because Sawtre had come from Lynn. The archbishop of Canterbury was intrigued enough to meet her in 1413 and 1417. She travelled also to the Holy Land, accompanied by a maidservant and a party of Norwich clerics. They sailed from Yarmouth to Holland and journeyed overland to Venice in the spring of 1414, where they took ship for Palestine, usually a voyage of three weeks if weather and pirates permitted. The fare of £15 on the Venetian state 'tourist' galley included food and drink. At Jaffa the Christians were met by Moslem officials who escorted them to Jerusalem on asses or mules. Here Franciscan friars acted as guides to the Church of the Holy Sepulchre and other places. Margery was overcome, and wept more in Jerusalem, with greater noise and emotion, than anywhere else, to the amazement of all. She returned to England in the spring of 1415 via Assisi and Rome. Two more pilgrimages abroad followed: she sailed from Bristol to the shrine of St James at Compostella, in north-west Spain, in 1417, and in 1433 she sailed from Ipswich to the Baltic, with her widowed German daughter-in-law, to visit Prussian shrines.

The Reformation

Was the English Reformation all the more easy for Henry VIII because of a growing popular detachment from the Church, if not a decline of religious belief? Enthusiasm for church building does seem to have disappeared after 1500, and the town's friaries were also running down before the Dissolution of the 1530s. When the Carmelites were forced to surrender their house, in 1538, there was only a prior and 10 monks, whereas there had been over 40 in 1377. Hillen mentions a falling away of offerings to Lynn's churches from the late 15th century, as the Benedictines at St Margaret's experienced. There is contradictory evidence, however. In 1517, for example, John Foster of South Lynn left instructions for masses to be sung at the *Scala Celi* in the Austin Friary after his death. To say mass here (the *Scala Celi* being a representation of a ladder to heaven) was believed to be the surest way to expedite souls from purgatory.

Some disillusion with the Church of Rome at Lynn was indicated by an anonymous local chronicler, who showed great interest in the Reformation. He talked of Luther before any other contemporary English chronicler: 'In this yere [1518] leutor wrot to leo the byshop of rome consarnyng pardons and other matters of relygyon for which cawse he was proclamed (trator) heretycke but by the mantynance of the duke of Saxton he preched and wrot styll agaynst the pope'. Luther had hung up his theses at Wittenberg in late 1517. Lynn's associations with the seaports of the Netherlands and Germany exposed the Norfolk town to the religious 'wind of change' in Europe. For 1538 our chronicler uses the phrase 'pylgiymes and Idolytrye forbyden' when telling of the dissolution of the Lynn friaries, and other references suggest Protestant leanings. In 1530 Bishop Nix of Norwich wrote his famous letter complaining about the reading of 'erroneous books in English' in his diocese, of which Lynn would doubtless have had its share. In 1528 a certain Robert Necton admitted to having taken New Testaments to Lynn.

Richards interpreted the Reformation at Lynn as a disaster for the townspeople. The dissolution of so many religious houses and the expulsion of 'such a multitude' of monks who 'must have had no small influence' in preserving 'social order and morality' convinced him of this. He referred to the burning of a Dutchman in the town for heresy in 1535 as an example of the social degeneration brought about by the Reformation. This unfortunate had 'probably' fled from religious persecution in his own country to Lynn because of England's reputation for generosity to 'the oppressed'. Richards was less interested in the events at Walsingham in 1537, where monks resisted the closure of their abbey. William Gisborough of Lynn was executed here for his part in this act of defiance. On the other hand, Simon Miller of Lynn was burnt in 1557 at Norwich for protesting about the Marian revival of Catholicism.

Queen Mary's Counter Reformation in the 1550s was popular in Lynn. Rood-lofts destroyed in the reign of Edward VI were replaced in 1558 and broken images 'mended' at some expense to the parishioners of St Margaret's. Elizabeth's succession, however, signalled a fresh impetus for reform, now cleverly associated with English nationalism. Roman Catholics came to be branded as traitors, friends of the Spanish foe. The printing of Bibles in English and the growth of literacy accelerated the growth of Protestantism, as did action by the state. In 1559 the rood-lofts and 'the images that were upon them' were again taken down from all Lynn's churches, and the steps up to the altars removed. Many 'popish relics' and mass books were burnt in the market-places in 1561. Furnishings and plate were sold to finance repairs.

Did Lynn's merchant rulers leave the townspeople in 'darkness' as Richards contends? Protestant preachers harangued market-day crowds in Elizabethan towns against Papism and immorality. Prostitutes were treated harshly at Lynn. They were stripped and pulled around the town in a cart like 'John Wanker's wife and the widow Porker' in 1587. Richards claimed that Protestant preachers were *not* appreciated in the town, citing the example of Baret, a local man whose ministry was 'lost' to Norwich. Lynn remained in 'a very dark and unimproved state' from the Reformation to the middle of the 17th century ('if not much

38. The Red Mount Chapel, or Chapel of Our Lady, was a wayside chapel on the pilgrimage route to Walsingham.

longer') according to the Baptist historian. The corporation did appoint lecturers or preachers like in other towns; two were appointed in 1619, one each for St Margaret's and St Nicholas', at a fee of £50 a year and a free dwelling, to preach on Sundays and other days prescribed by their merchant patrons. But, said Richards, only one lecturer was brave enough to attempt moral reform, Samuel Fairclough, and he was expelled for failing to use the sign of the cross in the ceremony of christening, apparently an excuse to rid Lynn of a preacher who was emptying taverns on Sundays, to the dismay of the town brewers.

It can be argued that the burning of so-called witches in the late 16th and early 17th centuries is best explained as a consequence of the Reformation, for the common people were being stripped of their traditional securities and had not yet accepted the new religion. Catholicism had not effectively attacked the old pagan attitudes. Misfortune in a difficult and hostile environment was seen by the native English as the work of Satanic forces, not the punishment of an omnipotent God, inflicted on individuals for no obvious reason. Catholic rituals, like crossing oneself, gave people the protection required in a world full of 'evil spirits'. Protestant preachers dismissed all this as superstitious nonsense, but to switch the explanation of misfortune from evil spirits to God's will was unwelcome and unacceptable to the poor. Did God always find labouring folk so wanting? Protestantism was a more comfortable religion for 'the middling sort', whose faith seemed rewarded by earthly success. Disaster for the nation or town was regarded as God's verdict on a sinful populace, as entries in the Hall Books about the plague in Tudor and Stuart times show. When individual citizens suffered for no apparent reason, however, here was the beginning of witch burning. Poor and old women were the usual victims. Their arguments with neighbours led to some inexplicable catastrophe for the latter, who accused them of making a contract with the devil.

Lynn did not escape the national sport of witch hunting. Margaret Read was burned in 1590. Elizabeth Housegoe was burned or hanged in 1598. In 1616 it was the turn of Mary Smith. She had been mistakenly accused by Elizabeth Hancocke of stealing a hen. Mary had retaliated by calling Elizabeth names and wishing 'a pox to light upon her'. Elizabeth soon fell ill. Her father sought the advice of a wise, or cunning, man, with knowledge of magic, who confirmed that she was bewitched. The 'magician' even purported to show the father the face of the witch in a glass, and gave him a recipe for 'Witch Cake' to counteract the spell. Elizabeth was soon better and happily married, but following a quarrel between her husband and Mary Smith her malady returned and a court case was brought against Mary. She had always had a bad reputation and other townspeople also made accusations against her. Mary confessed to having become a witch because of envy of her neighbours and temptation by the devil. She was hung in January. Her chief accuser, Reverend Roberts, 'one of the preachers of God's word for this town', was highly thought of. In January 1615 he was allowed 20 marks by the corporation for building a water pipe from the conduit to his house in the Tuesday Market Place. The house is adorned with the witch's heart.

The end of the Civil War coincided with a rash of witch trials in East Anglia, many instigated by the self-styled 'Witchfinder-General' Matthew Hopkins, an Essex lawyer. In 1646 Lynn's corporation sent for him; he was to be paid £15 a day for his work. Dorothy Lee and Grace Wright, however, were executed for witchcraft in the Tuesday Market Place before his visit and 'the witch' Dorothy Floyd cannot have been one of his victims, for she was hanged at Lynn in 1650, after his death in 1647. Popular beliefs about witchcraft were still current at Lynn in 1800: Richards complained about them. William Armes remembered in 1864 'the noted' Mrs. Sparrow, a 'wise woman' of the town who attracted men wanting her to find thieves that had robbed them or a girl for them to marry. Here was a woman with the 'magic' to do good; were there others less benevolent?

Puritanism and revolution

The fabrics of St Margaret's and St Nicholas' were well maintained in the early decades of the 17th century. New seating was also installed for the congregations to hear the long sermons directed at them. Repairs to both buildings were largely funded by the sale of their vestments and ornaments, as well as the bells and other pieces of St James'. Parishioners were apparently not so ready to be taxed for the upkeep of the churches as before, and some refused to pay the church rate in 1616. The churchwardens' accounts of St Nicholas' for that year record an annual income of £121 from rents on pasture in Gaywood and town tenements. It was insufficient and sums were borrowed from the corporation. Expenses this year included restoration of the chancel, a new bell rope, a key for the belfry door, painting the pulpit, mending the clock, communion wine, bread, oil and frankincense.

Expenditure on churches was increased during the 1630s as a result of the policies of Archbishop Laud. In 1634-5 his commissioners carried out a visitation of the Province of Canterbury, collecting information and tackling malpractices. Lynn received a good report:

> King's Lynn, April 13. Since the Court of High Commission took in hand some of their schismatics few of that fiery spirit remain there or in the parts thereabout. But there are divers papists, who speak scandalously of the Scriptures and of our religion. They are already presented for it, and I have given order that they shall be brought into the High Commission Court. The three churches in Lynn are exceeding fair, and well kept, and the three ministers are very conformable and agree exceeding well; only in the principal church called St Margaret's the communion table wanted [i.e. lacked] a rail, and at the upper end of the choir instead of divine sentences of Scripture divers saying out of the Fathers were painted. I have ordered these two things [i.e. put them in order]. The mayor and his brethren showed very great respect unto your Grace's Visitation in visiting of me and feasting me twice. They likewise went with me to the town quay where they caused all their ordnance to be shot off . . . In these parts divers parsonage houses have been ruined and much glebe land is embezzled. I have made a reference concerning these two things, wherewith the parties complaining are well satisfied.

It suggests that the merchants of Lynn had settled for supporting official policies of quashing extremism, Catholic or Puritan. Nor was money spent simply on entertainment. In January 1636 the corporation spent £48 on a new communion table and other 'ornaments' in the chancel of St Margaret's church, despite the fact that this was really a parish 'charge'.

Laud's policies, including the king's 1633 'Declaration of Sports' sanctioning traditional recreations and the order in 1637 that the communion table be moved to the east end of the church, which was to be raised on three steps and railed off, seemed to Puritans to threaten to reverse the reform of the Church. The bishop of Norwich made his support of the archbishop seemingly clear in a visitation question in 1638: 'Is your communion table enclosed, and ranged about with a rail of joiners' and turners' work, close enough to keep dogs from going in and profaning that holy place, from pissing against it or worse'. Rails had originally been set up for this utilitarian reason, not for kneeling against at communion. Persecution of Puritan writers and preachers encouraged their emigration. The Revd. Samuel Whiting (1598-1679) was born in Boston and after studying at Cambridge was private chaplain to Sir Nicholas Bacon and Sir Roger Townshend before becoming curate of St Nicholas' at Lynn. Hostility to his nonconformity drove him to New England, where his popularity as minister of the Massachusetts town of Saugus led its council to rename it 'Lin' after his adopted home.

During the Commonwealth Lynn's Puritan rulers attempted to impose a regime of strict religious observance on inhabitants whose lives had clearly been little affected by the Reformation. Days, such as Friday 10 October 1651, were 'sett apart' for 'publique humili-ations'. Shops and businesses were 'shutt' so that all citizens had the chance 'to seek God' at St Margaret's or elsewhere. 'All sortes of sinners' did 'abound', 'in particular' at Lynn, although 'the hand of God' had divided the nation 'by the sword' for three years.

39. View of St Margaret's church from the south, about 1680, after Henry Bell.

40. Henry Bell's view of the interior of St Margaret's before the destruction of the nave in 1741.

Drunkenness, pride, envy and wantonness were apparently rife. In December 1656 the corporation decided that the poor needed to be instructed in 'the principles of religion' because for the most part they were 'very ignorant'. All beneficiaries of the Poor Law had to attend St Margaret's every Friday.

After the Restoration the Anglican establishment curbed the religious sects, and over 2,000 radical ministers were forced to resign. In 1662 Reverend John Horne of All Saints' church at South Lynn was ejected from his living. He became the minister of the Presbyterians, who met in St Nicholas Street. When he received a licence to preach in 1673 the sect moved to the disused glass factory off Broad Street. The Presbyterians left this for a chapel in the same street, which the Congregationalists, or Independents, took over in 1803. The decline of the Presbyterians had been hastened in 1744 when several members seceded to the Baptists, started at Lynn in 1687 by Thomas Grantham of Lincoln, and assembling in private houses (and even the Town Hall) until a chapel was built in Broad Street. William Richards was their minister from 1776. The Quakers at Lynn were galvanised by a visit from George Fox in 1655, though he was chased out of town. Nine Quakers were thrown into prison in December 1663 after their meeting was discovered. The sect erected a meeting-house in New Conduit Street in 1774.

Religious toleration for Nonconformists was assured by the 'Glorious Revolution' of 1688, when the Protestants William and Mary arrived from Holland to lead the fight against the reactionary James II. The consequent Toleration Act of 1689 boosted Dissent, but Nonconformists were no more successful than Anglicans in converting townspeople to more than nominal Christianity.

The corporation continued in the 18th century to make unsuccessful efforts to change the behaviour of the townsfolk through reviving Sunday observance laws. Barbers were ordered not to trim customers on the Sabbath in 1718, 1727 and 1745, for example. A campaign to stop all 'worldly work' on Sundays was undertaken by the corporation in 1752, warnings being carried on posters in the market-places and reinforced by the town crier. In 1706 the corporation complained of 'notorious offences of drunkenness and profanity and cursing and swearing' being 'dayley comited' amongst Lynn's riverside labourers, but the threat of punishment was ineffective, for the porters were still 'taking God's Holy name in vain' in 1753.

Popular religion

Richards, a Baptist minister, was a stern critic of the Established Church, believing its clergy made little attempt to acquaint congregations with 'the real meaning' of Scripture because of their fear of losing control over 'the thinking' of the people. It is true that the literal interpretation of the Bible had potentially revolutionary consequences for a society shot through with injustice and suffering. He asserted that the labouring classes were 'unenlightened', and really in a state of 'mere heathenism', though, 'absurdly', all were considered to be Anglicans. He thought that the Methodists alone had as many 'regular communicants' as the Established Church. Of the 11,000 inhabitants in 1812, only 2,776 could have been squeezed into the three Anglican churches, and another 1,550 into the four Nonconformist chapels, so that 4,326 'places' were available each Sunday. Richards claims that no more than 3,000 attended Sunday services anyway. Over 8,000 townspeople were neither religious nor 'affected by any sound moral principles'.

Richards was in fact writing during an upsurge of religious zeal, encompassing more townsmen than ever before, although the pacemakers were the middle classes, especially tradesmen who had found Anglicanism wanting. Methodism, which began as an enthusiastic branch of Anglicanism, was strong at Lynn as it was elsewhere. When Mrs. Rachel Crawforth died here in 1818 she was said to be the oldest Methodist in England, having been a member for 80 years, first at Newcastle. She was certainly amongst the original Methodist congregation in the town. John Wesley had visited Lynn four times by 1788, when a chapel was built in Blackfriars Street to accommodate the growing band. It was replaced by a new and much larger edifice in Tower Street in 1812.

41. The Wesleyan Methodist chapel opened in 1813.

Congregations at this 'Methodist Minster' were always overflowing and the chapel was home for no fewer than 30 preachers in Lynn and district. Who followed these charismatic and energetic men? Thomas Folkard (alias 'Long Tom') was a barber who was usher at the chapel and kept 'the temperature right' by opening and shutting windows. James Burch, the High Street tailor and savings bank manager, was 'a staunch' Wesleyan and an 'upright man'. Another leading light at the Tower Street chapel about 1820 was the rope and sail maker, Mr. Linay. Daughters of the middling classes were also converts to Methodism, as the example of Maria Greeves (1793-1823) powerfully illustrates. She 'tried' Anglicans, Independents and Baptists before 'finding Jesus' with the Wesleyans. In January 1814 she spoke at her first 'love feast' and was 'sensibly affected'. Maria castigated all those who 'indulged' themselves at dances, taverns and the February mart. Her evangelical zeal brought her to charitable work amongst the poor as well as teaching Scripture to classes at Tower Street.

Divisions opened in the ranks of the Lynn Methodists, often because of conflict over the role of ministers, and chapels were started by the Reform, Association, New Connexion and Primitive Methodists. Primitive Methodism acted as a magnet to many of the town's labouring poor. Porters, sailors and fishermen responded to missionaries from Nottingham visiting Norfolk in the early 1820s. Mainstream Methodism was too stuffy for people who toiled on land and sea, and whose meetings were charged with intense feeling for Christ and of liberation from earthly bondage. Experiences of this kind sparked the 'ranting' so despised by Anglicans. A Wesleyan, William Armes, recognised the deep sincerity of these 'poor illiterate men' who followed Primitive Methodism at Lynn, such as the tiny labourer John 'Pin' Coulson, who marched to chapel in his long blue coat. The Lynn congregation met in a sail loft at the North End, and were bound together by Bellam, a local shipwright, who had been 'trained' in the Midlands. In 1826 they built a chapel in London Road, where three preachers were paid 10s. a week to tour west Norfolk. Camp meetings outside the South Gate demonstrated their success.

Methodism was not the only Nonconformist force to grip the hearts and minds of the middle classes of the town after 1800. The Congregationalists, or Independents, were recharged by Reverend John Allen of Hoxton, and a new chapel was erected in New Conduit Street by 1838. The Unitarians built their Salem Chapel in Norfolk Street in 1811 and were led by Robin Buscall, a shop manager, James Arrowsmith, an auctioneer, and a schoolmaster called Selby. After the death of William Richards in 1818 the Baptists continued meeting in their Broad Street chapel, built 1808, and in 1839 Thomas Wigner arrived among them and triggered an astonishing revival.

Born in Harwich in 1812 to a sailmaker and the daughter of a builder, Wigner attended Stepney College in London, where his family lived in poverty. Thomas was sent to Lynn to preach four Sundays by his mentor, Dr. Murch, and stayed 26 years as minister. Presents were showered upon him by the congregation, including a table-lamp, ink-stand, gloves, toast-rack and gold watch. His salary was supplemented by these gifts and the shares he held in several ships. Over 26 years his annual income averaged about £300, most of which was needed for the maintenance of his household. Wigner's first wife died in 1851 and his second in 1869, and he left Lynn with £20. Much of his time and energy was spent raising money to build the church still standing on Blackfriars Street. On the first day of the penny post in 1840 Thomas sent out 800 letters, which brought in about £100.

When the church opened in June 1841, about fifteen hundred people were 'literally crammed' inside, and 21 were 'converted', or 'decided for Christ'. One Sunday morning in 1841 a man was converted who had entered the building through curiosity. Even a 'reckless' master butcher, who had lost a leg falling from a cart during a drunken escapade, was 'won' in 1844. His conversion caused 'surprise and excitement' at Lynn. In August 1841 Thomas baptised an entire household of widowed mother, three daughters, prospective son-in-law and the family servant. In 1845 a lath render gave Wigner £65 towards the building debt as thanks for the conversion of his family, 'won to God' through his ministry. By early 1846 Thomas was baptising 15 persons every month by immersion in the church pool.

The Baptist congregation at Lynn was largely middle class, but Wigner did out-reach work amongst the poor; he gave lectures to sailors and drew good attendances. In the summer evenings of 1850 special services were held in the Walks. Wigner's mission extended to the towns and villages of Lynn's hinterland. A chapel was built at West Lynn. At Terrington Thomas preached in the kitchen of Mr. Kerkham's house and claimed conversions. Through the Norfolk Association of Baptists new chapels were built, and congregations revived, in Dereham and Downham. Wigner was involved in a 'good deal of work' in Suffolk and Cambridgeshire, as well as Birmingham and London. In 1850 a large Sunday school was built behind the Lynn church for £750. Wigner, who had feared that 'a building not congenial with our views would be erected and become an eyesore' if not 'a hindrance to our worship', cleared the debt in four years.

The Nonconformists were pioneers of Sunday schools in the town. The Wesleyans started one in 1797. The Independents established a school for 200 children in 1812 and the Baptists, in 1830, one for three hundred. The Primitive Methodists began operations in 1826 with two schools of children who had never been Sunday pupils before. Their schools had enrolled over 500 children by 1850, shepherded by 70 teachers, most of whom were young women. These children were given a prominent place in the Primitive Methodists' processions and open-air meetings, besides annual treats. In 1846 the first excursion from Lynn's new railway station took them to Downham and back. In September 1831 all the town's Sunday school pupils paraded through the streets to mark the 50th anniversary of the foundation of the movement by Robert Raikes.

The extent of Nonconformist influence in Lynn by 1851 can be assessed by the local findings of the religious census of that year, directed by the Registrar General, taken on the last Sunday in March. The clergy of all denominations were requested to record attendances at their morning, afternoon and evening services. Lynn had 15 churches and chapels, where 60 per cent of its 20,000 inhabitants could have been accommodated. The census recorded 10,045 attendances, some of which were obviously the same people recorded on the three different occasions. Roughly half were at the four Church of England establishments. Almost all the others were at Nonconformist services, although the small communities of Quakers, Jews and Catholics should not be forgotten. Indeed a small Catholic church had been built on London Road in 1845, designed by Pugin, after the fund-raising efforts of Father Dalton, a 'pleasant and agreeable' Jesuit. Lynn was not unique. English towns attracted thousands of rural migrants and ambitious tradesmen, anxious to be bound into fresh communities. Nonconformity offered a means to this, but it would be dangerous to emphasise the social-cementing role of the chapel as the main reason for the sects' success. There was also a yearning for religious experiences. Something of this electric spiritual atmosphere is suggested by the Lynn crowds pulled to hear two strangers preaching the second coming of Christ in 1843.

Not all labouring people were chapel goers, or Christians, in 1851. The absence of the urban poor from religious services in England and Wales on census day shocked Anglicans and Dissenters alike. But the figures were perhaps not so surprising to all, and the problem had long been recognised. The Bethel Union Society, meeting at the Independent Chapel at Lynn in 1832, decided to supply the sailors of 20 ships with books on history, morality and religion. Another meeting of religious activists at the Town Hall in 1843 discussed plans to appoint a Lynn missionary, dedicated to seeking the poor, hidden in dark courts or yards.

Anglican revival

The French Revolution of 1789 frightened English merchants and landowners into the restoration of their parish churches. Lynn was typical. St Margaret's and St Nicholas' were both repaired and 'beautified' at considerable expense, and evening sermons were organised at the mother church (Richards says they failed). Mass confirmations of Anglican youth were arranged at St Nicholas' chapel in 1794, 1802, 1813, 1820, 1827 and 1833, when the Bishop of Lincoln confirmed 2,000 children watched by big crowds.

It was a merchant from outside Lynn who jogged the local Anglicans into building a church for the labouring classes. Pews at St Margaret's and St Nicholas' were bought and sold for large sums of money, far beyond the pockets of labouring people, who stood at the back of the church, if they attended at all. The Church of St John the Evangelist, opened in 1846, provided 800 free places. The traditional pew system at St Nicholas' was abolished

42. St John's church, intended for the poorer classes, was built in Early English style in 1846.

in 1852, when finely carved medieval seating was destroyed. Anglican anxiety to open up their churches to the urban masses is well illustrated at All Saints' in South Lynn. By clearing away the old pews and replacing them with new seating and galleries in 1842, the capacity of the church was increased from 350 to eight hundred. Even the Methodist William Armes graciously acknowledged the revival of the Church of England, so evident by 1866:

> We have discharged our duty to the Established Church by noticing the erection of St John's Church and the National schools. We have only further to say in this behalf that to the credit of the Establishment, it may be added that they have recently put their houses in order at great cost; that they have now, in the dark Sabbath evenings 'lights in their dwellings', that the churches formerly gloomy and deserted are now attended; for all of which things every honest and upright Dissenter will rejoice with them.

Church rates were levied annually by each parish for the Established Church's schools, buildings, sextons, ringers, organists and wine. For St Margaret's in 1826-7 church rates were levied totalling £1,120. Nonconformist opposition was strong in 1843. Thomas Wigner had household goods distrained and sold because he 'objected on principle' to pay his rate of 11s., but a tradesman bought the property seized and returned it to him. Nonconformists attending the parish vestry at the Easter rate levying opposed it, demanding annual referenda. The motion to levy a rate in 1854 in St Margaret's parish was defeated by 364 to 220 votes in one such test of opinion. In 1868 Gladstone's Liberal government abolished church rates.

Lynn Jews

During the 18th century Jewish merchants in London began to take advantage of easier travel to settle in the more important provincial towns, including Lynn. According to Roth the Jewish colony in Lynn is of particular interest, its articles of foundation (1747) being the only set to survive in England. At this time services were held at the house of Jacob Levi.

Dutch influences were strong. One of the founders of the new Jewish community was Abraham Jones (1729-1811), who was a native of Holland. Several Lynn Jews were gold and silver smiths whose names (like Goldsmid) point to Dutch origins. When Daniel De Pass married Rachel Davis at the *Sun Inn* in Norfolk Street in 1815 it was a Dutch Rabbi who conducted the ceremony 'at which not less than fifty of the same people attended'. The synagogue in Tower Street had recently been sold to the Methodists, who demolished it for their new chapel. Not until 1826 was another acquired behind High Street, described in 1842 by the *Jewish Chronicle* as 'a pretty though small building'. A Jewish burial ground on the Millfleet was opened in 1811.

Thew remembers the Jews. Judah Hynes, an optician, and Mr. Jones, a silversmith, were the most prominent, running shops in High Street near the new synagogue. The rabbi 'eked out his living by acting as interpreter to the foreign sailors who frequented the port'. On a visit to the synagogue Thew found the congregation 'barefooted', but with covered heads, 'singing some of the songs of David in a strange land'. They teased the youth by looking through a small window, telling him they were hoping to see the Messiah coming. The ladies ran a charitable society for clothing Jewish orphans. Gratuities were also given to assist poor Jews in trade. In the 1840s the community slowly diminished as its members migrated.

A blocked Early English window in the tower of
St Nicholas' chapel.

Chapter Eight

Class and Culture

Self-help

The main purpose of the gilds of medieval Lynn was almost certainly the social and spiritual welfare of their members and their families. Death, illness, disability and other disasters all demanded more support than the households of most tradesmen and craftsmen could muster. The poor, however, were dependent on the charity of friars and merchants in times of distress rather than on the gilds of their masters. Richards recorded 31 gilds in 14th-century Lynn, including the five merchant gilds discussed in Chapter Five. Thirty-eight gilds contributed to a fund to help repair the town's defences in 1371 and 59 responded to a royal survey of England's gilds in 1388. The Black Death seems to have stimulated the foundation of gilds, whose members, men and women, were reacting to what seemed to be God's punishment. Lynn may have had more gilds by 1388 than any other English town save London and Norwich. Even if the average membership of each gild at this time was only 20, then some 1,200 people, or half the adult population, were enrolled in one or another.

Unfortunately there is no way to identify gild memberships since, with the exceptions of the shipmen, shoemakers, tailors and tilers, they did not obviously represent trade groups. The greater number of gilds preferred names indicating their religious character and affiliations, like the gilds of Saints John, Christopher, Margaret and Thomas. A little is known of some gilds, however. That of St Fabian and St Bastian boasted 38 members, having a membership fee of 2s. for men and 1s. for women. Wax was demanded to pay fines for breaking gild rules, implying that the membership was not poor. The gild of St Anthony seems to have been composed of taverners or publicans meeting in each others' houses. St James' gild is said to have been too poor to meet except for funerals at the chapel and on the feast of St James. Perhaps the most unusual of Lynn's gilds was that of St Francis, whose alderman, John Wells, was a Franciscan friar who governed both lay and clerical members with severity. The Young Scholars and Young Clerks started gilds dedicated, respectively, to St William, a Norwich boy supposedly crucified by Jews in that city, and St John the Baptist.

Richards compared these medieval craft and religious gilds with the benefit societies of his own day, 1812. The social organisations he described were new formations of the 'better-off' labouring classes. He counted over 20 benefit or friendly societies, meeting at various taverns. That based at the *Green Dragon* had more than 100 people in its annual procession around the town in June 1819. Their destination was St Margaret's church, where they were treated to a sermon before returning 'home' for their society dinner. Merchants had a paternalist relationship with these friendly societies, whereby they acted as 'bankers' for their employees' savings. One example was the 'Sailors' Friendly Society', based at the *Royal Oak*; its funds were managed by William and Thomas Bagge, who owned the pub and probably employed the men. In March 1835 a special meeting of the society took place at the *George and Dragon*, where 33 men signed a declaration (eight making a mark) that their funds, about £40, should be withdrawn and divided equally amongst the members.

If self-help of this kind was practised by a large slice of Lynn's labouring classes, then it would have been one of the forces promoting social stability among sailors, porters and others whose incomes were open to sharp fluctuation. The governing class was anxious to encourage friendly societies for this reason. The Savings Bank pioneered by a vintner, Edward Manning, opened behind a High Street shop in 1817, was a similar example of self-help being fostered from above. In 1843 the bank had over £57,000 deposited by 38 friendly societies, 40 charities and 1,763 individuals.

Town lodges affiliated to the great orders of British working people dedicated to mutual insurance against sickness and death appeared in the 1830s and 1840s. The Independent Order of Oddfellows celebrated their fourth anniversary in Lynn in 1842 with 300 members, and by 1845 had built a hall on the 'New Road' just to the east of the old town. The Ancient Order of Foresters and the Rechabites were both formed in Lynn in 1840. A natural ally of these benefit societies was the temperance movement, and each spring the latter two swelled the temperance processions through the town, with flags, banners and band, to St Margaret's for a service, followed by tea and cakes. The Lynn Temperance Association could bring hundreds of people onto the streets, according to a Norwich newspaper in 1840, when onlookers noted several former drunkards in its ranks. *White's Directory* for 1845 confirms that the 'Lynn Temperance Society' was 'very numerous'.

The Freemasons were led by Lynn's upper classes, its merchants, big tradesmen and professional men. Richards was puzzled by the 'fair and estimable characters' of many of Lynn's masons when their customs and ceremonies were 'so absurd', although masonry's charitable acts to the community outweighed its 'defects'. He said that the first lodge opened at the *White Lion Inn* in 1729, while by 1812 there were three lodges and 500 masons. Many processed from the *Maid's Head Inn* to St Margaret's in 1796 for a sermon by the Hebrew Professor at Cambridge. The tavern was still a masonic headquarters in 1818, when the funeral cortège of a shipowner named Thomas Burn escorted the body from there to the new burial ground of St James', through streets lined by 3,000 spectators. Freemasonry was far more open than it is today.

Labour power

In 1831 Lynn was home for 750 sailors, whose families were often left destitute during the long absences of the men at sea, unless merchants paid their wages to wives in advance. Odd jobs were performed by mariners waiting for a ship. In 1830 the spire of St Nicholas' was repaired by 'a hardy tar' who was seen swinging on the outside of 'the stately pile'. Boys from town and country were apprenticed to merchants for training as seamen. The Bagges took six or seven apprentices a year between 1774 and 1844. Several are recorded as having been drowned or killed at sea, while a few absconded, as James Russell did in London in 1823. Young mariners might make 20 voyages a year at 50s. a time once training was completed. Some found work on the whaling ships, the crews of which were protected from the press gang. When the *Fountain* sailed into Lynn from Greenland in August 1813 'the officer and men of impress' attempted to take some of its men, but were 'resisted', and 'the consequences had nearly been of a very serious nature'.

Sailors were often militant. In the summer of 1790 about two hundred sailors toured the town in triumph after a strike had forced merchants to raise wages. At the end of the French wars, however, the good wages at Lynn attracted many of the sailors discharged from the Royal Navy, and surplus labour led in 1814 to attempts by merchants to cut pay. The crew of the brig *Ocean*, about to sail for the Baltic, refused to work until better conditions were agreed, and occupied the vessel. Their leaders were arrested and escorted to the gaol in the Saturday Market Place, followed by a 'great mob' of sailors who 'processioned' the town with boxes to collect strike funds. An attempt to rescue the prisoners from the gaol was foiled by the mayor; Lionel Self apparently stood between 'the mob' and the door. A second attempt succeeded, however, and the German Legion was called to Lynn from Norwich to intimidate the sailors into submission.

Porters, the labourers at Lynn's riverside, were also numerous. Some belonged to distinct 'gangs' attached to one of the big merchants dealing in corn, coal and timber. Others were less fortunate, and formed a small army of casual labour without regular work. All depended on 'the state of the shipping', experiencing alternate spells of idleness and work described by the Town Clerk in 1833 as 'extremely laborious'. Simon Curry was one such porter. He told the Municipal Corporation Commissioners at the Town Hall in 1833 that his earnings might be 18s. or 20s. a week, but that sometimes he was a week or a fortnight without being employed; he had not earned more than 5s. 'this last fortnight'. Slumps in river traffic bred great hardship amongst these labouring people.

In 1830 the coal porters of the river displayed some degree of solidarity when their petition persuaded the merchants 'to equalise' work, to share what employment was available. They resorted to more traditional forms of protest to get the millers of Lynn to reduce the price of flour in 1830, assembling in the Tuesday Market Place. Demonstrations against food vendors in times of scarcity and high prices did not usually turn into strikes for better wages. Paternalism rather than conflict characterised relations between porters and merchants. In the winter of 1841 'the coalheavers' wrote to the merchants thanking them for their charity in alleviating distress. It was possible for porters to save money when trade was buoyant, however. A corn porter who had accumulated £30 was robbed of it all when his house was burgled in mart time about 1830.

1842 was the year of the 'General Strike', or Plug Plot, whereby the proletariat of the industrial towns of the North and Midlands struck against wage reductions and sabotaged mines and factories. Lynn sailors and porters agitated for better wages, the *Three Pigeons* in St James' Street being their strike headquarters. Sailors toured west Norfolk collecting strike funds, but were 'pounced' upon by magistrates. Over 800 men withdrew their labour and the port of Lynn was at a standstill in March 1842. The strike was broken when eight leaders were arrested by 100 special constables backed by rural police and dragoons brought from Norwich. In May a relieved corporation recorded thanks to the latter two groups for their aid when the town had been threatened 'by a serious riot'.

'The Grand National Consolidated Trades Union' was started in London and other large towns in 1834 to cement 'class solidarity' amongst builders, weavers, tailors, shoemakers and others. It soon collapsed because of lockouts by employers. The Lynn shoemakers employed in the workshops of Mr. Du Pass struck for better wages in January 1834, applying pressure by demonstrating outside his High Street house. Nothing seems to have been gained, however. The strikers were accused of heavy drinking and the mayor offered a £10 reward for information about those who had broken windows. Surprisingly little more is heard about the shoemakers. Independent craftsmen owning or renting their own shops were almost certainly active in labour politics at Lynn. The atelier of George Faircloth was a 'gossiping shop', with his wife making tea and the old man hammering at his bench. Like 'most' other shoemakers he was a 'great radical'.

Female participation in food riots and strikes should not be forgotten. When millers and farmers were assaulted at Lynn in 1801 and the *Duke's Head* was stoned by a crowd protesting against high bread prices, it is difficult to believe that women were absent. Hillen talks of local riots in 1815 over the Corn Bill introduced in parliament to protect the profits of landowners by prohibiting the import of foreign wheat. Norwich newspapers reported that there had been disturbances in the streets by the women of Lynn (Hillen's riots?) until the mayor had intervened.

Drink and Leisure

To a great extent the popular culture of Lynn had always been channelled through its taverns, of which there were 68 by 1804, often providing the names of the streets where they

43. *The Lattice House* was converted into a public house in 1714 and closed in 1919.
It is again a hostelry after restoration in the 1970s.

stood and sometimes distinguished by special clienteles. The *Three Crowns*, in Queen Street, was run by 'old master Seapey' and frequented by shipmasters before they aspired 'to the dignity of being called captain'. Sailors had their own taverns, like the *Town Arms*, *Royal Oak* and *Coach and Horses*, in the Saturday Market Place, where James Wiseman was famous for his serving of 'the early purl'. This was an early morning drink of hot ale flavoured with wormwood. Some taverns had a reputation for rogues and vagabonds; the *Spread Eagle*, for example, was conveniently situated just outside the East Gate, beyond the clutches of the town constables.

Gentlemen and tradesmen wandered into houses like the *Three Tuns* for hot chops and sausages as an early lunch. Many returned in the evening to drink brandy and smoke their long pipes, soon breaking into song, as Armes recalls of the *Rose and Crown* in South Lynn. Some publicans arranged annual dinners for tradesmen, selling the tickets around the town. Bowling greens were attractions at the *Crown Inn* and elsewhere, while cock fighting, skittles, darts and cards were also popular. Women were not excluded. The fisherwomen of North End enjoyed their own dinner and drinking parties every July at the *Black Goose*. Politics, auctions, inquests and dinners all attracted custom. William Richards and his friends celebrated the centenary of the Glorious Revolution in 1788 in one of the town's taverns.

The Quarter Sessions books for the 18th century are full of cases brought by the town magistrates to tame taverns identified as dens of drunkenness and immorality. In 1754, for example, Ann Pitts, wife of a hatter, was accused of keeping an ill-governed and disorderly house for her 'own lucre' and gain, allowing drinking, tippling, whoring, and misbehaving 'unlawfully' day and night by 'evil and ill disposed persons'. Prostitution, of which pubs were the hubs, was common. In 1812 Richards believed the general opinion to be that Lynn abounded more 'with that sort of sinner' than any other place of its size. In 1852 local doctors informed the inspector from the Board of Health that prostitution was more evident here than in any town known to them.

The Beer Act of 1830 torpedoed corporation efforts to police the growing number of drinking establishments, because it allowed anyone to start a beer shop on paying £2 for a licence. Pothouses sprang up throughout the town, and the Town Clerk blamed the act for increasing disturbances before the the Municipal Corporations Commission in 1833. He replied to the question about 'the moral condition of the town' that 'the morals of the people were generally improved' until 1830, since when they had 'retrograded'.

Initiatives by the corporation to enforce a closing time of 11 p.m. in drinking houses were not helped by the policemen who drank on duty at these same places. Perhaps their fault is indicative of the central place drinking occupied in the lives of townspeople of all classes, at work and play. How far drink was 'the opium' of an urban population subject to far greater hardships than known to most of us today is difficult to assess, but it should be emphasised that not all town taverns were centres of drunkenness, as the official sources tend to suggest. The warmth and community spirit found in them were a liberation from the slum housing and hard labour which were the lot of thousands.

Sport and leisure activities were encouraged by the lay and ecclesiastical authorities of medieval Lynn. A kind of football was played some Sundays on the sands to the north of St Nicholas' chapel and at South Lynn. Priests served as referees, but the game was robust and violent, leading to injury or worse. About 1300 John Godesbirth fatally wounded a fellow player with a dagger and fled to sanctuary in St Nicholas'. He was captured while trying to escape, but nevertheless was allowed to go abroad. Archery was a more controlled sport. Edward IV ordered all towns to set up public butts for popular enjoyment and exercise on Sundays and holidays — the contribution of English archers to victories at Crécy (1346), Poitiers (1356) and Agincourt (1415) is legendary.

Bulls and bears were baited at Lynn. A tax of 40d. was imposed at the tolbooth on every imported bear in 1242, and a 'berman' called William Gun is mentioned in 1315. Bull baiting was in decline before 1800 as farmers and butchers lost interest in sponsoring the sport. Baiting before slaughtering, with dogs lacerating the animal, was a normal fate for bulls. It was almost certainly staged in both market-places: the chamberlain paid Adam Martin 4s. for 'a bull rope' in 1679, and Thomas Sommersby, mayor 1743-4, remembered a ring in the middle of the Tuesday Market Place 'for bull-baiting'.

Cock fighting was also popular. In 1769 the *Duke's Head* had a cock room with 'deal furniture for fighting cocks', showing upper-class interest. The lower orders were just as enthusiastic. 'Bandy Green' was a shoeblack and cock fighter said to be represented in the picture of the Lynn peace celebrations of 1814 with a cock under his arm. Boxing was another attraction. In October 1830 a banker and a sailor started a contest for a sovereign on the Common Staithe, to the delight of townspeople. Young men and boys seem to have shot game on the outskirts of Lynn at this time, despite warnings against poaching. During hard winters, ice-skating on the Ouse was common. Armes talked of how the skaters 'glided gliby' before the marshes were drained.

44. This drawing of John Green by W. White in 1818 shows him reading a poster for his favourite sport, cock fighting. He was a shoeblack who sold his wife with a halter around her neck for a gallon of beer. Bull baiting near the Red Mount Chapel is featured in the background.

Northenders used the Ouse for leisure more than other townsfolk. In July 1794, four pilots gone for 'recreation' in a boat drowned after becoming incapable through drink. Summer activity on the river was usually more sensible than this. Lynn merchants patronised an annual regatta, the highlight of which was racing by fishing smacks. Coal and corn porters had their own competitions in rowing boats, using the Eau Brink Cut after 1821. The Ouse banks were thronged by excited crowds, and others took to the water in their own boats, zig-zagging to avoid the racers. The festivities lasted several days, and included evening firework displays at the *Crown Tavern* in Church Street and other public houses. In September 1841 a Mr. Gypson produced extra holiday fun by lifting off in a hot air balloon.

Lynn's eccentric characters also provided popular amusement. Miss Mary Breeze, who died in 1799 aged 78, was as good a shot 'as any in the county', and her hounds and favourite mare were killed and buried with her. In 1815 David Stokes fell into the well at South Lynn workhouse and was drowned; he had been made drunk on a visit into town and was trying to wash after a fall. Stokes was one of these 'half witted original characters too frequently to be met with in large towns' who inevitably became 'the butt and ridicule of the unfeeling and vulgar part of the inhabitants'. Others entertained less cruel citizens. 'Dicky' Braithwaite was a failed attorney who turned to poaching and walked the streets in shooting costume. 'Cuckoo' had been a drover, and attempted to sell matches, but depended on begging coins in exchange for 'a song of spring'. 'Billy Boots' was a shoeblack said to be the son of a nobleman, but too proud and unforgiving to accept his father's gifts.

Winter Festival
The February mart was the heart of Lynn's Winter Festival. It lasted two weeks and embraced all social classes. Once Christmas had passed, townspeople began speculating on the attractions of the mart as carpenters sprang into action making booths and stalls. Excitement mounted as handbills proclaimed the rich variety of human and animal species about to descend upon the town. Gangs of children followed the first great caravans that entered, bringing, by 1800, elephants, lions, bears, horses, monkeys, clowns, actors and simple tradesmen. On 14 February at one o'clock the red-robed mayor led the corporation from the Town Hall to the Tuesday Market Place where he declared the fair open. In 1815 the opening of the mart coincided with market day and fine weather, so 'a deal of fashionable and genteel company was in town'.

People from town and country packed the market-place once the fair had opened, looking for clothes, and household goods as well as entertainment, including 'naughty' sideshows. By 1815 Lynn's Methodists and other religious groups were expressing disapproval of 'worldly' persons 'indulging themselves' at the mart. It was still a popular event where ladies and gentlemen of the town and district mingled with the populace without any sense of embarrassment, though they had a 'special' day in the mart, as did their servants. Carriers from the villages transported bubbling young women dressed in bright colours and displaying big cotton umbrellas; men walked miles into Lynn to 'show off' new white hats and baggy trousers in the mart throng. Many must have spent a week's wages in one day of beer, women and song. The 'Johns' and 'Marys' of the villages were often easy game for the experienced urban criminals or 'swell mobs' at the mart, too.

A band, or waits, was started by the corporation in medieval times to play music around the streets each morning between October and March and at official functions such as the installation of the mayor. Each musician was provided with a blue coat and silver chains on which the arms of the borough were suspended. The band seems to have disappeared before February 1656, when the waits of Cambridge were invited 'to wayte' on the mayor and corporation at the mart because the town was 'wanting of their own waytes'. In August 1657 'waytes' or 'loude musick' was again required to attend the corporation and mayor in their 'solemnity' and 'to walke the streets in the winter nights according to the ancient custome of this Burgh'. A certain Francis Ebbison was paid £20 to go to London to negotiate with a company willing 'to embrace' Lynn as waits. He was unsuccessful, and in August 1658 £5 was sent to Richard Lowe and his company at Ipswich to come to Lynn and play at the mayoral election. The four men agreed to become Lynn's waits at £16 a year.

Hillen says that the Gildhall in King Street was first used as a theatre in 1592. Before then it seems certain that troupes of actors on circuit from Norwich or London performed in the yards of inns. Players were denounced in the Elizabethan period as 'rogues' and 'vagabonds', on the grounds that drama weakened popular attachment to Church and State. In 1572 and 1597 parliament condemned touring companies of players. To be safe from prosecution players required the patronage of a great man and licence to perform from local magistrates. The corporation of Lynn favoured the theatre. In 1616 it decided to contact the 'Chancellor of England' to win privileges for 'the companyes' yearly 'resorting' to Lynn. In 1627 the corporation gave £9 12s. to the 'King's Players'. Had they endured a bad season in the town?

Lynn's records then fall silent on the theatre until the 18th century. In 1765 the corporation borrowed £400 to make 'a commodious theatre' inside the medieval St George's Hall, partly a response to the canvassing of the Norwich Company of Comedians, already regular visitors at mart time. The Gildhall was also used by local amateur players; in April 1759 the young gentlemen of the grammar school staged *Adelph of Terence* before a packed audience, rapturous in their applause.

A magnificent proscenium supported by timber posts gave the new theatre an Elizabethan look. Tickets for upper and lower boxes cost 3s. and 4s., respectively. Those for the pit were priced at 2s., and the gallery 1s. Constables were posted outside to impose order on the confusion of traffic, and inside to curb a rowdy gallery, the occupants of which loved to

45. The town theatre, built in 1813 and destroyed by fire in 1936. The Greyfriars tower is in the background.

shower the pit with nuts and fruit. Servants were obliged not to mix too freely with their superiors in the theatre.

Big houses during the French wars led the corporation to start a campaign for a larger and more modern theatre. St George's Hall was sold as a warehouse and the new theatre, in the shadow of the Greyfriars' tower, opened in February 1815, playing every night during the mart and at least 40 nights until March. The boxes were packed by merchants and gentry, whose carriages crowded the streets outside. Tradesmen and others of a middling rank were placed in the pits, while the lower orders sat on benches in the gallery. Even here a seat cost 1s., or a day's wage for a labourer. The theatre was let for £200 in the first season to the actor-manager Mr. Brunton, formerly of Drury Lane.

Brunton's successful stewardship of the playhouse lasted for five years, he providing dramas, musicals and comedies. Successors included members of the Fisher family, who toured the theatres of East Anglia. The theatre was making losses by the 1830s, however, because of the decline of the mart and opposition from increasingly puritanical citizens. Thew commented: 'The theatre in my early days was to me tabooed, but I can remember secretly gaining admission there, and hearing that queen of ballard singers, Mrs. Waylett, in some of her favourite songs'.

Seasonal celebrations were important to the townspeople. Christmas saw gifts of coal and money to the poorest citizens from the charitable bequests of Lynn merchants. For the more fortunate the Christmas market was full of meat and the coaches heavily loaded with presents. The mart and theatre soon followed. May Day was celebrated by dancers around the Maypoles clad in fancy costumes. In 1682 two new poles were set up, one on the Tuesday Market Place, the other at St Ann's Fort. From 'time immemorial' the children had toured the streets on May Day, with flower garlands and sounding horns, but in 1835 the corporation prohibited it. The popular celebration of 5 November with fireworks and ringing church bells was also being discouraged.

Adult education

Richards declared in 1812 that Lynn was not 'much distinguished' for its literature or libraries, apart from the collection of books in St Margaret's, over 1,700 volumes, long neglected by the 'great families' of the borough. The corporation library at this church was founded in 1630 and enlarged by the addition of the library started at St Nicholas' chapel in 1617; Dr. Thurlin of Cambridge University donated numerous volumes in 1714. Its books were mainly on medicine and theology. In 1658 the corporation expressed concern over the disorder of the library, from which books had gone missing, and in 1671 the master of the grammar school was appointed library keeper at 20s. a year. Nevertheless, by 1753 two of the 'most valuable' books, Phelps Ogilby's *Africa* and *America*, were in poor condition, and cost 40s. to be rebound. It was not until 1773 that the corporation accepted that St Margaret's library was 'hurt' by being open to the chancel.

In 1797 the Lynn Subscription Library was started behind a shop in High Street. By 1812 it boasted 1,400 volumes and 100 members, paying an annual subscription of a guinea. The management committee was dominated by booksellers, clergymen, doctors and tradesmen. In 1834 about £38 was spent on the purchase of books from Whittingham's High Street shop. Another room was built adjoining the library in 1835 to improve its facilities. Books were now being despatched to country members via local carriers, though volumes were often lost and special bags had to be provided for them. The administration of the library was lax: Thew says that the surveyorship of Lynn's scavenging department and the care of the subscription library were always seen as 'the proper refuges for otherwise unrecognised merit'. In 1837 a 'very respectable' and 'methodical' old gentleman, who always carried 'a huge umbrella', was appointed manager of the library rooms, a local celebrity named

John Skippon. Thew continued: 'The collection of books was a valuable one, but the library had other attractions; in the evening the room was the happy hunting ground of all the town gossips and quidnuncs, many times to the great scandal of good Mr. Skippon'.

A Lynn 'Mechanics Institute' is recorded in *White's Directory* of 1836, with a library of 400 volumes and 60 subscribers. It had been founded in 1827. Artisans and tradesmen also paid 5s. a year to attend lectures on subjects like 'Natural Philosophy' and the 'Constitution of England'. The master of the grammar school was among the lecturers. In 1845 the institute moved to more spacious premises in Purfleet Street with the aid of its patrons, who included the bishop of Norwich and Lord Bentinck. Something of the motivation of the Tory establishment in directing adult education can be appreciated by the fact that in about 1830 radical publications, such as the famous unstamped newspaper *The Poor Man's Guardian*, were on sale in the town. The Stamp Acts were a device to raise newspaper prices beyond the pockets of labouring people, discouraging the dissemination of revolutionary writing. Journals more acceptable to the corporation were available in a newspaper and billiard room opened over the Saturday Market House in 1827.

The earliest Lynn newspaper was *The Lynn and Wisbech Packet*, produced weekly by two printers in 1800 at 6d. a copy. Most of the news was poached from the London press and juxtaposed with a few local items and advertisements. The paper was distributed over much of East Anglia, but competition from Norwich, Ipswich and Cambridge publications led to its demise in 1802. The first successful paper printed in Lynn appeared in 1841, when John Thew opened his High Street offices. *The Lynn Advertiser and West Norfolk Herald* took full advantage of the reduction of the newspaper stamp from 4d. to 1d. in 1836, and advances in printing technology. The premier edition of 1,000 copies was given away free and the Tory sympathies of its owners moderated until it was safely launched. *The Lynn Advertiser* appeared every Tuesday, price 2d., focusing more on local news from the late 1840s, although national politics and sensations were still prominent. The telegraph brought 'hot news' to the town after 1848.

In 1842 the Lynn Conversazione and Society of Arts was launched, its objectives being to stimulate 'taste' for literature, science and art, and 'useful improvements and innovations'. The annual subscription of 7s. 6d. emphasises the middle-class character of the society, which first met in the Town Hall. Here papers were delivered and debated. The conversazione was behind the museum founded at Welwick House in South Lynn in 1844. Visitors to it needed introductions from the small circle of subscribers. Natural history was the most substantial section of the museum.

The Lynn Ecclesiological Society was also started at Welwick House in 1844. Clergy and professional men, and their wives, fascinated by the architecture of the English medieval church joined this society, which collected a valuable library. Thew was a member: 'What little knowledge I have of Norman arches, early English windows, the mysteries of mouldings, and perpendicular transoms (a well-known architectural 'bull') dates from thence'.

Interest in the arts and sciences was not confined to Lynn's intelligentsia. The band of the Music Society played Haydn and Mozart in the Assembly Rooms and St Margaret's to large audiences, like the 400 who attended its seventh concert in 1832. Madame Tussaud displayed her collection of 90 public characters in the Assembly Rooms in May 1819, citizens being charged 1s. each for entry. The Market House in the Tuesday Market Place was also useful. In 1842 a Mr. O'Connell gave a lecture on astronomy there to a packed audience. Gardening was becoming more of an art and science, and in October 1840 The West Norfolk and Lynn Gardeners' Association for Mutual Instruction met for the first time. Its programme included lectures on the economy of the vegetable kingdom.

Much of this activity at Lynn was promoted by the growing band of big shopkeepers, who had the time and resources to develop other interests. According to Richards in 1812, some of the town's tradesmen were 'known' to be as rich as local 'gentlemen', or merchants, who were 'really' tradesmen, too. In Chester in 1815 it was not uncommon for tradesmen to leave between £100 and £500 in wills, some amassing fortunes of over £1,000. Lynn was no different. Thew talked of High Street shopkeepers in the early 19th century investing their savings in property, pictures and wine. This shopocracy was not new: plenty of evidence from 18th-century wills and property deals tells of tradesmen whose wealth was invested in all kinds of cultural furniture. When Mr. Wardell died in 1791, for example, he left an abattoir in Madd Lane and a house full of plate, linen, glass, clocks and books.

Town schools

The religious houses and gilds of medieval Lynn provided schools for boys and girls whose parents wanted to give them educations. Urban provision of this kind was common. An important educational initiative sprang from a leading member of the Holy Trinity Gild who died in 1510. Thomas

46. The Athenaeum was opened in 1854 to accommodate Lynn's cultural organisations.

Thoresby's will talks of a school in which a priest would teach six poor boys grammar and song, so that they could form a chantry choir. His wishes were not followed up by the corporation until 1534. A Cambridge Master of Arts was appointed to be master of the grammar school in the Charnel chapel next to St Margaret's church. Perhaps it was the threatened closure of the monastic schools at Lynn that jogged the corporation into action.

Tudor and Stuart urban oligarchies were increasingly anxious to improve educational provision in their towns. Borough government required lawyers for smooth operation; commerce depended increasingly on paperwork; good Protestant clergy were needed to consolidate the Reformation. The corporation accordingly provided scholarships to allow six scholars from the grammar school, at any one time, to attend Cambridge University. Boys were given a three-year trial at the school to show their academic worth before being allowed to complete the six years of study seen as necessary for acceptance at university. The core of the curriculum was Latin, Greek and Hebrew; boys were expected to have basic literacy on entering the school.

Lynn Grammar School was called the 'Free School' because a classical education was provided gratis to the sons of borough freemen. Other parents had to pay for their sons' places, effectively denying the poor training for the professions. Tradesmen and farmers who were not freemen were also frustrated by the lack of grammar school places for their children. This exclusiveness and the narrow curriculum damaged the school. In 1746 the corporation described it as 'at a low ebb' after 'flourishing' for a long period. The master then had a salary of £40 a year and a free dwelling. In 1755 there were just three boys and a master, but the school revived in the 1760s, and a new boarding house for 24 scholars was built in St James' Street in 1768.

In 1812 the grammar school had few free pupils and the master was allowed to supplement his income by taking more fee-paying students. William Armes was a pupil about this time and remembered the scholars selling books, slates and pencils to buy sweets, cakes and pea-shooters. In the 1820s the corporation rebuilt the school in St James' Street. The classics-laden curriculum, which left the boys 'uninstructed' in the 'more useful' branches of learning, was criticised by the corporation in 1839. Even in 1854 there were only 34 scholars and three masters at the school.

The Writing School was started by the corporation in 1630 above the shambles in the Saturday Market Place. In 1654 William Barnard was chosen to be a scholar at this public school to learn to read, write and cipher with five other poor boys. These six charity children nominated by the corporation were usually boys who had been left the responsibility of a single parent. The writing school contained 11 scholars in 1670. Between 1664 and 1693 it was directed by a capable master called George Osborne, who also taught arithmetic and navigation. His son left the grammar school in 1669 for Emmanuel College, Cambridge, on a corporation scholarship. The school was still strong in 1734, when William King, 'a poor boy', was 'put to school' as one of the charity children.

A writing school was not sufficient, and Alderman Brown in 1737 proposed one to teach English language and reading. He told the corporation that there was 'a very great want of a schoolmaster in this town to teach children the rudiments of the English tongue', and he moved for the provision of one. The Town Hall was enthusiastic for 'so useful and beneficial [a] design', and two rooms near the writing school were found for it. The need for a more literate workforce was probably the reason for Brown's initiative. In July 1752 Thomas Robertson was made master 'of the English school for poor children to read' on the nomination of the mayor 'as hath been usual'. When he died in 1756 he was replaced by William Elstobb, commissioned to teach English to all children sent to him, and to three poor children nominated by the mayor.

The failure of the grammar school to satisfy the educational demands of the district's middle classes is apparent from the number of private academies founded in the 18th century. Norfolk newspapers carried their advertisements. In 1812 Richards ridiculed the social pretension of teaching music, drawing and other 'genteel accomplishments' to the children of the relatively inferior classes. He saw these boarding and day schools as aping the education suitable only for the children of squires, merchants and 'opulent farmers'. It is clear from the directories of the 1830s and 1840s that such establishments were thriving at Lynn. In 1836, for example, there were 15 boarding schools and over 20 other private academies in a town of 15,000 people, some specialising in music, language, drawing or other disciplines, such as navigation. Thew described the characters teaching at Beloe's School in New Conduit Street, 'at which half the county of Norfolk was educated'.

A charity school for girls was opened in Lynn in 1792, its mistresses teaching about fifty pupils reading, sewing and spinning. The project was started by a meeting of ladies at the Town Hall. Richards was amazed that so large a town as Lynn had no similar school for boys. The large financial obligations seem to have been the obstacle, and the schooling system promoted by Joseph Lancaster, whereby one or two masters used older pupils as monitors to instruct the younger, offered a solution. The famous educationalist was invited to speak at the Town Hall as part of a campaign to open a school, and action thereafter was swift. The corporation allowed the subscribers' management committee to use the old mill house by the Millfleet for their school in 1808.

Charity school pupils were required to read the Psalms and recite the catechism before the management committee. A visit to St Nicholas' chapel each Sunday was compulsory. The religious overtones, however, should not obscure the utilitarian character of the school. Of the 226 boys at the school in 1812 at least 25 were ready for examination in 'good writing'. The master was 'always' receiving requests from tradesmen for his pupils, and in 1832 over 70 boys left the school for jobs.

1833 was a turning point in the history of popular education in England, because the state began to make grants to the two voluntary school societies founded at the end of the French Wars. The 'British and Foreign' had emerged from Joseph Lancaster's 'Royal Institution', to co-ordinate the schooling efforts of Nonconformists, and the 'National Society' was begun by Dr. Bell to propagate popular education according to the tenets of the Church of England. The charity schools for boys and girls became a National school for 500 pupils when a new building was erected for £1,400 in 1849. This, St Margaret's school, was within easy reach of the parish church. The congregations of St John's and All Saints' also raised the 50 per cent of school building costs required to qualify for state grants. South Lynn was the fastest growing part of the town, and in 1831 a room in Coronation Square had been fitted up as an infant school for 200 pupils by local ladies as 'a useful auxillary to the lower orders of society'. A purpose-built school was erected in 1852. The corporation supported all these Anglican schools with small grants of land and money.

The Nonconformists would not be left behind. A public meeting led to a subscription for a British school for 500 boys and girls, which opened in Blackfriars Street in 1842. In 1866 Aitken looked back on a schooling revolution in Lynn:

> Thirty years ago the scholastic establishments in the town were confined to the Grammar School, then but scantily attended, the Lancastrian School, and a few private academies for either sex. Now the Grammar School is well attended, and in lieu of the Lancastrian we have a British and three National schools, in which both boys and girls are educated in a far more efficient manner than was formerly the case, so that it is no means a common thing to find a lad, even of the lowest rank, who cannot read and write; indeed an errand boy who is not possessed of these accomplishments has but a poor chance of employment.

His remarks emphasise how literacy had become vital to the development of commercial and cultural life in English towns. Yet school was not compulsory and attendance was irregular. Not all children of labouring families acquired even a basic education. Of the five million people between the ages of three and 15 in England in 1851, only two million had undergone a spell of day schooling. No more than one child in 12 was a Sunday school pupil in Lynn in 1851.

Chapter Nine

The City State

Medieval politics

From the 12th century the merchants of Lynn struggled to turn their growing economic strength into the political mastery of the town. This irresistible force met an almost immovable object in the bishops of Norwich, the lords of Lynn until 1537. To quicken the erosion of this ecclesiastical overlordship the merchants petitioned the kings for 'freedoms'. Medieval kings courted the loyalty of the expanding urban populations to counter baronial power and to milk the towns of ships, men and money, the resources needed for war. Borough status, and further degrees of independence from the bishops granted in a series of royal charters, was the reward of the merchants of Lynn for such support. Finally, when Henry VIII dispossessed the bishops in 1537, the corporation owed allegiance only to the crown.

Postan describes medieval towns as islands of freedom in a feudal sea of landowners and their bondsmen. Yet the bishops were the strongest and most reactionary of urban as well as rural lords, as the political history of medieval Lynn shows. The Wash seaport was amongst England's biggest towns when King John obliged the bishop of Norwich to make concessions. In 1204 Lynn's first royal charter granted borough status, or self-governing powers, exercised through its merchant gild. The following year Bishop de Grey granted the men of Lynn the liberties enjoyed by the burgesses of Oxford in another charter. Some historians interpret John's charter as Lynn's equivalent of Magna Carta of 1215, as English urban communities began their long march to democracy.

These charters established an oligarchical town government, inseparable from the merchant gild of the Holy Trinity, the members of which carefully controlled local political life by the creation of burgesses. The alderman, or senior officer, of the merchant gild took the initiative in the formation of a mayoral electorate of 12 jurats and acted as the mayor's deputy. Robert, son of Sunolf, is the first mayor whose name is known; he was chosen in 1220 and 1223. The mayoral electorate of 12 was later enlarged by a further 12 to govern with the mayor and his deputy as the Community of Lynn. They elected Lynn's two M.P.s, and appointed officials to safeguard the town's defences and public health, and enforce trading regulations. Disputes were settled in the mayoral court in the gildhall.

Nevertheless, the charters granted by King John and de Grey had created an unequal system of power sharing in Lynn rather than given complete freedom to the borough. The bishops remained lords of the town, and were given permission by the crown to levy taxes on the townspeople, while mayors were, on election, to be presented for approval at the nearby episcopal palace of Gaywood. It would be a mistake to cast the mayor and bishop as always bitter rivals, however, for the former sought 'good lordship' from the latter. Not all the bishops of Norwich were as unpopular as Bishop Despenser. In 1377 he insisted that the borough official who went before the mayor with the wand tipped in black horn at both ends, a symbol of authority, should walk before him. He ignored warnings to avoid a confrontation and his procession was broken up by an angry crowd of artisans who attacked it with stones and clubs. The bishop retreated to the refuge of St Margaret's priory, and the king made the town pay a heavy fine for the outrage.

The running of borough government depended on money. The main sources of income for the borough treasurers, or chamberlains, were the port tolls, rents of various houses, shops and lands owned by the town, and taxes occasionally levied for the upkeep of the banks, dikes and walls vital to Lynn's welfare. Municipal services, salaries and civic entertainment drained the treasury, while loans to the crown were also a burden. In 1403 Henry IV borrowed over £300 from the borough, which was not repaid until 1425. To ensure borough finances were healthy the Holy Trinity Gild served as banker to the community. It was owed £160 in 1337, £500 in 1408, and the enormous sum of £1,214 in 1421. Public expenditure of this order demonstrates how far the merchant rulers of Lynn had 'taken charge' of their town. The expense of their challenge to the bishop's liberties in the royal courts resulted in heavy taxation of the townspeople, however.

Of the urban orders at this time the merchant oligarchy was labelled the *potentiores*, below them were the artisans, or *mediocres*, and the labourers, or *inferiores*. In 1406 John Oxford led the popular party of *mediocres* and *inferiores* against the *potentiores* in riots and unlawful assemblies pressing for a more democratic constitution. The rebel leaders were imprisoned. Trouble flared up again in 1411, however. The popular party insisted that the £458 spent fighting the bishop's liberties in Lynn should be paid by the last five mayors rather than found by more taxes. Bishop and king commanded the conflict to be settled by the appointment of a commission of 18, to include seven *potentiores*, five *mediocres* and six *inferiores*. Not surprisingly, this commission created more burgesses, all of whom were to join in the election of the mayor in August 1411. In 1412 Henry IV recognised this new constitution by charter. The popular party even nominated one of the town's two M.P.s.

The *potentiores* successfully counter-petitioned the king for the restoration of the old constitution, receiving another charter. In 1415 disgruntled burgesses left the gildhall to whip up support in St Margaret's church, returning to defy the royal mandate that Robert Brunham continue as mayor. Brunham was forced to administer the oath to the popular candidate for the office, John Bilney. There were more riots in 1416. To prevent crowds gathering the *potentiores* ordered all non-burgesses to remain at work.

To defuse opposition to their supremacy the *potentiores* decided to give a role in local politics to the *mediocres*. A common council of 27 burgesses was introduced, three men being elected from each of Lynn's nine wards. The bishop approved this new constitution in 1420. The charter of 1524, however, restored an oligarchical arrangement by reducing the common councillors to 18, appointed by the 12 aldermen, who were elected by these same eighteen.

Bishops of Norwich had long exercised the administration of justice, on which so much authority and income depended. Two courts served Lynn: Steward Hall, at the south-east corner of the Tuesday Market Place, heard cases on Wednesdays and Saturdays; Monday Hall in the Saturday Market Place had been recovered from the prior of St Margaret's by Bishop de Grey in 1205. Debt, trespass and assault were among the cases determined in these courts. The bishop had his own gaol, too. He also retained the court leet held each year in the Monday Hall, when his steward took the view of frankpledge, at which the community swore to uphold law and order and appointed officers to police the town. His right to do so was acknowledged by the mayor and burgesses in 1309. In 1347, however, another dispute between bishop and mayor over the view of frankpledge led the king to order the sheriff of Norfolk to seize it until a settlement was made. The king's court decided for the bishop in 1352, and he then farmed out the court leet to the town.

Clerks and ecclesiastical officials could not be convicted in secular courts. Other criminals had the right to take refuge, or sanctuary, in churches and, after 40 days, to confess and be banished from the kingdom rather than face trial. In 1479 the coroners of Lynn (Simon Pigot and John Burbage) removed a certain John Williamson from sanctuary, but were obliged to restore him at the behest of the bishop. Coroners were royal officials under the sheriff. Their main tasks were to hear inquests and to keep pleas for the crown ready for the county justices who held assizes in the gildhall. By 1413 the borough also had its own justices of the peace with royal authority to command the bishop's steward to hand over

47. A section of the town walls demolished in the 19th century.

citizens charged with crimes. The bishop, however, controlled nominations to the commission of the peace.

Medieval Lynn was very attractive to criminals because its harbour and markets offered richer pickings than most towns. The highways to Norwich and Cambridge were also dangerous. In 1417 Margery Kempe was afraid to travel to Bristol because of the gangs of thieves on the roads. Lynn taverns and brothels were often the scenes of bloody fights. Deaths and woundings involving European sailors can be found in the borough coroners' inquests of 1302-4. On one occasion a German sought sanctuary in the Dominican church to avoid punishment. Children could be at risk, too. Capgrave records a shocking tale: three beggars kidnapped three Lynn children and mutilated them to win the pity of the crowds of London. The father of one of the youngsters discovered his child on a visit to London and rescued it; the beggars were hung.

There is only fragmentary evidence for the town's involvement in the civil wars of medieval England. When King John died in 1216 his nine-year-old son Henry was left facing the barons rebelling against him. An invasion by King Louis of France strengthened the opposition forces. The merchants of Lynn wavered in their allegiance to the crown following John's death, no doubt hoping to avoid attack, but volunteers from the town fought the barons on Henry's behalf near their Ely stronghold, only to be routed. Lynn displayed greater loyalty to Henry in his later war with the barons, led by Simon de Montfort. Ely was again the East Anglian headquarters of the rebels, who attacked Lynn in Easter week 1266, but were repulsed at the gates. Murage, a tax on commerce to pay for building town walls, was granted in 1266, 1294, 1300 and 1339.

The kings of England not only tried to subjugate Wales and Scotland, but France, too. The campaigns of the Hundred Years War (1337-1454) were frequent and costly, and Lynn was milked for ships, men and money. In 1337-8 the town furnished the king with at least seven ships, and paid the wages of the press-ganged crews. Edward III required the borough to send 100 men to Portsmouth to join an expedition to Gascony in 1345. In 1347 he assembled 748 ships and 15,000 men at the siege of Calais; Lynn contributed 16 ships and 482 men. It is almost certainly correct to assume that local men fought at Crécy (1346) and Agincourt (1415). Fear of French invasion brought royal orders for Lynn to strengthen its defences, and in the late 1330s large sums were spent on walls, banks and ditches.

In 1377 parliament granted the king a poll tax of 4d. for every person over 14 years old, to cover war expenditure. Lynn's 3,127 taxpayers contributed £52, little less than Norwich and much more than Yarmouth. Edward already owed the borough £550. The graduated poll tax granted to his successor Richard II in 1379 was more equitable in principle, but its yield was disappointing, and no provision was made for grading in the next one, of 12d. per head on everyone over 15, granted in 1381 to pay for campaigns in Scotland and France. Moreover the collectors provoked hostility by their insensitivity. Only 1,757 paid this tax in Lynn.

Rumours of more taxation brought revolt. Wat Tyler led thousands of men to London to parley with the king, while Geoffrey Litster gathered a peasant army at Mousehold Heath, outside Norwich. Several hundred were from Lynn and West Norfolk: glovers, tailors, weavers, bowyers and labourers had left Lynn behind John Spayne, a shoemaker. This violent band murdered Flemings and robbed 'gentlemen' on their way to join Litster. The rebel army pillaged Norwich, but was dispersed outside North Walsham by the forces of that bellicose cleric, Bishop Despenser. Litster was captured and beheaded, pieces of his body being sent to Norwich, Yarmouth and Lynn for display.

The city state

The real power of the corporation families rested in their domination of the town's economy as merchants, brewers and bankers, but the corporation was the agency through which this domination was consolidated and promoted. In 1833 its annual income was £6,609, divided more or less equally between property and taxation. Farmland owned in west Norfolk totalled over 1,500 acres, whilst houses, warehouses and granaries were let to 92 tenants. Revenue from market, port and other taxes fluctuated according to the level of commercial activity. Most of this income was absorbed by property maintenance, official salaries and entertainments. The corporation was not too upset by the reform of municipal government in 1835, despite the fact that about 800 householders were enfranchised. The merchants of Lynn were too entrenched. They continued to win seats in the three new wards and to control the town. Radical business and professional men were sometimes elected to represent new forces in the Town Hall, but not until Lynn's traditional maritime economy collapsed, after 1850, did its merchants find political power disappearing, too.

Between the Henrician charter of 1524 and the Municipal Corporations Act of 1835 the government of the town was closed to all save its minority of rich merchants. The mayor was elected every 29 August, a branch of flowers being offered to the nominee by a messenger if he was absent from the Gildhall — sometimes this involved a long journey. Refusal to accept the branch incurred a fine of about £50. The 12 aldermen who nominated the mayor from their own number were irremovable except for misconduct: in 1731 John Rudkin was dismissed for disclosing corporation secrets and accusing members of the hall of piracy. Any vacancy occurring in this magic circle was filled from the 18-strong common council,

48. The doorway to the Trinity Gildhall, added in 1624.

all chosen by the aldermen from the borough's freemen. The freemen were the corporation's safe constituency outside the Town Hall; there were 257 in residence in Lynn in 1832, and 70 living outside the town, all traders, mariners or professional men. The majority had qualified as sons or apprentices of freemen, though some had purchased the privilege from the corporation. A registration fee was paid after an initiation ceremony in Latin that Richards, in 1812, thought absurd.

The corporation played host to the 'secondary' merchants and large tradesmen of Lynn at banquets, balls and concerts at the Town Hall, much enlarged by the building of the elegant assembly rooms in 1766. There were three highlights to this exclusive social calendar: the king's birthday, the festivities associated with the February mart, and the installation of the new mayor on 29 September. The mayor was expected to pay for entertainments and dinners, although he was made an allowance of £200 for the purpose. In 1819 and 1829 William Bagge spent over £400 on these three events each time. Mayor making in late September was the most significant of them. The French aristocrat de la Rochefoucauld gave an account of that for 1784, to which he and the gentry of west Norfolk were invited:

> After a procession through the town and a service in the parish church we sat down to table. There were three tables: one for the two mayors, at which all the men sat; alongside, in the same room, was a ladies table, with the two mayoresses at its head; and in another room was a third for the unmarried young men and women. . . . The dinner was magnificent: meat in great quantities; plenty of game, though at that time it was still quite scarce; fowls in abundance and likewise venison, which is known to be the dish most highly prized by the English.

This annual spectacular at the Gildhall played a vital role in the politics of the town, whereby Lynn's merchant rulers asserted (or reasserted) their domination of it. Armes remembered the scene: flags and flowers decorated the candle-lit Town Hall; two tables ran from the great south window through to the card room, where the mayor presided in scarlet robes; 300 guests, including the merchants, local gentry, M.P.s and others 'high caste' people only for this occasion, the men immaculate in blue coats with large bright buttons and white waistcoats set off by black silk stockings, their ladies equally resplendent. The bells of St Margaret's greeted the carriages of guests alighting at the steps of the Gildhall. The crowd in the market-place cheered the guests until it was time to fire the gun nearby:

> This was done when the mayor inside proposed a toast and of course all the loyal people outside rejoiced for so auspicious an event; the guns fired and the people shouted and the sound rang through the old Hall, and no doubt the mayor elect resumed his seat deeply impressed with the people's loyalty; and the people, having no programme, and therefore ignorant of the terms of the toast, did nevertheless rejoice that a King had been given to reign over them and that his majesty was so comfortable on the occasion.

The corporation reinforced its 'majesty' by parading through the streets on these 'special' occasions. Armes emphasises the impact made on the people by processions of this 'colourful host', inspiring 'homage' or 'admiration'.

Lynn's merchants ran the town on behalf of the crown, and royal events were good opportunities to cultivate the loyalty of the inhabitants to local and national figures of authority. In 1660 the proclamation of the restoration of Charles II in London led to Lynn's rulers acknowledging his 'undoubted birth right', and 29 May was kept as a special day in the town calendar to 'solemnise' it. Barrels of beer were provided for the populace and a bonfire lit in the Tuesday Market Place, while church bells pealed and the guns of St Ann's fort were fired. Three hundred maidens dressed in white paraded the streets, and the corporation marked the occasion by processing through the borough dressed in their scarlet robes to St Margaret's for a sermon, and back to the Town Hall for a banquet.

The town's records are silent on the thinking of the corporation in the months leading to the 'Glorious Revolution' of 1688. There was opposition to the Catholic James II at Lynn: in March 1689 the mayor offered a reward for information leading to the arrest of those responsible for breaking his statue in the Tuesday Market Place. The revolution was soon accepted in Lynn, however, and in 1745, when Bonnie Prince Charlie's Scottish army was expected to march into East Anglia, corporation grandees set an example by wielding spades to help strengthen the town's defences. The centenary of the Glorious Revolution was celebrated by Lynn's merchants and Norfolk aristocracy at banquets and balls.

The coronations of the first three Georgian kings (1714, 1727 and 1761) brought the familiar celebrations in the Tuesday Market Place. George III's birthdays were also marked by 'every demonstration of public joy' and firework displays. At the accession of George IV in February 1820 the corporation walked from the Town Hall to the market cross to declare the good news from its balcony. Beer, wine and cakes were distributed to the crowd and church bells were rung as usual, but no bonfire was allowed because of the danger to the mart booths. Some compensation was made in July at the coronation, when 'a whole' bullock was roasted and bread and ale, fireworks and music provided for thousands of townsmen and country people.

When Bishop's Lynn became King's Lynn in 1537, the corporation was invested with the authority of the crown to enforce law and order through several courts. The Quarter Sessions gave the mayor and his fellow justices the power of life and death; jurors, drawn from 96 names in a hat, were mainly merchants and tradesmen. Petty sessions, dealing with lesser crimes, were held by the town's magistrates three or four times a week. The county assizes were also held in Lynn, and the king's justices treated to gifts of wine and sturgeon. These courts were held in the Gildhall of St George. In 1727 the corporation leased the building to a painter called John Cooper for a peppercorn rent provided he painted the new seats for the justices and gilded the king's arms.

A new court in 1537 was the Gildhall court, presided over by mayor and recorder, to hear civil and criminal cases of a less serious nature. It met Wednesdays and Saturdays, replacing the courts of the bishops, but was 'seldom used' according to Hillen. Property disputes, assaults, malicious speeches and debt were the most common suits there. The need for a more rigorous approach to the problems of debt thrown up by such 'a large and populous town' led to a local Act of Parliament in 1772 to set up a new court to deal with debts of more than £2. The Court of Admiralty was granted by James I in recognition of the expense of maintaining sea defences and marks. Through it the corporation exercised jurisdiction over a wide area of sea adjacent to the port. The court leet continued, now held every six months, in the Market Cross, and the piepowder court was now held at mart time in 'the roome' next to the Custom House on the Tuesday Market Place.

Lynn's two market-places were the hubs of both crime and punishment. Here were the shops, inns and markets where public squabbling, assault and theft were most likely to occur, and here big crowds could gather to watch the awful consequences of crime for those tempted to it. Pillories and whipping posts punished slanderers, drunks, vagrants and thieves. A new whipping post was erected in the Saturday Market Place in 1745 and used as late as 1847. A new pillory was set up in the Tuesday Market Place in 1655, where 'the old one' had stood. A woman found guilty of disturbing the peace or being 'a common and public scold' and 'sower of discord' was liable to be ducked. In 1742 Jane Baxter was ducked for keeping 'a disorderly house'. New ducking stools were set up by the Purfleet near the Custom House in 1621 and 1709. The Purfleet was the scene of the punishment of a man 'drawn through' the water for 'unnatural acts' at the *Boar's Head* about 1800.

The charter of 1537 confirmed that the town could keep a gaol. In 1615 the rooms under the Town Hall ('now a storehouse') were converted into a prison. The building of a new gaol next to the Town Hall in 1784 released these cells for the house of correction, the destiny of the violent, beggars and runaways from the workhouse. The facilities impressed James Neild on his tour of inspection of English prisons in 1812, when only two prisoners were being held. In January 1819 nobody was in prison, to the amazement of Norwich newspapers when Lynn was such 'a large and populous town'. Nor did the mayor have to buy anyone the usual Christmas dinner given to inmates.

Street lighting was seen as one way of deterring criminals. Lynn's 1701 Poor Law Act contained a clause obliging householders to display a street light. In 1753 a fresh initiative at enforcing it was taken because of 'outrages and disorders' committed in Lynn, supposedly encouraged by darkness. Similar clauses were included in the Paving Acts of 1803 and 1806. The establishment of a watch house under the Town Hall in 1808 was evidence of borough concern for better policing. The rapid growth of Lynn's population made imperative the creation of a more professional force, but in 1833 Lynn was served only by the traditional constables, selected 'from the class of secondary tradesmen' according to the mayor, supplemented by the four sergeants-at-mace, the sword bearer, the mayor's beadle and five night watchmen. Small salaries were paid under Peel's 1829 act, and uniforms had been adopted, but the men were still part-time.

Murder was not frequent at Lynn. In 1531 a maidservant was boiled alive for the murder of her mistress, the poor wretch being dunked in the cauldron until dead. This barbaric law was repealed in 1548; Lynn appears to have been the only place outside London where it was enforced. Betrayal of this kind by servants was regarded by the upper classes as tantamount to treason. In 1730 Mary Taylor had been the accomplice of George Smith in the robbery and murder of her mistress at the *Queen's Head*, in High Street. Both were executed in the Tuesday Market Place before a large crowd, Smith being hung 17 yards from the spot where Taylor was burnt at the stake. In 1754 William Chaplain, hung for murder, was the first man 'known to be hung in chains in this town', or gibbeted, his body left to rot in an iron frame. This fate descended on a language teacher at the grammar school: Eugene Aram had murdered Daniel Clarke in Yorkshire about 1743; in 1758 he was arrested at Lynn and hanged and gibbetted at Knaresborough.

Between 1676 and 1783 Hillen recorded only nine hangings at Lynn for robbery, ranging from shoplifting to robbing the royal mail. Despite the existence of over 200 capital offences in the 18th century, such drastic retribution for crimes against property was obviously rare. The most savage occurred in 1708 when two children, Ann and Michael Hamond, were executed for petty theft. It is significant that townspeople were repelled. Thunder and lightning are said to have accompanied the hangings outside the South Gate; the hangman is said to have died within two weeks; his widow was ducked three years later. Public opinion would clearly not have tolerated regular executions for cases of theft where no violence was committed. The execution of children for theft was unthinkable by the 19th century. In 1839 five boys were fined 15s. each for stealing strawberries from a garden in South Lynn, and the three who could not pay were imprisoned for a month. Adults, too, were being treated more leniently. An old and notorious sheep stealer called Thomas Ruddenham was sentenced to death in 1819 but reprieved. So, also, was Ann Clark, whose death sentence for attempting to kill her husband was in 1814 commuted to transportation. Capital punishment was still applied to rapists, like the infamous Watts, whose victim in 1831 was a girl of only seven years. The last public execution in Lynn was in 1802, when a soldier was hanged for forgery.

The habitual thief was most likely to end on the gallows. Charles Holditch, the son of a Lynn merchant, had a cavalier and extraordinary criminal career cut short in 1750, when he was twenty-five. He made many journeys to London and back by road and sea, taking every opportunity to steal clothes, horses and money. At Lynn he fraternised with the young

49. A painting of the two Hamond children before their horrific hanging in 1708. The South Gate is in the background.

50. The East Gate was a target of the parliamentary army during the siege of Lynn in 1643.

customers of the disreputable *Town Arms*, next door to the Town Hall itself. Prison sentences in Lynn and London failed to deter him, and Holditch not only rejected his father's help but tried to rob him. Charged with attempted murder, which he admitted after sentence, he was condemned to death at the Quarter Sessions and taken by cart to the gallows outside the South Gate through streets lined with spectators. Robert Fox was condemned for robbing and beating a young Jew called Isaac Levi on the road from West Winch, and asked to see the Baptist minister at Lynn hoping his repentance would warrant a reprieve. He was hanged close to the scene of the attack, however, without Richards making any intervention. Richards had welcomed the conversion, but believed a public execution would both deter and educate: 'A violent death is intended to alarm and amend the morals of the lower classes of the community'.

Quarter Sessions books for the 18th century tell much about Lynn life and labour. Masters wishing to discharge 'drunken' or 'idle' apprentices were more common than apprentices being maltreated by masters, though some absconded perhaps because of maltreatment. Numerous alehousekeepers failed to get a licence or allowed their pubs to become dens of people 'of evil name and fame'. There were many complaints of stench and filth from slaughterhouses and pigsties. Farmers from neighbouring villages sometimes sold meat so bad that they 'endangered' the health of 'the King's subjects'. Petty thefts of clothing and money warranted transportation to America or a whipping at the Market Cross. Violence and assault are also recorded, and Lynn merchants were among the victims. A sailor called James Bane badly beat George Hogge and did him 'other wrongs', for example.

Lynn's crime rate always soared in the two weeks of the February mart. The town was 'thronged with suspicious looking faces'. In 1816 two men and five women were imprisoned for robberies at various shops and booths in the mart. They were part of a very large gang that 'infected' the town. In 1830 the mart was invaded by pickpockets, of whom one was 'a thief of the tribe of Judah', called Mr. Moses, who was caught with false sovereigns. Market days pulled in the thieves, too. In 1774 three men befriended a farmer who lost 28s. by 'the trick of cutting cards', so that 'the detection of sharpers' was soon a newspaper item. Lynn's big shops were also irresistible. In 1821 Thomas Robertson was shot by a High Street shopkeeper in the act of stealing, and the notorious 'bad character' of the intruder confirmed the verdict of 'justifiable homicide'. Ships moored on the Ouse were other treasure troves for the criminal. In 1815 two men who broke into a vessel were given six months' prison with hard labour instead of transportation 'so that others be deterred' and because they were 'so young'.

Lynn and the Civil War

The ambition of Charles I to build up a fleet was one of the important causes of tension between the people and the crown before the Civil War. In 1634 the king revived the ancient levy of Ship Money, by which coastal towns and counties had furnished ships for the navy. It was an unpopular tax. In 1636 the sheriff of Norfolk had to collect £8,000, of which Norwich was required to find £1,100, Lynn £300, Yarmouth £220, Thetford £30 and Castle Rising £10, the county paying the remainder. Norfolk was asked to raise £7,800 in 1637 and again in 1638. At Lynn in 1635 aldermen were appointed collectors 'for the King's ship of War', of 800 tons. The sheriff's assessment of Lynn's share of Ship Money was always opposed. On one occasion 16s. was returned by the town to the widow of a man who had paid Ship Money shortly before his death. In late 1636, when the plague was destroying trade, the king was petitioned for supplies for this 'now distressed town'. In February 1637 Lynn's assessment was reduced from £300 to £250, and a further £50 reduction was the product of a second petition.

Parliament and crown both realised the strategic importance of Lynn's port and position as gateway between the north of England and East Anglia. So did the corporation, which tended towards parliament. In September 1640 a platform was ordered to be made at St Ann's Fort, and ordnance to be mounted 'in the usual places' for the 'better defence' of the town. By January 1642 gunpowder had been stored at key locations about the town: Market Cross, six barrels; St Ann's Fort, three barrels; Trinity Hall, four barrels; and Red Mount, five barrels. Every inhabitant was allowed to buy two or three pounds of powder. In September 1642 a messenger was sent to Boston for an engineer to repair the town walls. Parliament instructed Lynn to prepare its defences and keep armed men on the walls in October 1642. Drawbridges were set up at east and south gates. London also advised shows of strength by Lynn's volunteer force of 1,000 men, led by Captain Slaney. In December parliament was asked for more money for the defences and for 10 cannons in 'these troublesome and dangerous tymes'. About £400 was granted.

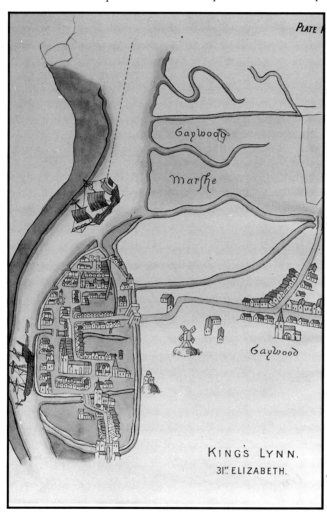

51. The first known map of Lynn shows the town and its defences about 1588. The defences were strengthened during the Civil War.

The gentry of west Norfolk were royalists, and exerted a good deal of influence on those members of the corporation who were also sympathetic to Charles I. In March 1643 Cromwell rushed from Lowestoft to order the mayor to arrest 13 local gentlemen who had designs on Lynn. They either escaped, however, or were allowed to go free. Sir Hamon Le Strange of Hunstanton led a successful coup attempt at the Town Hall in August 1643, and installed himself as governor of Lynn for the king. His garrison took possession of 40 guns and 1,200 muskets, as well as 500 barrels of gunpowder, collected to fight the royalists, and Toll and Percival, Lynn's two Puritan M.P.s, were put under house arrest.

The following siege of Lynn was organised by the Eastern Association, a military alliance of the eastern counties formed to raise forces against the king. It was slow to act, partly because the harvest was the priority for most communities, and the Earl of Manchester, in charge of the forces to retake Lynn, grew impatient. The royalist press claimed that he had 'as much hope of Heaven's gate as to enter Lynn'. The siege began on 28 August and Manchester took three weeks to frighten the town into surrender, on 16 September.

The Hall Books are silent on the siege of Lynn. All we have is an entry in August about the 'dangerous times', and the information that 'a great company of strangers are now come to this Burgh', who were to be resisted. While the Association's army blockaded Lynn on land, the Earl of Warwick's warships patrolled the Wash. Only one royalist vessel got through. Manchester's task was little eased, however, because Lynn had strong fortifications and a well-equipped garrison. The royalists were defiant. When summoned to surrender they sent the earl 25 of their names 'lest you should forget to plunder us when you have taken our town'. Different sources give differing estimates of the size of Manchester's forces, but the figure of 18,000 infantry and cavalry is ridiculous: he had no more than 8,000 under his command at the end of the siege, including reinforcements.

Among the latter was a new battery of cannon. It was decided to use these to soften up the town, which might surrender without the need of an assault, and the bombardment was started from West Lynn. According to one contemporary observer the parliamentary gunners kept the town 'in continual alarm and did so terrify the people with their shot and granadoes' that they dared not stay in any houses 'that were towards that side'. The shot was daily 'flying' into the houses in the Tuesday Market Place. The shrieks of the women and children were said to have carried well beyond the town walls. The most dramatic hit was a cannonball that smashed through the west window of St Margaret's on Sunday 3 September, scattering the congregation in panic though without loss of life. It is unlikely that many civilians were killed by the batteries, but they terrorised the population and did considerable damage to property.

The decision of the royalist garrison to surrender avoided a bloody end to the siege. They had failed to attract help, and there was the nightmare of the town being sacked or even destroyed. An honourable surrender would also relieve the stranglehold on the local economy. There remained hawkish royalists who wanted to maintain the struggle, but the doves among the garrison opened the gates, and men were killed in the confusion. Manchester marched his troops to the Tuesday Market Place through streets lined with women, but with men conspicuous by their absence. He established his headquarters at the mansion of Thomas Toll, who had escaped arrest some days earlier, and ordered a service of thanksgiving for the peaceful conclusion to the siege and sermons to be given for the townspeople every morning. His other priority was to seize the armaments of the royalists and arrest their leaders. Sir Hamon Le Strange was held responsible for the damage inflicted during the siege and his estates and property in west Norfolk were sequestrated.

Until September 1644 Lynn was the most important garrison town of the Eastern Association, where munitions were stored for parliament's forces. Vessels from London landed their military cargoes at Lynn for distribution inland by river barge. Some merchants made big profits as contractors to parliament. Bartholomew Wormell sold Dutch munitions to the garrison worth £8,000, for example. The opportunity for this kind of war profiteering disappeared when the fighting moved west and south, however. Quartering the garrison placed a burden on Lynn from the first. In January 1645 Alderman Toll travelled to Norwich to complain of 'the great amount of money imposed on this town' following the special levy to pay soldiers and other charges. Lynn's tradesmen accumulated debt because the army could not pay for the supplies it needed. Financial assistance had also to be given to the wives and children of Lynn men in 'the state service' and aged parents whose sons had joined the army. The families of sailors were becoming discontented as impressment continued. Parliament attempted to calm the seething townsfolk in 1648 by ordering 2,000 oaks to be sent to Lynn for the repair of buildings damaged in the siege of 1643. Tradesmen were paid the money owed by the garrison in 1649.

Foreign wars

The war with Spain in the late 16th century was the first of a series of conflicts which closely affected Lynn. In 1588 most of the 'best' ships of Lynn were off Iceland or Holland when the call came to supply vessels against the approaching Armada. The *Mayflower* of 150 tons and 70 men, under Alexander Musgrave, was available, and £100 was collected in April to fit her for war. Three of the town's waits were also assigned to this 'shipp of warre' to make 'the noyse' of waits. A pinnace (a small two-masted vessel) accompanied the *Mayflower* to the English Channel. Two other Lynn ships, of 90 and 60 tons, appear to have been with the fleet fighting the Spanish. The destruction of the Armada was not the end of the Spanish threat, however, and in 1589 five other Lynn ships strengthened the Royal Navy, while in 1599 the Privy Council asked the mayor to send two or three ships to guard against further Spanish designs. Sometimes the town requested help from the county to meet crown levies for warships. The Lord Lieutenant agreed in 1596 and 1601.

Spain controlled the Netherlands, and its ambassador in London regarded Lynn as an ideal harbour for an invasion from across the North Sea. The Armada of 1588 could have sailed up the Ouse. In 1587-8 it was ordered that a fort be built 'at the croche' (a mile from Lynn, where the channel was narrowest) at the charge of the inhabitants and 'to be furnished with ordinance and ammunicion by them'. There is no evidence that the fort was built. St Ann's Fort, at the mouth of the Fisher Fleet, already existed; it had been erected about 1570. In 1626 it was considerably developed, the crown providing 12 cannons. Better defence was needed against the increasing aggression of the Dutch and Dunkirk pirates.

By the middle of the 17th century the Dutch Republic had emerged as England's main rival for command of the seas and, therefore, international trade. The Dutch lost a major naval engagement with the English off Lowestoft in 1666, when the gunfire was 'distinctly heard' at Lynn. A second Dutch defeat in 1666 led to victory celebrations at Lynn on 25 August, bonfires and fireworks entertaining the townspeople in the evening. Another Dutch war soon followed. In 1672 the government agent at Lynn, Bodham, told London that the war gave 'general satisfaction as to the ground of it', despite being 'prejudicial' to trade by 'occasioning' the price of grain and wool to fall. A month later 100 men had enlisted at Lynn, and 'this day was at this place a very religious observance of the day in fasting, praying and preaching' in order to bless his Majesty's navy 'and for the good success against our enemies'.

At Lynn war and peace were proclaimed by the mayor on the steps of the Town Hall. He was then escorted by soldiers and musicians to the Market Cross, the health of the sovereign sometimes being drunk halfway, at the Custom House. Defeats of foreign armies or fleets were always celebrated by ringing the bells of the churches of Lynn and west Norfolk. Following the Treaty of Utrecht in 1713, marking a triumph over the French, the guns of St Ann's Fort were fired and a firework display bigger than 'yet ever was seen in Lynn by the present inhabitants' was staged. There were enthusiastic addresses to the crown from the corporation in 1759 when the French had been beaten in India and America, and British arms were successful 'in every quarter of the globe' due to the sagacity of the king and his ministers, with the clear 'sanction' of the 'Great Disposer of All Events'. A Protestant and free nation had been victorious over Popery and tyranny.

England's wars against rival European powers drained Lynn and other ports of men and resources. The press gang established 'a rondy', or headquarters, at a tavern in a poor part of the borough like North End. It might trudge 20 to 30 miles a day looking for likely lads. Sailors, sailmakers and ship carpenters were obviously the prizes, rather than the incapable mob hastily pressed by the navy here in 1755, taken to Portsmouth and dumped ashore. Resistance from individuals was hopeless. A town constable assisting the impressment of a mole catcher at South Lynn in 1757, however, was smashed on the head with the man's molespade. The constable's fractured skull was 'mended' by a surgeon for 10 guineas, but he was deemed too disabled to keep his post. Not all the Lynn men who fought in the army or navy had been impressed. In 1755 the corporation tempted able-bodied seamen to join the navy by offering a bounty of 20s. to each recruit. Volunteer soldiers got two guineas.

The Lynn Loyal Volunteers were created in 1794 to repel invasion by Revolutionary France. About £6,000 was collected from the wealthiest citizens to support over 500 infantry and cavalry, commanded by Edward Everard. These men remained on the alert for years, apart from the short period of peace in 1802-3. Everard was himself under the authority of the Norfolk Lord Lieutenant, the Marquis Townshend, who recruited William Bagge of Lynn as one of his deputies. Lynn's volunteer army consisted of seven companies led by captains and drilled by sergeants like William Millington, who was paid 1s. 6d. a day between 1803 and 1806. The force was proud and serious. In 1794 it was presented with colours by the ladies of Lynn in the Tuesday Market Place before going to St Margaret's for a sermon, followed by a field exercise and dinner at the *Crown, Globe* and *Duke's*.

There was a separate volunteer force enrolled for South Lynn under a Captain Middleton. Its men were allocated a two-wheeled cart for camping gear like tents and kettles. No women or children were to accompany the South Lennensians once they had marched to meet the foe. Muskets and cartridges were to be supplied from the army barracks at Norwich, but no drums. Too many of Middleton's volunteers wanted to be officers, others failed to attend drills, and some dropped out and ridiculed former comrades. A French invasion of Norfolk was expected. Middleton and his 120 men were to march as soon as they received news 'by signal or otherwise' of the enemy's appearance 'in force off our coast'. Red flags on churches and big houses were to signal a French landing.

Although there was never a landing, the enemy appeared in large numbers in the town as prisoners of war. A large camp was established in 1797 at Norman Cross near Peterborough for 7,000 men. Prisoners were marched or shipped from Yarmouth to Lynn where they were accommodated in a large warehouse near the river. From this transit point they were taken via the Fenland waterways to Norman Cross. About 1,500 Frenchmen passed through Lynn in 1797, and over 350 Dutchmen in 1798. The Treaty of Paris in 1814 led to 4,617 prisoners making the return journey from Norman Cross to Lynn for despatch to Dunkirk.

In 1792 a crown proclamation against popular meetings and 'seditious' writings highlighted English upper-class fear of the French Revolution. Lynn's corporation responded with an address to the king supporting the constitution 'as established at the Glorious Revolution' with a promise to suppress 'all attempts to interrupt the public tranquility'. A well-attended meeting at the Town Hall sent off this patriotic message. People who failed to display sufficient loyalty to the crown were subject to harassment. When William Curtiss refused to stand for the national anthem at the theatre in King Street a fracas followed. There were revolutionary-minded persons about, however. In the winter of 1795-6 the mayor was threatened by an anonymous letter with an uprising by 869 'parsons', who would burn Lynn unless food prices were lowered and corn exports stopped.

The visit of John Thelwall is testimony to the existence of Lynn radicals. Thelwall was a leader of the London Corresponding Society, which attempted to organise popular forces for reform of the British political system. He was arrested following the suspension of the Habeas Corpus Act in 1794, but found not guilty of treason at the Old Bailey. After this he toured the provinces to rally support, and frightened urban élites tried to stop him. Thelwall published a pamphlet about 'the outrages' committed against him in East Anglian towns. On the Saturday night of 12 September 1796 he was to address an audience at the *Globe Inn*, Lynn, but the crews of two ships sabotaged the meeting. They surrounded the building, breaking windows and hurling bricks inside. One attacker tried to fire a gun. Thelwall wrote to the deputy mayor to demand protection from 'ruffians' and 'assassins' who had 'hunted' human beings as if they were 'wild beasts'. This was a 'Church and King' mob set in motion against republicans.

Throughout the French wars no opportunity was missed by the corporation to create an image of George III as 'the warrior leader', despite his physical and mental handicaps. Messages were frequently sent to London, expressing the loyal sentiments of the borough on royal birthdays, recovery from illnesses or escape from assassins. Of special importance was the jubilee of the king in 1809, for which the merchants of Lynn staged another patriotic display. Richards was not impressed:

> In the month of October this year, the memorable Jubilee took place, which was kept and solemnised here with the greatest hilarity and exultation, as if the commencement of the present reign had been the introduction of the very millenium itself. It was a political manoeuvre; and not the first to which the British public have been the dupes.

To remind the inhabitants of the solid character of the British constitution and its champions, street names were changed in 1809 to include 'King', 'Queen', 'Norfolk' and 'Nelson'. Richards found this ludicrous, and wondered whether the name of the town itself might be altered!

In 1808 the corporation banned expenditure on Town Hall entertainments for seven years because of the parlous state of its finances. Victories over the French were such a relief, however, that some celebration was essential. In December 1813 over 200 guests met at the Town Hall to feast in recognition of the triumph of allied forces over Napoleon. Gratitude that the urban masses had not followed the example of their Parisian counterparts brought special treats for the populace. In July 1814 a grand festival marking the return of peace was held for 6,000 people in the Tuesday Market Place, with dinners, music, fireworks and, outside the East Gate, rustic sports. The propertied classes of Lynn subscribed about £1,000 for this spectacular entertainment.

Borough politics

In 1558 Lynn was among 100 English boroughs electing representatives to sit in parliament. The town was one of five Norfolk parliamentary boroughs returning two members, all under the influence of Thomas Howard, 4th Duke of Norfolk, the most powerful man in the nation. Landed gentlemen were anxious 'to be elected' to the House of Commons by important towns like Lynn, to enhance their role at court; urban rulers expected political benefits from having high-status representatives. At the same time, however, the merchants of Lynn found aristocratic interference in their affairs irksome, and preferred to select parliamentarians from their own corporation. When the Duke was beheaded for treason in 1572 they took the opportunity to return two local men: the town's recorder, Sir Robert Bell, and the merchant John Kynne.

In 1672 Lord Townshend, Deputy-Lieutenant of Norfolk, exerted pressure on Lynn to accept as M.P. the king's Solicitor-General, Sir Francis North. This sparked hostility among Lynn's merchants and Norfolk gentry alike opposed to the extension of court patronage. The local rivalry between merchants and gentry for the Lynn seats resumed. In 1675 Simon Tayler lost an election to Robert Coke of Holkham in a contest costing the latter £10,000. In 1677 landed interlopers were repelled when Tayler and John Turner were sent to the House of Commons instead of a Coke and a Walpole. The merchants of Lynn were ready to align themselves with a Walpole after 1702, however, in the shape of Norfolk's rising star, Sir Robert (1676-1745).

Opportunities for urban disorder were limited by legislation. In 1714 the Septennial Act increased the timespan between parliaments from three to seven years. Elections allowed freemen to be rewarded for their loyalty and the crowd to display its preferences. Social tensions were nicely discharged in the Lynn parliamentary contest of 1747. Richards, writing

52. A dinner for 6,000 citizens was given in the Tuesday Market Place to celebrate the return of peace in 1814 after the long war against France.

in 1812, quoted an eyewitness that it was 'fierce and violent' and the taverns were open all day for the people to get drunk. The three candidates for the two Lynn seats spent over £2,000 apiece. Horace Walpole (the son of Sir Robert), M.P. for Lynn before resigning in 1767, hated the hustle and bustle of Lynn's elections:

> It is plain I never knew for how many trades I was formed, when at this time of day I can begin electioneering, and succeed in my new vocation. Think of me, the subject of a mob, who was scarce ever before in a mob, addressing them in the town hall, riding at the head of two thousand people through such a town as Lynn, dining with above two hundred of them, amid bumpers, huzzas, songs and tobacco, and finishing with country dancing at a ball and sixpenny twist!

The most significant parliamentary contest in 18th-century Lynn was in 1768 when the Turners were attacked by a militant party of merchants. Charles had abused his position as Collector of Customs at Lynn. Sir John had seemingly identified with the absolutist politics of George III. His support at Westminster for the crown's proposal to introduce general warrants, or arbitrary house arrest and search, enraged townspeople. Turner was opposed by Crisp Molineux, a West Indian plantation owner who promoted his candidature by emphasising that his private wealth would make him independent of the crown. Most parliamentarians were 'not worth £10000 a year' he triumphantly told a friend. In February 1768 at least 13 men favouring Molineux were admitted to the borough freedom. Lynn freemen living in London were also courted by the anti-Turner forces at a dinner at the *King's Arms* in Cornhill. Friends of Sir John countered by supplying freemen with groceries and coal, largely at the expense of George Hogge, who spent £6,000. Hogge told over 100 freemen meeting at the *Nag's Head* to plump for Turner — plumping was using only one of a freeman's two votes, increasing the chance of the election of a particular candidate.

Polling by the 310 freemen began at 11 a.m. on 21 March in the Tuesday Market Place, where the hustings, or platform, was erected. The mayor declared the result in the Town Hall at 5 p.m. Thomas Walpole was first with 200 votes, Turner next with 174, and Molineux defeated with a hundred and fifty-nine. Sir John was finally ousted when George Hogge withdrew his support. Molineux had given him turtles and rum, describing him privately as 'the sole author of my miscarriage' now 'lamenting' the fortune spent. In 1774 Thomas Walpole and Molineux were elected without a contest.

After the defeat of Napoleon parliamentary reformers saw a democratic legislature as the key to the alleviation of social distress. In December 1816 a meeting of the inhabitants at the Town Hall petitioned parliament for public spending cuts and a reform of the House of Commons. At the great parliamentary reform meeting at Spa Fields in November 1816, when Henry Hunt and other democrats had shown tricolours, one of the orators was Dr. John Watson. He had practised as a surgeon in Lynn, where his wife and children still lived. He was soon in custody, but the Home Office was also in pursuit of his son, Camille Desmoulins Watson, who had encouraged radicals in the capital to storm what he regarded as England's Bastille, the Tower of London. Police from London assisted the mayor of Lynn to search for him, hiding somewhere 'in the eastern stews'.

Parliamentary reform was again in the wind in the early 1830s, when there was severe economic depression. Unrest among the half-starved agricultural labourers of southern England, 'led' by the mythical 'Captain Swing', affected most of the villages around Lynn, and threshing machines were smashed, cattle maimed and ricks burnt. Landowners and farmers meeting at the *Duke's Head* in December 1831 offered rewards to anyone helping to find 'those responsible for the fires'.

A meeting in the Town Hall in May 1832 gathered over 1,000 signatures for a petition to the House of Commons demanding parliamentary reform. In June news arrived to a packed and torch-lit Tuesday Market Place that the House of Lords no longer opposed the Reform Bill. A posse of fisherwomen dressed a bust with a blue jacket to represent Earl Grey and chaired it through the town. The tradesmen dined at taverns and founded a Political Association.

How much change to town politics did the Reform Act of 1832 bring? Male householders rated at £10 a year were enfranchised. New voters registered in 1832 totalled 583 and, together with the freemen, the local electorate was now 836 in all. The fact that 2,323 houses are recorded in the town in 1831 illustrates the limitations of the act. A substantial body of small property owners had been enfranchised, however, and by 1841 Lynn boasted 1,144 voters as a result of the town's expansion.

Lynn Liberals were unprepared for the general election of 1841 and failed to attract a candidate. The Conservatives, led by Sir Robert Peel, won an impressive national victory. Peel came subsequently to believe, however, that Britain's urban and industrial millions would turn revolutionary unless grain could be imported cheaply and to wish to repeal the 1815 Corn Laws curbing imports. This was popular in Lynn as elsewhere: in 1839 over 100 members of the Lynn Working Men's Association supported the *People's Charter* for parliamentary reform and repeal of the Corn Laws. When the laws were repealed in 1846 Peel faced opposition from within his own party, many landed members of which feared the loss of protection to British agriculture. The Protectionists found an able leader in Lord George Bentinck, M.P. for Lynn.

The Conservative Party was broken up and the government fell; Bentinck invited Disraeli and other 'Tory flowers' to Lynn where Peel's fall was celebrated in the Market House.

When Bentinck died suddenly in 1848 the corporation found another Tory aristocrat to represent them in the son of the Earl of Derby. Lord Stanley's big test arrived with the general election of 1852. Lynn's merchant families were losing influence to new banking and railway interests. This new Peelite and Liberal bourgeoisie, with little sympathy for reactionary Tories, was personified by Daniel Gurney. It was already represented by Lord Jocelyn, but he was too conservative for many tradesmen opposed to the deferential society all conservatives upheld. Their champion was Robert Pashley, a London lawyer. The three candidates canvassed hard in hot July days. Stanley saw all 1,100 electors and concluded that their politics were simply determined by like or dislike of 'leading persons' in the town — a gross exaggeration for he knew that popular opposition to him was growing because of fears that a Tory government would restore the Corn Laws.

Stanley only just managed to foil an electoral pact between Pashley and Jocelyn that would have put him in third place. With the rump of 112 'malleable freemen' still

53. Lord George Bentinck, M.P. for Lynn 1828-48, political patron of Benjamin Disraeli and leader of the Tory revolt against Sir Robert Peel.

part of the electorate, however, the odds shifted against the radical, who got 385 votes to Stanley's 550 and Jocelyn's 637 votes. Popular reaction to the defeat began in the Tuesday Market Place, where the hustings were fired. The crowd then funnelled through the High Street to the Saturday Market Place and burnt the hustings there, too. Police were called in from outside Lynn to help the town's regular and special constables to arrest 'the rioters'. When the tumult subsided the mayor adjourned the last meeting of the election to the

Tuesday Market Place. Here Pashley claimed the support of the overwhelming majority of townspeople, including women, and interpreted the riot as a legitimate protest against an unjust political system.

College Lane with the Town Hall.

Chapter Ten

Lynn since the Coming of the Railways

The fabric of the town

Harrod's directory for 1868 reported that Lynn was a thriving port and market town with well paved streets and 'excellent' shops. Recent local improvements such as the covering of the Purfleet had contributed much to this opinion. The fall in population during the 1850s and 1860s from 20,000 to 17,000 had killed off house building, but civic buildings still tell of the town's solid prosperity in these mid-Victorian years. Opposition from many ratepayers to public expenditure was overcome by the money of the town's aristocratic parliamentary spokesman, Lord Stanley. He believed in 1853 that local energies had been directed 'into plans of improvement mainly projected by myself', listing the Athenaeum, Baths and Corn Exchange. He boasted how he had 'rapidly taken and carried through' plans 'long advocated' by Lynn's liberals without success. Tory paternalism, or the noble lord's desire for a safe and grateful constituency, was a factor in the development of the ancient borough.

The Athenaeum, on Baxter's Plain, completed in 1854, was of Italianate style. The Baths, of 1856, still standing on the riverside, are a modest amenity, but the same classical influences are apparent. A new pilot office and tower was attached to the building in 1865. East of old Lynn the London Road was also being built up. In 1861 the County Court, of yellow brick in 'the humble palazzo' style often adopted for such official edifices, was erected near the Greyfriars Tower. Grey brick was used by the Primitive Methodists for their chapel in similar Italianate style built on the adjacent plot in 1859. Secessions from other congregations led to the erection of the Union Baptist chapel in Market Street, also in 1859 — contemporaries regarded it as 'a creditable addition to the public buildings of the town', perhaps impressed by the only Nonconformist chapel with a spire. It became the town museum in 1904.

Anglicans disliked the bold building of the Nonconformists, not least because of the prominent sites of the new chapels. Part of their response in the 1850s and 1860s was several schools for the children of the working classes in Tudor Gothic style, of which St Margaret's, on the Millfleet, was the largest. This style was also chosen for the new St James' Workhouse. It may be significant that the workhouse was the largest of all Lynn's civic buildings in these years of mid-Victorian 'prosperity', although it does not gainsay the rising living standards of most townspeople. The Savings Bank built in 1859 in St James' Street confirms that Lynn's population was becoming a little richer if a little smaller.

Probably the most prestigious location in Lynn was taken for the erection of the Corn Exchange in 1854. The Market House of 1830 was demolished to make way for it. The Exchange was as symbolic of the commercial lifeblood of Lynn as the Cotton Exchange is of Manchester. Its classical façade is the work of a local stonemason. He topped the attic with a representation of Ceres, the goddess of corn. The building running west to the Ouse behind this façade is of unimpressive brick. Inside, iron pillars against the walls support the glass roof (not the original), all *avant-garde* in 1854, soon after the Great Exhibition in the Crystal Palace. Pevsner describes the Corn Exchange as 'jolly but vulgar' and typical of its kind.

Lynn's population began to rise as large industrial enterprises associated with the new docks and railways developed in the suburbs of the old town. The main shopping streets were much altered by the building of department stores to tap the consumer demand generated by rising real incomes. The merchants' houses of the riverside quarters were converted for other uses. The Girls High School occupied a fine mansion in King Street in 1891. In 1869 Gurney's Bank took over Hogge's house in the Tuesday Market Place. The Saturday Market Place lost its Georgian shambles in 1914 to allow the restoration of the north porch of St Margaret's church. A preference for the Gothic over the Classical style of architecture had also been apparent in Gilbert Scott's 'restoration' of the interior of the parish church in the 1870s, destroying the nave of the 1740s. He was also architect of the new spire at St Nicholas' chapel, erected in 1869.

The expansion of the town was now most intensive along the line of London and Railway Roads and the streets leading onto these broad Victorian thoroughfares. The Roman Catholics remade their Pugin church; the Methodists built and rebuilt chapels. St James' Hall and Assembly Rooms, built on the site of the medieval chapel in 1887, were destroyed by fire in 1906, rebuilt, and burned down again in 1936. The Technical School, erected in 1893 in Neo-Gothic style with the help of grants from local and central government, still stands. The Stanley Library of 1884 was soon found to be too dark and cramped, but the borough could not afford a new building. Civic leaders persuaded the steel baron Andrew Carnegie to provide the money, over £5,000, for a new library. It was built in Neo-Gothic style close to the Greyfriars Tower and opened in 1905.

Suburban growth had broken through the line of Lynn's medieval defences by 1900. The communities of North and South Lynn acquired their own chapels and schools, while ribbon development along the Lynn and Gaywood Roads indicated another suburban thrust, to the east, where a new grammar school was built in 1906. This population movement was hastened after the First World War. Slum clearance in the 1930s drove the corporation to build 1,000 houses on land at North and South Lynn as well as at Gaywood. A large secondary school was opened at Gaywood in 1939. Private housing was also projected at Gaywood and the Woottons, auctioneers tempting buyers with the 'frequent' bus service to Lynn and good electricity and water supplies. Gaywood was 'absorbed' by Lynn in 1935. Across the Ouse the hamlet of West Lynn was also becoming more of a suburb of the borough. A concrete structure replaced the old iron bridge in 1925.

The old town did not escape further redevelopment between the wars. Small shops began to disappear in the face of competition from the department stores built in the High Street by big city firms: Marks & Spencer and Burton the tailor, both of Leeds, are notable examples from the 1930s. The Lynn Cooperative Society erected an impressive headquarters in Norfolk Street in 1928. That year a fire gave Lloyds Bank the opportunity to construct a modern establishment of classical design in the south-east corner of the Tuesday Market Place. Another fire in 1936 destroyed the theatre in St James' Street, allowing its replacement by a cinema opened in 1939. A purpose-built post office of Neo-Georgian style was also opened in 1939, on Baxter's Plain, the Athenaeum being demolished to make room for it. Off the main shopping streets Lynn's historic buildings were forgotten and neglected, save by a few who fought for preservation orders. Wartime bombing of the town was, fortunately, not heavy.

Ancient buildings of all sorts survived in Lynn's riverside streets and market-places in 1950, but many were vulnerable to the elements, decay and random demolition — the collapse of a medieval house in St Nicholas' Street during a gale in February highlighted what was a formidable problem. The town lacked the resources to restore, convert and maintain them because of the general crisis gripping Lynn. Lynn was in danger of stagnating unless it expanded, but the clinching of an overspill agreement with the Greater London Council in 1962 made Lynn's revival possible.

Between 1962 and 1975 public and private building added 4,400 units to Lynn's housing

54. High Street looking south, in the late 19th century.

stock, as the borough's population climbed from 28,000 to thirty-five thousand. The new housing was concentrated to the north-east of the old town by new housing estates at Gaywood and the Woottons. The centre of the town experienced profound upheaval. Half of it was demolished to accommodate the supermarkets and car parks required to service the new suburban population. Protests against the destruction of old but sound housing were to no avail. In 1965 the mayor hoped that Lynn's 'big leap forward' could progress after official delay and indecision had left the town full of derelict streets. Lynn's riverside streets and two market-places became an 'historic core', presumably barred to the developers. To be restored by a more prosperous borough? The concept has more or less justified demolition outside the 'historic core'. It is sad to report how much of Lynn's Victorian heritage has been bulldozed, including important historical sites.

The rescue of some of the town's ancient buildings has continued since the Second World War, however. In 1945 St George's Gildhall was in bad condition. This large medieval structure was restored by donations and grants before being safeguarded by the National Trust. It is again a theatre, and is the focus of the annual Lynn festival of music and the arts. The Greenland Fishery was also restored after 1945 by the Norfolk Archaeological Trust. The delapidated Hampton Court was saved for a second time in 1958 (the first time was in 1939). To complete the restoration of this medieval complex local activists formed the King's Lynn Preservation Trust. Official grants and the proceeds of the sale of restored properties have allowed this charitable body to keep up its work in Lynn. The borough council responded to the Chesterton Report of 1964 by the conversion and occupation of Georgian houses in Queen Street — the houses have since reverted to domestic use. The Hanseatic Warehouse opposite Hampton Court was restored by the county council for local

55.   An aerial view of Lynn just before the destruction of several streets for the shopping precinct of the 1960s. The density of occupation behind the frontages of the principal streets is clear.

government offices in 1972. Preservation Trust, borough council and determined individuals have rescued buildings in all parts of the borough. The designation of a Lynn conservation area in 1972 indicated that the drive to build anew, so evident in the 1960s, had run out of steam.

Redevelopment of Lynn in the 1960s destroyed much of its intimate and historic street pattern and snuffed out the atmosphere of a country town. If the full town expansion plan had been implemented this redevelopment would have been even more drastic. Justified criticism continues to be made of how far one of England's best known historic towns has been sacrificed to shoppers and car parks, when Dutch and Belgian equivalents have been treasured. Yet an important slice of Lynn's rich urban fabric remains and sympathetic housing developments and conversions are repopulating the town centre.

The port of Lynn

The declension and almost total extinction of the nautical business to which Lynn owed its prosperity during several centuries was caused by the introduction of the railway system diverting the course of traffic into new routes, and for a while leaving this and other ancient mercantile entrepots stranded, as it were, high and dry. In course of time, 'the iron hand', as it has been called, was extended hither, with the effect, not so much of reviving the old as of favouring new branches of trade, both inland and maritime; and Lynn has gradually become one of the most important railway centres in the eastern counties.

J. D. Thew (1891)

During England's railway mania of 1844-5 the Lynn and Ely Railway Company received its Act of Parliament, and the line between the two ancient cities was opened in October 1847 amidst great celebration. Connections to the northern industrial towns and to London via Ely were seen by contemporaries as the salvation of the port of Lynn. Fear of Wisbech taking its traffic had been strong. In 1847 Lynn was also linked to Norwich and Yarmouth. Another railway station was established at South Lynn in 1862 to handle new lines to the Midlands and North through Sutton Bridge, Wisbech and Peterborough. Lynn's first station had been rapidly constructed in timber in a field just to the east of the built-up area. It was not thought to be a grand enough building for such an important town as Lynn, particularly when Sandringham became a royal residence, and was rebuilt in 1872.

The Lynn to Hunstanton railway is a good illustration of how even a short line promoted economic and social change. The Le Strange family of Hunstanton ensured land was available for its construction, to develop a resort 16 miles north of Lynn. The total cost of the railway was only £80,000. Turntables, wire fencing and other equipment were purchased in Birmingham, Liverpool and Cardiff, but station building and other work was subcontracted to Lynn craftsmen. The railway was laid by a small army of navvies, paid at local taverns. Fatstock, manures, coal and agricultural implements were transported on the line, and Hunstanton expanded rapidly after the opening of the railway in 1862. Growing numbers of townspeople took holidays at or day trips to the seaside, while access to Lynn's markets and shops for the communities along the line was easier, to the consternation of village tradesmen.

The railway age robbed the port of Lynn of its geographical advantages, however, as coastal and river traffic was lost to the new system. The tonnage of coal imported into Lynn coastwise dropped from 242,000 tons in 1848 to 159,000 in 1855, and it fell further when Ely was linked to Midland coalfields by the railway in the 1860s, and Ipswich also received a connection to London, allowing Bury St Edmunds to be supplied more cheaply than by river. River traffic was killed off: in 1853 toll receipts on the Little Ouse, which allowed barges to travel between Lynn and Thetford, fell dramatically when the latter town was reached by the railway.

William Armes condemned the merchants of Lynn for neglecting the harbour, but admitted that the Wash port had 'suffered' because of the railways. His *Port of Lynn* of 1852 is nevertheless an optimistic book which presents the port as the natural outlet of the industrial Midlands. Coal brought by rail and ship could also be used for manufacturing. Glass was an obvious potential product because of local sand. Lynn's economic development was delayed until the dock and railway company was set up in 1865, with £88,000 share capital, to construct the Alexandra Dock. Large steam ships were almost impossible to load when they had to sit awkwardly on the mud of the Ouse.

Dock and railway together changed Lynn's fortunes. Only 37 ships used the Alexandra Dock from July to December 1869; in the second half of 1870, when rail links had been made, this figure increased to 327, and over 500 vessels a year were in dock by 1876. Success encouraged the construction of the Bentinck Dock, completed in 1883, with warehouses and railway. The port was now advertised by its owners as being in an ideal position to trade with the industrial Midlands, northern coalfields and London, all in easy reach by rail. Steam tugs, a deep channel into the port, and its warehouses for grain, oil cake and guano were also featured. There were twice-weekly steamship services to Hamburg, too. The King's Lynn Steamship Company, founded 1873, of which Lewis Jarvis was the leading promoter, holding £3,000 worth of shares of the total capital of £8,500, played a central role.

The port now suffered setbacks, however. A full warehouse adjacent to the Alexandra Dock was destroyed by fire in 1880. The opening of the Bentinck Dock coincided with a slump in the British economy. Tonnage handled fell from 148,000 in 1883 to 96,000 in 1887. The dock company profits had been a mere £2,527 in 1882 and, by 1887, it was virtually bankrupt. One casualty was the steamship company, but its relaunch as the Lynn and Hamburg Steamship Company in 1888 reflected a revival of trade. New warehouses were built on the dock sides. But more misfortune struck in 1889 when a steamer from Baltimore carrying maize to Lynn ran aground in the channel to the port, threatening sea traffic. The corporation was forced to borrow £20,000 to remove it in 1893. This disaster led to the Lynn Conservancy Act of 1897, whereby a board representing local interests was appointed to safeguard the river, dealing with lights, beacons, buoys, tolls and the removal of wrecks.

Because of its agricultural hinterland Lynn remained reliant on trade in primary products like corn, coal and timber, but there were changes in its direction. Far more corn was now imported than exported through the port; Britain's expanding cities demanded vast amounts of foodstuffs and home farmers were turning more to meat and dairy products. The grain brought to Lynn from North America was either milled locally or sent direct to other towns by rail. Animal feedstuffs were produced at the Boal Mills owned by R. and W. Paul, at the mouth of the Nar. Only the chimney of this complex remains today, isolated in a car park. Several flour and oil mills were put up near the Ouse, such as that in Queen Street built by Henry Leake in 1899.

British farmers were also using increasing amounts of natural and artificial fertilisers. Guano was imported into Lynn from South America. Most town merchants dealt in manures of various kinds. Raw materials for the production of high-quality fertiliser were landed at the Boal Quay. French sulphur, German potash and Moroccan phosphates were taken by rail to the plant of the West Norfolk Chemical Company at South Lynn. This co-operative company, owned by farmers, was managed from its opening in 1872 by Thomas Brown. It established research laboratories and trial farms to improve crop yields. The 'Manure Works' developed into one of the town's biggest factories and employers. Some fertiliser was exported from Lynn to Europe, including artificial products and coprolite, fossilised excrement rich in calcium phosphate. Sand from the pits at Castle Rising was also exported.

56. The Fisher Fleet at North End before it was truncated by the construction of the Alexandra Dock.

57. The Alexandra Dock soon after its opening in 1869. The importance of the railway to the harbour is demonstrated by the way the dockside tracks are crowded with railway wagons.

Lynn had imported huge quantities of coal before the railways took most of the traffic, but the railways then allowed the port to benefit from the growing volume of coal exports from the Midland coalfields. At the same time pit props for British mines were imported through Lynn from the Baltic, and the timber trade received a boost from farm building in the 'golden' 1850s and 1860s. In 1864 Pattrick and Thompson began dealing in timber and building materials on the Common Staithe. Once the Alexandra Dock was constructed the firm moved to its edge, acquiring a new saw-mill and timber sheds, as well as offices fronting on the Tuesday Market Place.

The First World War disrupted Lynn's North Sea trade and the government took control of the docks. Prospects for growth after 1918 seemed good. The hinterland of the port was widened by the development of motor transport, forcing the railways to face stiff competition for freight. Lynn companies purchased fleets of lorries. The port was also convenient for the distribution of petroleum to inland towns, and in 1923 the Anglo-American Oil Company began building storage tanks at Lynn docks ready for the first cargo of petroleum in 1925. British Petroleum and Shell Mex Ltd. constructed their own depots in 1928. The port was still too distant from the industrial regions of the nation to attract exports of industrial goods, however, and ships sailed with general cargo or in ballast.

Official guides of about 1950 describe the port of Lynn as 'somewhat declined' since the coming of the railways, despite being 'well situated' to link Europe and the industrial Midlands. William Armes' dreams had remained unfulfilled, and the future looked bleak. What changed the outlook for this ancient port was Britain's expanding European trade. By 1986 total cargo through the enclosed docks exceeded a million tonnes, an all-time historic tonnage, and further growth took place in 1987. The docks passed into the ownership of the British Transport Docks Board in 1963 following the break-up of the British Transport Commission into separate undertakings for railways, docks and waterways. The B.T.D.B. was privatised in 1983 and the docks are now owned by Associated British Ports, a subsidiary of Associated British Ports Holdings plc.

B.T.D.B. pursued a policy of investment, with new cranes, quay reconstruction, provision of roll-on/roll-off facilities for the Washbay Line Hamburg service, and other schemes. This policy has been continued: a container and timber terminal opened in 1984 and cargo-handling equipment has been modernised, for example. In 1988 A.B.P. proposed a scheme for development of berths on the river frontage, and these plans have just been given parliamentary approval. Although Lynn's port is in a highly competitive field, facing rivalry from Boston, Wisbech and Yarmouth, among others, its future should be bright.

Grain and foodstuffs, notably malting barley, are still the main exports from Lynn, as the silos on the town's skyline tell. Of the 550,000 tons of grain exported in 1981, about 440,000 were shipped to ports in northern Europe. Occasional exports of machinery, scrap and sand should be noted. Lynn's exports are far less significant than its imports, however, to emphasise a problem felt for at least 150 years. Port development is retarded by poor road and rail communications.

Petroleum from Humberside and Southampton is by far the largest import into Lynn, from where it is distributed inland. Steel from Europe is another cargo, and fertilisers and animal feedstuffs. Timber from Russia and Scandinavia is a substantial import, as it has been for centuries. Czechoslovakian motor vehicles are shipped to Britain via Lynn, and the port handles miscellaneous cargoes from all over the world, despatched to it from the great harbours of western Europe.

Lynn's industrial revolutions
The building of railways and docks allowed Lynn to undergo an industrial revolution, the main motor of economic growth being the servicing of British agriculture. Farmers demanded

feedstuffs, fertilisers, machinery and traction engines. The latter were supplied by Lynn's three greatest engineers, whose factories developed all kinds of other products, too: Frederick Savage, Alfred Dodman and Thomas Cooper.

58. Frederick Savage (left) driving an early chain-drive traction engine.

Frederick Savage (1828-97) moved from Dereham to Lynn in 1851 to make iron and wooden rakes, cake-breakers, steam-powered drills and threshing machines. With investment from farmers Savage was soon able to build a traction engine called the 'Juggernaut'; it crept along at 3 m.p.h. pulling threshing machines or ploughs, or delivering coal or manure. Savage's success was ensured when his machinery won praise at the Agricultural Show at Lynn in 1864. The business was transferred to St Nicholas' Street, where it received a boost from the construction of the Alexandra Dock. Savage was employed to build hydraulic coal-drops and cranes for the dock company, and new machinery for the Albert Oil Mill, owned by Walker and Sons, at the dockside. Savage also turned his attention to Lynn's February mart, and the construction of fairground roundabouts was a preoccupation of the firm by the 1880s.

The St Nicholas' Street site was too cramped to allow the firm to expand, and nine acres of land reclaimed from the Ouse in 1853 were bought from Sir Lewis Jarvis. The new St Nicholas Ironworks was finished in 1873, and 450 men were employed there, making machinery exported to Germany, Romania and the British colonies. Ploughs and traction engines manufactured by Savage were exhibited at shows in Paris and Brussels, winning medals and recognition of his engineering skills as well as new orders. Diversification continued and in 1888 Savage began building digging machines for Darby of Essex, of which

20 were completed at Lynn. The firm was also approached by Americans to build motor cars, but the Boer War stopped the investment.

Savage died in 1897 and his two sons reorganised the firm as Savage Brothers Ltd. One of their most interesting developments was the steam wagon, but unfortunately this was not the modern and successful invention the company badly needed. Profits failed and in 1910 it went bankrupt. The St Nicholas Ironworks was closed, but was reopened by a consortium brought together by Lynn's M.P. The steam-powered technology of Victorian England had been cleverly used by Savage, but the switch to the new technology of the internal combustion engine and electrical engineering was difficult. The company had not possessed sufficient capital to build motor cars, for example. The First World War demonstrated the skills of the workpeople, who built aeroplanes with French engines, and top secret work and ship repairs were carried out for the Admiralty during the Second World War. These interludes could not stop the gentle decline of the company, however, and the St Nicholas Ironworks was finally closed in 1973, and completely demolished.

Savage's greatest rival was Alfred Dodman (1832-1908), owner of the Highgate Ironworks, built in 1875 on the line between the railway station and the Alexandra Dock. He specialised in boilers for hospitals, breweries, mills, laundries, locomotives and ships, and many were exported to India and South America. Special 'colonial' boilers were adapted to burn wood and refuse from mills and sugar plantations. His company also made pumps and cranes, and his customers included Lynn industrialists and Fenland farmers. It is surprising that he seconded a town council motion in 1877 to limit the use of traction engines on the highways, but perhaps Savage's machines were the target since Dodman built traction engines, too. The last one was supplied to Fryson of Soham in 1915.

In 1897 Dodman turned his business into a limited company with a capital of £14,000. In 1902 the Admiralty placed Alfred Dodman & Co. Ltd. on its list of contractors, providing extra prestige for the firm. After Dodman's death it continued to prosper under the management of Alfred Crisp, the former works manager, despite a serious fire in 1913. In 1931 the company took over E. S. Hindley & Son of Dorset, and the business transferred to Lynn. At this time Dodman's was making food-processing and canning machinery as well as high-speed vertical steam engines for driving machinery.

During the Second World War Dodman's won Admiralty contracts, including refitting a captured German motor vessel. After 1945, however, the firm began to face difficulties. Manufacture of equipment for the North Sea oil and petro-chemical industry was a positive change of course. In 1972 the title of the company was changed to Dodman Engineering Ltd., and a move to the Hardwick Industrial Estate was planned, but the slump of 1973 forced the firm out of business. The plant was sold to Bead Engineering, former Dodman employees, and the factory demolished in 1977.

Cooper Roller Bearings plc remains one of the town's biggest employers. The company was started by Thomas Cooper in 1894 to make mechanical diggers. The digger he designed and patented was simply a traction engine with digging equipment attached to the rear. Dozens were sold to west Norfolk farmers and exported to Europe. A few, retained by the firm for hire to farmers, pulled three trailers (for spares, coal and water, and a caravan for the driver). This heavy load produced exceptional wear on the engine, and the problem led to Cooper's development of the split roller bearing to reduce friction in its wheels. He achieved it by reboring the hubs and inserting short lengths of mild steel between them and the shafts.

The early years of the firm saw other engineering achievements. Cooper designed and built motor cars powered by a 22 hp four-cylinder, two-stroke engine, which were exhibited at Olympia in 1909. Production of cars was stopped by the Great War, however, as the factory was flooded with government orders for munitions. Up to 1,000 bombs were being made each week, as well as naval shells and bearings. The workforce grew sharply, from about fifty in 1900 to over 300 in 1918. Between 1919 and 1939 Cooper's became an important manufacturer of split roller bearings, which are needed for machinery of all kinds from marine engines to nuclear power stations. Jodrell Bank telescope runs on Cooper split roller bearings. Millions have left the Wisbech Road works since 1918. The firm has also established three subsidiary companies abroad in recent times. The factory at South Lynn continues to be modernised, with computers assisting in production.

Lynn's economy was strengthened between the two World Wars by new food industries exploiting its rich agricultural hinterland. State subsidies after 1918 encouraged sugar beet cultivation in eastern England. A processing factory was built at South Lynn, beside the Ouse. The fruit and vegetables of the Fenlands and west Norfolk made Lynn an ideal centre for the new canning industry. Beaulahs Canning Ltd. was established in 1932 at North Lynn and employed about 250 workers during the summer peaks of production. In 1933 Lincolnshire Canners Ltd. of Boston built a factory on the Ouse at West Lynn. Both companies relied on fleets of lorries to collect fresh produce and to deliver the canned peas, beans, potatoes, plums, strawberries and other foods.

The growth of the food industry at Lynn was stimulated by the relaxation of the post-1945 controls on the British economy. 'Campbells U.K.', a multinational company based in the U.S.A., arrived in 1958, drawn to Lynn by the copious supply of local vegetables for soup making. It was also interested in a labour force used to handling agricultural produce, plentiful water supplies and the docks and railways. The size of its Lynn plant was doubled in the first two years, and the workforce soon numbered over 500, peaking at about a thousand. Mechanisation has slowly reduced this, however. Not only had the firm become a large employer at Lynn by 1962, but it increased the confidence of the borough council, out to tempt other companies to the town.

The overspill agreement of 1962 initiated a new phase in the town's economy. Plans to increase the population from 25,000 to 50,000 in 20 years necessitated industrial growth, and London firms were attracted by building grants, cheap land and the relatively low labour costs of the district. Food, refrigeration, clothing, chemicals and light engineering were strongly represented by the 50 companies offering 5,000 new jobs in Lynn between 1962 and 1971.

The borough council laid out its principal industrial estate at Hardwick, to the south of the town, where Campbells had set up. Food-producing firms included Master Foods, a division of Mars U.K. Ltd., with sister units in Europe and a headquarters in the U.S.A. Meat has become as vital to the factory as potatoes and rice because of moves into frozen ready meals; it is also Britain's largest manufacturer of fresh pasta. Frigoscandia Ltd. has erected the biggest cold store in Britain, with a substantial vegetable processing and repacking plant, which is still expanding. Lynn's canning industry has been eroded by frozen food technology.

The diversity of Lynn's second industrial revolution at Hardwick and North Lynn deserves some emphasis. The manufacture of commercial refrigerators is the speciality of Foster (U.K.) Ltd. and Williams Ltd. Fertiliser plants founded at North Lynn have compensated for the closure of the 'Muck Works' in 1966. Berol Ltd. left London in 1968 to rebuild its main factory in the town, making pens and high-quality art materials. Jaeger established its distribution centre at Lynn in 1967, from where its clothes are sold worldwide. Josiah Wedgwood revived one of the borough's ancient industries, glass-making. The Dow Chemical Company arrived at Lynn in 1957 to manufacture herbicides and insecticides, mostly for export. Porvair is another multinational company, whose microporous plastic materials are exported to 35 countries. The manufacture of plastic valves and mouldings for the pharmaceutical and other industries is the business of Bespak plc.

The introduction of London and American international companies to Lynn contrasts with the 'home grown' enterprises of Victorian origin which have now disappeared. Brewing had stopped before the overspill agreement with the G.L.C., however. When W. & T. Bagge was sold to Steward & Patteson of Norwich in 1929, a deal which included 75 tied houses, it was rightly recognised as 'an important change'. All the town's breweries were now owned by Norwich companies, and Morgan's closed the last of them in the late 1950s. Only the maltings on the Millfleet built in 1868 by Elijah Eyre survives of this large brewery.

Town society and politics

Although Lynn's population was stagnant in the century after 1850, merely rising from 20,000 to 25,000, its social and political structure was remade. An industrial society of capitalist and worker had more or less replaced that of merchant and labourer by 1900. Frederick Savage, a captain of industry whose statue was erected before his death, had become Lynn's chief citizen after 700 years of merchant princes. Paternalism remained important, however.

Not all Lynn's upper crust was Tory and Anglican. Alfred Jermyn, of the big department store, a Methodist and a Liberal, was elected mayor in 1897 and knighted in 1919. The lesser businessmen also tended to be Nonconformist and Liberal: their newspaper was the *Lynn News and County Press*, which gave the label 'Tory thraldom' to the domination of the big industrialists over their employees. The *Lynn Advertiser* answered on behalf of the establishment.

Liberal working men in the town tried to take advantage of the political rights bestowed upon them by the Parliamentary Reform Act of 1867. In 1868 the Liberals swept to power at Westminster, 'though Lynn returned two Tories as usual' in a contest marked by rowdyism. Tory party agents were guilty of bribery, dispensed through public houses, especially in North End, where Liberals feared to tread. A by-election in 1869 gave Lynn's Liberals another chance, but by 1,051 votes to 1,032 their champion, a Wisbech merchant named Young, was beaten. This time the fishermen were Liberals and might have saved him 'but for a foul wind which kept them out in the Wash'. In 1880, however, after the Ballot Act of 1872, which made voting secret, the Liberal William Folkes topped the poll, although a Tory took the second Lynn seat. National issues were probably more important than local ones, but a local factor favourable to the Liberals was the bitter opposition of the North End fisherfolk to plans for a dock which might destroy their livelihood.

The election of 1885 was a disappointment to the Liberals. Lynn had been reduced to one seat in the Redistribution Act of that year, and Folkes lost to a Tory. The Conservatives had worked their election machine very hard, and were accused of mass bribery. The new north-west Norfolk constituency, however, was won by the champion of the newly enfranchised agricultural labourers, Joseph Arch. He went to the count at Lynn Town Hall in a donkey cart to show how his supporters had overcome the superior means at the disposal of the Tories to get people to the widely-scattered polling stations. His victory was a bad omen for upper-class Liberals, most of whom joined the Conservatives.

As national unions began to flex growing industrial muscles just before the First World War, their organisers began to rally Lynn's working class. Because Lynn was an important railway centre it is not surprising to find a strong branch of the National Union of Railwaymen. Lynn's railwaymen were in the vanguard of proletarian politics in the town. Some thirty of them formed a local co-operative society in 1888 and when Lynn's Socialist Society was founded in 1897 the railwaymen were represented.

Normal Lynn life was disrupted by the Great War. The blackout altered habits such as evening shopping; football was restricted to games by local teams against troops billeted in the town; a prison camp was established on the recreation ground. The New Year's

59. Children lead the Peace Festival Procession at Lynn on 19 July 1919 to celebrate the end of the First World War.

resolution broadcast by the local press was 'I will be a man and enlist today'. In January 1915 bombing by a zeppelin killed two people in Bentinck Street, proving to the *Lynn News* that the German war machine was without 'moral purpose'. In 1919 the paper thought the high price Germany paid through the Treaty of Versailles for 'the second greatest crime in the history of the world' was justice 'at last' for 'the organised murders by bomb at Lynn'.

The Representation of the People Act of 1918 allowed two million more men and six million women to vote for the first time. The *Lynn Advertiser* believed that the men and women of the town had 'no sympathy' with the Bolshevism and pacifism preached by leaders of the Labour movement such as MacDonald, but its 'red scare' politics had little impact and the Labour candidate lost only narrowly in the new constituency, which included north-west Norfolk. Lynn's Trades and Labour Council, the local Trades Council and Labour Party combined, made progress in 1919, and Raby and Bunnett were elected to the town council for South Lynn. Unions representing 3,000 workers in the town sent delegates to the Trades and Labour Council in 1925.

During the Depression unemployment became as critical an issue as housing. The T.L.C. petitioned the town council to start public works to provide jobs for the unemployed, and a swimming bath resulted. National Assistance was given to the unemployed at the Labour Exchange, under the direction of an advisory committee on which the Labour Party was represented, but many people had claims rejected. Demonstrations against unemployment arranged by the T.L.C. were not very successful because of 'the apathy' of the unemployed. In 1932 the town's unemployed did form an organisation and acquired premises in Church Street with the help of local businessmen. Employed men were also allowed to join this 'Workers' Club', whose main attraction was its recreational facilities. The patronage of 'a small committee of influential local gentlemen' was lost when the club refused to give up its bar. These civic leaders found rooms in the Methodist Church on Railway Road for a 'Social Service Club and Gymnasium', which provided teaching in carpentry and boot repair, newspapers and games. The mayor opened it, declaring that he thought that the unemployed in Lynn 'are the best behaved in England'.

Housing and health were inseparable. Although some had moved to council housing at South Lynn provided under the Housing Acts of the 1920s, the poorest families still inhabited yards off the streets of the old town. Dr. McIntosh, the local Medical Officer of Health, condemned the rabbits and poultry kept in the backyards of Lynn's working class as health hazards. The 'usurping' of the horse by the motor car had done more than 'anything else' to clean up Lynn by 1933. Infantile diarrhoea had completely disappeared, for example. Yet the Ministry of Health found maternity facilities wanting in Lynn, where infant mortality was well above the national average.

Children handicapped by ill health and poverty were those least likely to get the full benefits of schooling. A dual system of education existed in 1933. Provided, or 'council', schools maintained by local authorities had taken great strides since the Education Acts of the late 19th century had made schooling compulsory and free. Voluntary, or Church, schools had catered for the majority of children before 1914. In 1933 only a minority of Lynn children were in such schools. At a conference of the National Union of Teachers at Lynn, borough officials spoke of their good relations with teachers and Church schools. Popular feeling against education had 'decreased' since the war. Educational expenditure per child in Lynn, however, at about £10 a year, was still one of the lowest of all local authorities in England. Over 2,800 children enjoyed the services of 89 teachers in 1933.

In 1942 Pratt thought that universal education had improved 'the habits and manners' of townspeople, despite the lack of parental control he now saw. What else did this schooling achieve? Only a minority of children progressed from elementary to secondary education at Lynn where two grammar schools took scholarship pupils. Most working-class children left school at fourteen. Domestic service was still the lot of many girls.

Young people with the means to pay the fees had the opportunity to develop skills by enrolling for evening classes at the Lynn Municipal Technical Institute. Speech Day in 1933 witnessed 50 students receiving prizes in commercial and engineering subjects. Over 400 attended classes. Distinguished guests called for Lynn employers to help with the fees asked of their employees who wished to obtain qualifications. The Institute was renamed the County Technical College in 1956, then having over 300 full-time students who had progressed from the secondary modern schools established by the 1944 'Butler' Education Act. New buildings were opened on Tennyson Avenue in 1961. Evening and day release students were still the majority.

Life in Lynn was profoundly affected by the Second World War. Over 1,000 Lynn men were in the forces by the end of 1940, but there was little change in the early months, apart from the large number of evacuees sent from London — 1,150 by January 1940. The rough manners and dirty appearance of many London children shocked Lynn's respectable citizens, who had known little of the degree of slum life in Britain's large cities. Once German bombing began in earnest the number of evacuees rose to 3,000; some Lynn

60. The Millfleet became Lynn's bus station soon after it was covered over in 1897. St Margaret's School (1849) is clearly visible.

True's Yard, North St.

61. True's Yard in the 1930s. It is now being restored as a museum dedicated to Lynn's fisher folk.

householders took up to six children. The tensions generated by the need to accommodate so many Londoners eased as the war progressed: most were able to go home in 1942 and 1943.

There had been an early rush in Lynn to build public and private shelters against the expected air raids. The fact that the town was not heavily bombed convinced locals of German plans to invade through Norfolk ports. Nazi bombing was indeed irregular and spasmodic, with only one or two planes involved. The biggest raid was in June 1941, but the most serious was in June 1942, when a bomb destroyed the *Eagle Hotel* in Norfolk Street just before closing time, killing 42 local residents and servicemen.

The social consequences of the war were most serious. A high proportion of Lynn's younger adult males were absent, but hundreds of servicemen were billeted in and about the town, whilst teenagers found parental control diminished. The *Lynn News* was alarmed by the extent to which local girls 'pestered' soldiers, as the number of court cases arising from relations between the two mounted. Venereal disease became a problem, too, the Lynn press calling for an end to the 'hush-hush' attitude to it so that treatment could be provided for its victims. This was the seamy side of wartime Lynn. Even more disastrous, to the editors of the two papers, was the erosion of Britain's 'Christian Heritage' by the break-up of so many marriages through the absence of husbands. Nevertheless the British birth rate increased in 1942 for the first time in several years, and many new marriages were made towards the end of the war.

Lynn women enjoyed a new status because the manpower shortages led to them doing many jobs, such as driving commercial vehicles, delivering mail and bus conducting, formerly 'man's work'. To allow women the freedom necessary to help the war effort, the Ministry of Health encouraged the provision of nurseries; the purpose-built nursery of 1944 in Lynn continues today. The local press also talked of a 'social revolution' generated largely by the combined pressure of war taxation and rationing, whereby the living standards of 'all classes' were more uniform than ever before.

News of the 'Welfare State' being planned in London was becoming frequent in Lynn's newspapers by 1943. The Workers' Educational Association organised a series of lectures about it, although the mass of townspeople paid little heed. Only 44 citizens attended one of its sessions in March 1943, whereas over 800 packed the Theatre Royal to see the Tarzan film the same afternoon. This did not discourage the *Lynn News*, which warned its readers that democracy would not work unless the individual played as great a part in the life of the state as did the state in his. Society must become 'a great family' in peace as it was in war.

Notes on Lynn's cultural history

Church attendances fell at Lynn as elsewhere in England in the 20th century, yet there was little warning of it in the reign of Victoria. Congregations at St Nicholas' chapel in the 1860s were 'very large'. St Margaret's church was less popular until 'the restorations' of the 1870s cleared the internal clutter. Nonconformists continued to build chapels, though none was large enough to accommodate the thousands who wanted to hear Charles Spurgeon, the famous preacher, who visited the town in 1857. Over 2,600 people attended two sessions at the Corn Exchange. Anglicans and Nonconformists alike were anxious to provide recreational and educational facilities for young men and women. Three bodies driven by the Christian leaders of Lynn involved hundreds of young people: the Forward Association, the Christian Association and the Church of England Young Men's Society. Ministers extolled the virtues of religious observance and healthy exercise as antidotes to the evils of life, among which the public house still loomed large. The Salvation Army arrived in Lynn in 1881.

The Christian character of Lynn society, however was becoming weaker rather than stronger. At Christmas 1903, if 'large numbers' attended services, many people preferred 'amusing themselves at football and other Sunday pastimes'. It is easier to record this decline of church and chapel attendance than to explain it. Pratt declared in 1942 that the 20th century was 'too materialistic and mechanical'. The improvements in health and living standards had been among the most remarkable developments of his long life in Lynn. Had prosperity dampened religious enthusiasm? The failure of the Sunday School Union to stop a fall in membership between the wars suggests another factor. Compulsory schooling at public expense was rapidly ousting the Church from the educational domain.

Liberals and Nonconformists attacked England's public houses, which they believed were the mainsprings of many social evils, disease, crime, prostitution and poverty. In 1892 Lynn's 'Vigilance Committee', campaigning to close as many as possible, commissioned a map to emphasise the great number of houses licensed to sell alcohol: 180 for 18,625 people, or one for every 100 inhabitants! The Licensing Act of 1902 triggered official action. The licensing justices reported on the sanitary condition of the licensed houses in the borough in 1903, after visiting 165 of them. Most were health hazards, no less than 110 of those inspected having sanitary defects. They were particularly concerned that many public houses in Lynn 'almost' seemed to have been constructed 'for the purposes of prostitution', with their small back rooms and back entrances. They wanted to close 25 at once. Their contention that Lynn had too many pubs was based on commercial as well as moral grounds. The harbour now accommodated fewer if bigger ships, and there were consequently fewer sailors, while the porters who moved the cargoes were no longer paid in pubs. Houses near the river had therefore lost custom. The railways bought people into Lynn on market days, so the many small inns depending on stabling facilities had less trade. The Licensing Consolidation Act of 1910 was used by the corporation to close a number of squalid beerhouses, and between 1906 and 1916 at least 59 licensed houses were closed in Lynn as 'unnecessary', and the owners were paid compensation.

The Society of Arts and Sciences was launched in 1913 at the Town Hall amidst declarations of the need to encourage 'taste' for the arts and sciences, and to promote original investigation. The mayor wished the society success, and said proudly that 'it looked as if Lynn was taking steps to keep pace with other towns in such matters'. Others agreed that it would bind together 'the intellectual men and women' of Lynn. Historians, scientists and painters, mostly, of course, part-time and amateur, had not been numerous enough to form their own clubs. Borough officials, customs officers, estate agents, business-men and lawyers constituted the leading lights of the society, whose membership had climbed to over 200 within six months.

Farm labourers and fishermen in East Anglia kept a rich tradition of folk songs, which was beginning to disappear in the late 19th century under the impact of universal elementary education. Vaughan Williams was acutely aware of the heritage being lost, and a visit to Lynn in 1905 was highly significant for the development of his music. He met Harry Cox, a farm labourer who possessed an immense repertoire of folk songs which the BBC recorded in the 1930s (some were variations of music hall numbers, others of ancient origin). Williams was most influenced by the music of the North End fisherfolk, whose songs told of sea tragedies and legendary heroes. James Carter captivated him with his version of a song about a pauper boy farmed out to a cruel sea captain — *The Captain's Apprentice*. Its references suggest Lynn as the source. At the Lynn workhouse Williams met other fishermen and sailors who helped him collect at least 30 North End songs. Of his music shaped by this experience, *Norfolk Rhapsody* and the 'Sea' and 'Pastoral' symphonies must be included.

The tradition of public holidays associated with victories and royal anniversaries con-tinued through Victoria's reign. Her jubilees in 1887 and 1897 were celebrated at Lynn with programmes of church services, old English sports, fireworks, dinners and exhibitions. A children's ward was added to Lynn hospital. Sadness at the queen's death in 1901, however, soon turned to joy at the coronation of Edward VII, the 'squire of Sandringham' and Lynn's 'friend and neighbour'.

Lynn's special relationship with the royal family began in 1862, when the Prince of Wales purchased the Sandringham estate, about six miles outside the town. The royal residence at an enlarged Sandringham and the opening of the Lynn to Hunstanton railway were likely to mean new fame and fortune for the town, which could now take even more pride in its 300-year-old 'regal title', as the local press proclaimed. When the prince attained his majority that year flags decorated all the town's public buildings and shops closed at six to allow assistants to share the evening fun. Then Edward married Alexandra of Denmark! The wedding day sparked 'great rejoicings' at Lynn. Pratt's earliest recollection was going to see the royal train at Lynn station in March 1863 when it brought the royal couple to Sandringham; the engine was painted white and 'profusely' decorated with flowers. Once installed at Sandringham House the royal party drove into Lynn, on a Tuesday when the streets were full of people 'up to market'. Lynn's prospects did appear to improve after the royal settlement at Sandringham. In 1869 the Prince and Princess of Wales boarded a steamer for a very short trip into the new Alexandra Dock, to declare it open. The restoration of St Margaret's church in 1874 was undertaken as a thank-offering for the prince's recovery from illness.

More holidays and shorter working hours (in 1884, for example, Lynn shops stopped opening until late) gave townspeople more leisure time. Sporting clubs proliferated: angling, bowls, cricket, cycling, football, rowing, sailing, swimming and walking were all popular in 1900. People 'thought nothing' of walking to Hunstanton and back. There was skating on the pond at the waterworks and Fenland dikes in the great frost of 1881. Pratt believed that the conversion of the marshy meadow in the Walks into a recreation ground in 1902 met a real need. An attempt was made in the late summer of 1862 to revive a recent spectator sport at Lynn: horse racing. A big grandstand was erected on the old bed of the Ouse at West Lynn. The organisers were extremely angry at the decision of the Great Eastern Railway Co. not to run special excursions for the event, but on the afternoon of 10 September the rain stopped and about ten thousand people descended on West Lynn. In race week other entertainments were staged in the town, including comic operas and a circus.

Football was rapidly becoming the most popular spectator sport. Lynn Town was started in 1878 by a team from the Church of England Young Men's Society. In the 1900-1 season the mayor and 400 spectators travelled by train to Dovercourt to see their club draw 1—1 with Crook Town in the F.A. Amateur Cup Final. The club's 'highest ambition' was dashed in the replay. In 1906 Lynn Town played Aston Villa in the F.A. Cup before a 40,000 crowd in Birmingham, and lost 11—0. The decision to play the draw away gave the club gate receipts of £270 for the erection of a new grandstand. The borough could not sustain its footballing success, however, because it was too small to support a professional club. Since 1945 Lynn Town has employed part-time professionals to compete in the Midland and other leagues.

Railways tempted townspeople to seek recreation away from home. The *Lynn Advertiser* declared in 1851 that perhaps no result of the railways was more 'wholesome' than the means it afforded 'of giving change of air and scene to our working population'. That year excursions were arranged from Lynn and other East Anglian towns at cheap rates to allow people to visit the Great Exhibition at the Crystal Palace in Hyde Park. Six million Britons attended it. In the same month the second Lynn Races attracted no fewer than 20,000 people; the Great Northern Railway had offered excursions to them. At least 280 townspeople took advantage of the cheap day return ticket from Lynn to London for the second Great

62. The proclamation of the annual mart by the mayor in 1908.

Exhibition in 1862, but the price, 10s. first class, 5s. covered wagon, deterred many others. About 1,300 enjoyed a cheap day excursion to Hunstanton in August 1868, and there were also excursions to Matlock Spa, Holkham Park and London that year.

Pratt, who was born in 1859, lived through the period when the February mart gradually lost all trace of its ancient bazaars, becoming 'mechanised', with steam roundabouts built by Savage. He remembered, also, strolling players staging melodramas. The mart was still 'one of the great events of the year', and continued to attract crowds from town and country after 1918. Raby mentioned how road improvements and bus services allowed rural folk to flock into Lynn. Their shoddy clothes and broad Norfolk accents that he knew as a boy had been changed by better wages and communications. Lynn's contribution to the funfair was marked in 1933 when the Showmen's Gild arranged a luncheon at the Town Hall to commemorate Frederick Savage.

Moving pictures could be seen at the mart as early as 1910. Between the World Wars four cinemas were operating in the town. In 1928 East Anglian Entertainments Ltd. rapidly erected the Majestic in Tower Street, the 'last word in luxurious picture-theatre' in the eastern counties and 'as good as any' in London, boasted the local press. With its clock tower and porticos this imposing building made the town 'proud', the mayor told its first audience. The cinema was an addition to 'healthy amusement', and attracted citizens away from the public house. The film shown at the opening was *Ben Hur*, an orchestra playing throughout.

Epilogue

Lynn grew rapidly from humble beginnings in the 11th century to become one of the largest towns, and most important seaports, of medieval England. For centuries Lynn was the principal outlet to the sea for some of England's richest counties, benefiting from its site at the mouth of a major river system. The town became a cultural centre for the gentry and aristocracy of its hinterland, but ruled by the merchant class which dominated its extensive overseas, coastal and inland river trade. These men and their fellow citizens left a rich heritage of fine buildings, domestic, civic and ecclesiastical, despite the destruction wrought at the Reformation and by subsequent redevelopment. Yet Lynn was also a market town pivotal in the economy and society of west Norfolk and Marshland, whose tradesmen and labourers shared in national social developments, such as the growth of Nonconformity in the late 18th and early 19th centuries.

The coming of the railways and the revolution in ship design described in the preceding chapter, however, rapidly destroyed Lynn's geographical advantages. A period of population decline ensued and the political and social hegemony of the merchant class was broken. The railways, nevertheless, brought also an industrial revolution to Lynn and new docks saved the port. By 1880 the town's leading citizen was no longer a merchant, no longer a Turner, Hogge or Bagge, but an industrial entrepreneur, Frederick Savage. Lynn grew slowly, breaking through the line of its medieval defences. There was again danger of stagnation as the industries founded in the Victorian era began to fade, despite new food-processing firms set up in the 1920s and 1930s, but careful planning in the post-war period has brought an influx of population and a second industrial revolution, far more diverse than the first. Although the port is no longer central to the economy of the town, the docks flourish through growing trade with Europe. Lynn can look to the future with confidence.

Bibliography

Primary sources
Space prevents detailing of all the primary sources used in compiling this book, manuscript and printed, at record offices and other locations, but the short review below should be of assistance to both general reader and research student.

King's Lynn borough archives, the Town Hall
The Hall Books from the 15th to 19th centuries have been read to provide all sorts of valuable information recorded as the town's merchant rulers transacted civic business. These volumes are Lynn's 'town council minutes'. A range of other sources have been used, including borough quarter session books, charters, revenue accounts, deeds and tax assessments, offering the historian an impressive wealth of raw material.

Reference might be made here to the Heritage Centre. The Regalia Rooms occupy the undercroft of the Gildhall of the Holy Trinity where the 'Treasures of Lynn' can be seen, including the famous King John Cup. In the Gaol House of 1784, adjacent to the Town Hall, can be found the Heritage Room, telling the story of Lynn through displays on its river, trade, buildings and people.

The Local History Library, King's Lynn Public Library
This library contains a great variety of primary sources for the local historian, of which Acts of Parliament, official reports, directories, newspapers, censuses, parish registers, poll books, maps and photographs have all been valuable. The publications of the Norfolk Record Society have been useful, while volumes of medieval material from the borough archives, translated and printed, have facilitated research.

King's Lynn Museums
Lynn's two museums are home for rich collections of drawings and paintings by local artists. Much of interest pertaining to Lynn's industrial heritage is kept here. The trading accounts of the *Jane*, sailing between Lynn and Newcastle in the early 19th century, feature in Chapter Two.

King's Lynn Custom House
Books of correspondence between Lynn's customs officers and their superiors in London in the 18th and 19th centuries reveal fascinating aspects of trade and smuggling. Unfortunately, all the furniture and records once held in Bell's elegant building of 1683 have been removed, and the Custom House has been sold.

The Norfolk Record Office, Norwich
The Bradfer-Lawrence collection held here has an extensive section on King's Lynn as well as on the Bagge family. Deeds, wills, inventories and business papers tell a great deal about Lynn merchants in both private and public roles. Parish and Poor Law records of the town have also been consulted.

The County History Library, Norwich City Library
Norwich and Norfolk newspapers for the century 1750-1850 have been mines of information about Lynn and West Norfolk. (The *Lynn Advertiser* was not launched until 1841.)

Miscellaneous sources
Sources concerning medieval Lynn have been easily accessible through the printed calendars published by the Public Record Office, which is also the home of the Port Books for Lynn, beginning in 1565. The Bodleian Library at Oxford has a minor collection of manuscripts of some significance to Lynn historians. References to Lynn can also be found in the catalogue of the Cholmondeley (Houghton/Walpole) papers deposited in Cambridge University Library. Several private individuals have kindly allowed me to study sources in their possession.

Secondary sources
Below I have listed most of the books of consequence to this history as a guide to the reader who wishes to know more. A few of these secondary works are largely presentations of primary sources. Some unpublished theses used by the author are also included.

King's Lynn and East Anglia
Aiken, J. W., *Reminiscences of Lynn* (King's Lynn, 1865)
Anderson, G. H., *Inns and Taverns of Lynn* (King's Lynn, 1933)
Apling, H., *Norfolk Corn Windmills* (Norwich, 1984)
Armes, W., *The Port of King's Lynn* (King's Lynn, 1852)
Armes, W., *Memories of Lynn* (King's Lynn, 1864)
Armstrong, Col. J., *The History of the Ancient and Present State of the Navigation of the Port of King's Lynn* (London, 1766)
Badeslade, T., *History of the Ancient and Present Navigation of the Port of King's Lynn* (London, 1725)
Beloe, E. M., *Our Borough, Our Churches* (Cambridge, 1899)
Bidwell, W. H., *Annals of an East Anglian Bank* (Norwich, 1900)
Bradfer-Lawrence, H., 'The Merchants of Lynn', in Ingleby, C. (ed.), *A Supplement to Blomfield's Norfolk* (1929)
Braithwaite, D., *Savage of King's Lynn* (Cambridge, 1978)
Browne, P. (ed.), *Domesday Book: Norfolk* (Chichester, 1984)
Burnet, W. P., *Handbook of King's Lynn* (King's Lynn, 1846)
Carter, A., and Clarke, H., *Excavations in King's Lynn, 1963-1970* (London, 1977)
Cornford, B. (ed.), *Studies Towards a History of the Rising of 1381 in Norfolk* (Norwich, 1984)
Coulton, G. G., *Four Score Years: An Autobiography* (London, 1945)
Darby, H. C., *The Medieval Fenland* (Cambridge, 1940)
Darby, H. C., *The Draining of the Fens* (Cambridge, 1940)
Defoe, D., *Tour Through the Eastern Counties* (reprinted Ipswich 1984)
Digby, A., *Pauper Palaces* (London, 1978)
Evans, H., *The East Anglian Linen Industry* (London, 1985)
Gifford, A., *George Vancouver: A Portrait of his Life* (King's Lynn, 1985)
Gordon, D. I., *A Regional History of the Railways of Great Britain, Volume 5: The Eastern Counties* (Newton Abbot, 1977)
Greeves, J., *Maria's Legacy or the exposition of a Suffering Christian delineated in a memoir of the late Miss Greeves of Lynn* (London, 1823)
Grice, E., *Rogues and Vagabonds* (Lavenham, 1977)
Gourvish, T., *Norfolk Beers from English Barley* (Norwich, 1987)
Harland, M. G. and H. G., *The Flooding of Eastern England* (Peterborough, 1980)
Harper, C. G., *The Cambridge, Ely and Lynn Road* (London, 1902)
Heard, N., *Wool: East Anglia's Golden Fleece* (Lavenham, 1970)
Hillen, H., *History of the Borough of King's Lynn* (Norwich, 1907)
Holcombe Ingleby, *The Treasures of Lynn* (London, 1924)
Holditch, C., *The Life and Transactions of Charles Holditch* (King's Lynn, 1750)
James, E., *King's Lynn and the Glass-making Industry* (Norfolk Museums, 1979)
Jenkins, S., *The Lynn and Hunstanton Railway* (Oxford, 1987)
Ketton-Cremer, R. W., *Norfolk in the Civil War* (Norwich, 1985)
Linnell, C., *Some East Anglian Clergy* (London, 1961)
Mackerell, B., *The History and Antiquities of King's Lynn* (Norwich, 1738)
Mason, R., *The History of Norfolk* (London, 1884)
Miller, E., *The Abbey and Bishopric of Ely* (Cambridge, 1969)
Marchant, J. (ed.), *A Frenchman in England in 1784* (Cambridge, 1933)
Meech, S. B. (ed.), *The Book of Margery Kempe* (Oxford, 1940)
Moore, A. W., *Dutch and Flemish Painting in Norfolk* (H.M.S.O., 1988)
Owen, D. (ed.), *The Making of King's Lynn: A Documentary Survey* (Oxford, 1984)
Parker, V., *The Making of Kings Lynn* (Chichester, 1971)
Pevsner, N., *The Buildings of England: North-West and South Norfolk* (Harmondsworth, 1977)

Powell, E., *The Rising in East Anglia in 1381* (Cambridge, 1896)
Pratt, J. H., *Recollections* (King's Lynn, 1942)
Raby, J. W., *The Alloted Span in King's Lynn, 1879-1949* (King's Lynn, 1950)
Richards, W., *The History of King's Lynn* (King's Lynn, 1812)
Smith, A. H., *County and Court: Government and Politics in Norfolk, 1558-1603* (Oxford, 1974)
Spelman, H., *The History and Fate of Sacrilege* (London, 1632)
Summers, D., *The Great Ouse: The History of a River Navigation* (Newton Abbot, 1973)
Stirling, A. M., *Coke of Norfolk and his Friends* (London, 1912)
Taylor, W., *The Antiquities of King's Lynn* (King's Lynn, 1844)
Taylor, W., *The Pictorial Guide to King's Lynn* (King's Lynn, 1844)
Thew, J. D., *Personal Recollections* (King's Lynn, 1891)
Wale, H. J., *My Grandfather's Pocket Book, 1701-1796* (London, 1883)
Wallis, J. P. R., *Thomas Baines of King's Lynn* (London, 1941)
Wigner, J. T., *A Brief Autobiography* (1894)
Williams, N. J., *The Maritime Trade of East Anglian Ports, 1550-1590* (Oxford, 1988)
Wilson, R., *A History of the Libraries of King's Lynn, 1797-1905* (London, 1970)
Wren, W. J., *Ports of the Eastern Counties* (Lavenham, 1976)
Young, A., *General View of the Agriculture of the County of Norfolk* (London, 1804)

General
Abell, F., *Prisoners of War in Britain, 1756-1815* (London, 1914)
Barbour, P., *The Three Worlds of Captain John Smith* (London, 1964)
Beardwood, A., *Alien Merchants in England, 1350-1377* (Cambridge, Mass., 1931)
Beresford, M., *New Towns of the Middle Ages* (London, 1967)
Borsay. P., *The English Urban Renaissance* (Oxford, 1989)
Bowden, P. J., *The Wool Trade in Tudor and Stuart England* (London, 1962)
Brown, J., *The English Market Town* (Marlborough, 1986)
Burgess, F., *England and the Salt Trade in the Later Middle Ages* (Oxford, 1955)
Carus-Wilson, E. M., *Medieval Merchant Venturers* (London, 1969)
Clark, P. (ed.), *The Early Modern Town* (London, 1977)
Clark, P. (ed.), *The Transformation of English Provincial Towns* (London, 1984)
Edward Cook & Co. Ltd., *Soap: The History of Cooks, London* (London, 1915)
Corfield, P. J., *The Impact of English Towns, 1700-1800* (Oxford, 1982)
Davis, R., *The Rise of the English Shipping Industry* (Newton Abbot, 1972)
Edelen, G. (ed.), *The Description of England by William Harrison* (New York, 1969)
Edmonds, A., and Day, B., *Witchcraft and Demonism* (London, 1970)
Ellis, A. R. (ed.), *The Early Diary of Fanny Burney, 1768-1778* (London, 1889)
Flenley, R. (ed.), *Six Town Chronicles of England* (Oxford, 1911)
Gentleman, T., 'England's Way to Win Wealth', in *Harleian Miscellany*, iii (1809)
Gras, N. S. B., *The Evolution of the English Corn Market from the Twelfth to the Eighteenth Century* (Cambridge, Mass., 1915)
Green, A. S., *Town Life in the Fifteenth Century* (London, 1894)
Green, V. H., *The Universities* (London, 1969)
Hoskins, W. G., *The Age of Plunder: The England of Henry VIII, 1500-1547* (London, 1980)
Hoskins, W. G., *Local History in England* (New York, 1984)
Houlbrooke, R., *Church Courts and the People During the English Reformation, 1520-1570* (Oxford, 1979)
James, M. K., *Studies in the Medieval Wine Trade* (Oxford, 1971)
Lloyd, T. H., *The Medieval English Wool Trade* (Cambridge, 1977)
Nef, J., *The Rise of the British Coal Industry* (London, 1932)
Open University, *Course Books for A322: English Urban History*, (Milton Keynes, 1977)
Owens, W. R., *Seventeenth Century England: A Changing Culture* (Open University, 1980)
Plumb, J. H., *Sir Robert Walpole* (London, 1956)
Power, E., and Postan, M., *Studies in English Trade in the Fifteenth Century* (London, 1933)
Rogers, A., *Approaches to Local History* (New York, 1977)
Roth, C., *The Rise of Provincial Jewry, 1740-1840* (London, 1950)

Salzman, L. F., *Building in England to 1540* (Oxford, 1984)

Scarisbrick, J. J., *The Reformation and the English People* (Oxford, 1984)

Schazmann, P., *The Bentincks: The History of a European Family* (London, 1976)

Seeley, L. B., *Horace Walpole and his World* (London, 1895)

Smith, T., *English Gilds* (London, 1870)

Stone, L. and J., *An Open Elite? England 1540-1880* (Oxford, 1986)

Vincent, J. R. (ed.), *Disraeli, Derby and the Conservative Party* (Hassocks, 1978)

Wailes, R., *The English Windmill* (London, 1977)

Whitney, J., *Elizabeth Fry* (London, 1937)

Willan, T. S., *River Navigation in England, 1600-1750* (Manchester, 1938)

Willan, T.S., *The English Coastal Trade, 1600-1750* (Manchester, 1938)

Winstanley, M. J., *The Shopkeeper's World, 1850-1914* (Manchester 1983)

Unpublished Theses

Allison, K. J., 'The Wool Supply and the Worsted Cloth Industry in Norfolk in the Sixteenth and Seventeenth Centuries', Leeds Ph.D. (1955)

Battley, S. M., 'Elite and Community: The Mayors of Sixteenth- century King's Lynn', State University of New York Ph.D. (1981)

Caroe, L., 'Urban Change in East Anglia in the Nineteenth Century', Cambridge Ph.D. (1965)

Glover, E. C., 'King's Lynn 1400-1600: Developments in Civil Government', London M.Phil. (1970)

Hayes, B. D., 'Politics in Norfolk 1750-1832', Cambridge Ph.D. (1957)

Metters, G. A., 'The Rulers and Merchants of King's Lynn in the Early Seventeenth Century', University of East Anglia Ph.D. (1982)

Patten, J. H. C., 'The Urban Structure of East Anglia in the Sixteenth and Seventeenth Centuries', Cambridge Ph.D. (1972)

Stephens, D. G., 'Parliamentary Elections in King's Lynn during the Age of Reform, 1821-1837', Birmingham B.A. Diss. (1959)

Withers, R., 'The Public Library of King's Lynn, 1905', Open University B.A. Diss. (1977).

Index

All Saints' church, 4, 16, 97, 101
All Saints' Street, 13
Allen family, 29, 38, 41
Archaeological Surveys, 3, 4
Armes, William, 16, 22, 34, 36, 55, 94, 114, 121, 140
Assembly Rooms, 12, 112, 136
Athenaeum, 135, 136
Augustinian friars, 4, 89

Bagge family, 12, 16, 27, 19, 32, 37, 39, 56, 65-9, 103, 121, 146
Banks: 56-8; Gurney's, 21; LLoyd's, 136; Savings, 55, 98, 104, 135
Baptists, 22, 97-9, 135, see also Richards, W.
Baxter's Plain, 1
Bell foundry, 44
Bell, Henry, 11, 46, 65, 69
Beloe, E. M., 72
Benedictine Priory, 1, 8, 88, 90, 116
Bentinck, Lord George, 133
Bishops of Norwich, 1, 61, 95, 112, 116, see also Losinga, Turbe, de Grey
Blackfriars (Dominicans), 4, 88
Blackfriars: Road, 16; Street, 16, 98, 99
Boal Quay, 36, 71, 140
Boston, 28, 37
Brewers, 36-9, 62, 65, 119
Browne family, 13, 21, 33, 34, 38, 52, 56, 65, 67, 68, 81
Burney: Charles, 68, 69, 70, 71; Fanny, 69, 70
Butchers, 46, 48, 49

Cambridge, 18, 19, 21, 28, 29, 104, 109
Capgrave, 75, 90, 118
Carmelites, see Whitefriars
Case, Philip, 21, 56, 65
Chapel of Our Lady: Millfleet Bridge, 9; see Red Mount Chapel
Charles II, 11, 121
Checker Street, 16
Cinemas, 136, 154
Civil War, see War
Clifton House (Queen Street), 13
Cloth industry, 9, 21, 23, 24, 42, 46
Coal: 28, 29, 45, 73, 105, 139; for paupers, 81
Coke (of Holkham), 65, 130
Common Staithe Quay, 10, 47, 52, 64, 107

Conversazione, 55, see also Society of Arts and Sciences
Cooper Roller Bearings, 144-5
Corn: 46, 73, 83, 105, 140; Repeal of Corn Laws, 132, 133
Corn Exchange, 135, 150
Courts: 117, 122; Admiralty, 122; County, 135; Gildhall, 122; Leet, 47; Quarter Sessions, 48, 197, 122; Piepowder, 51, 122
Crime, 51, 123
Cromwell, Oliver, 33, 126, see also War
Custom House, 11, 27, 30, 65, 67, 69

Defences: flood, 9, 18, 75; military, 8, 119, 126, 128, 136
Defoe, Daniel, 13, 19, 27, 52, 73
De Grey, Bishop of Norwich, 4, 49, 116
Docks: 140, 142; Alexandra, 140, 152; Bentinck, 140; see also Shipping
Dodman, Alfred, 143, 144
Domesday Book, 1
Dominicans, see Blackfriars
Dowshill Gate, 8
Dugdale, William, 19
Duke's Head, 11, 21, 32, 38, 83, 107

East Gate, 8, 34, 39, 41, 42, 46, 80
Edward III, 23, 90, 119
Edward IV, 49
Elizabeth I, 11, 84, 92
Ely, 12, 18
Everard family, 12, 27, 48, 65, 67, 72, 129
Executions, 92, 123
Eyre, Elijah, 39

Fairs: 49-53; Sturbridge, 49, 53; Cheese, 53
Fells Warehouse, 4
Fens: 18, 19, 34, 152; drainage of, 28
Ferry, 76
Folkes, William, 81, 146
Fire: engines, 76; Great Fire (1331), 3, 75
Fishing, 34, 35, 49, 75, 83, 86, 99, 108, 132, 146, 151
Fleets, 78, 80, see also Purfleet, Millfleet
Floods, 75, see also Defences (flood)
Friars, 4, 36, 89, 92, see also Augustinians, Blackfriars, Greyfriars and Whitefriars

Gaol, 104, 122

Gates, 8, 127, *see also* Dowshill, East Gate and South Gate
Gaywood: 1, 41, 136; Bagge estate, 67; bishop's palace, 116; church, 1
Gaywood, River, 8, 18, 35, 39, 42
George II, 12
George III, 122, 131
Gildhalls, *see* Trinity Gildhall and St George's Gildhall
Gilds, 41, 56, 61, 77, 88, 103, 113, 116
Glass manufacture, 44, 140
Great Ouse, *see* River Ouse
Greenland Fishery, 10, 137
Greyfriars (Franciscans): 4, 89, 91; tower, 4, 89, 136

Hampton Court, 5, 10, 137
Hansa, 23
Hanseatic Warehouse, 6, 12, 24, 137
Health: 76-8, 80; Black Death, 22, 59, 73, 76-7; Board of, 80, 107; epidemics, 76; and housing, 80, 148; N.H.S., 150; plague, 77, and fairs, 51; quarantine, 25, 77
Henry I, 3
Henry III, 8, 24, 118
Henry IV, 117
Henry VIII, 8, 61
High Street, 52, 53, 55, 112, 113
Highwaymen, 58
Hillen, Henry, 16, 92
Hogge family, 12, 21, 27, 29, 65, 69, 72, 82, 132
Hospital, Lynn & West Norfolk General, 81, 152,
Hull, 9, 24, 28, 32, 73

Ipswich, 9, 28, 32, 109, 139

James I, 44, 122
Jermyn, Alfred, 144
Jews, 52, 56, 90, 100, 102, 103, 125
John, King, 23, 49, 61, 116, 118

Keene, Sir Benjamin, 65
Kempe, Margery, 59, 61, 76, 90, 91
Kettlewell Lane, 8
King Staithe: Quay, 84; Square, 13
King Street, 4, 5, 10, 12, 35, 58

Lattice House, 6, 37
Libraries: Carnegie, 136; Stanley, 136; Subscription, 111; *see also* St Margaret's church and St Nicholas' chapel
Lincoln, 36
London Road: 14, 16, 99, 135, 136; Catholic church, 100, 136

Losinga, Herbert (Bishop of Norwich), 1, 3
Lynn: 1; meaning of, 1; from Bishop's to King's, 112; *see also* South Lynn, North Lynn, West Lynn
Lynn Advertiser, 53, 55, 112, 146, 147
Lynn Law (navigation), 19
Lynn News, 146, 147, 150

Mackerell, Benjamin, 12, 13, 39, 46
Market Cross, 12, 46, 122
Market Lane, 4
Markets, 122, 139, 151, *see also* Saturday Market, Tuesday Market
Mart, 109, 125, 153, *see also* fairs, Tuesday Market Place, Markets
Mary, Queen, 92
Melchbourne family, 59
Methodists, 16, 109, 135
Millfleet, 34, 39, 41, 115
Mills: 39, 41, 42; oil, 42, 44, 140
Molineux, Crisp, 27, 33, 71, 132
Monasteries, Dissolution of, 4, 62, *see also* Benedictines, Augustinians, Blackfriars, Greyfriars and Whitefriars
Museum, 135

Nar, *see* River Nar
Nelson Street: 1, 5, 65, 67; No. 15, 13
New Conduit Street, 32, 34, 97
Newland: 1; Survey, 3, 42
Newspapers, 52, 54, 56, 105, 112, 123, *see also* *Lynn Advertiser* and *Lynn News*
Nicholas of Lynn, 89
Nonconformists: 16, 97-100, 146, 151; schools, 115, 136; *see also* Baptists, Methodists, Wesleyans and Quakers
Norfolk Street, 2, 13, 51
North End, 73, 81, 99, 106, 108, 128, 146, 151, *see also* Fishing

Ouse, *see* River Ouse

Pepys, Samuel, 34
Pirates, 27, 119
Plans of Lynn: Woods 1830, 16; Bell's Groundplat, 41, 42, 44; West Prospect, 42
Poor Law, 81, 84-7, 97, *see also* Workhouse
Population: 73, 75, 76; and Church, 16; increase, 17; of South Lynn, 14; and water, 39
Post Office, 136
Priory (St Margaret's), *see* Benedictines
Public houses, 36-9, 103, 106, 107, 125, 132, 146, 150, 151
Purfleet, 1, 18, 33, 80, 135

Quakers, 16, 97, 100
Quays, *see* Boal Quay, King Staithe Quay, Common Staithe Quay,
Queen Street, 1, 4, 5, 10, 13, 137

Railways: 139; excursions, 139, 152; harbour, 71; Lynn & Ely Railway Co., 16, 139
Red Mount chapel (Chapel of Our Lady), 126
Red Register, 59
Reformation, 91-4, 113
Restoration, 121
Revett family, 64
Richard II, 32
Richards, William, 12, 16, 27, 39, 78, 86, 88, 97, 103, 107, 130
River Gaywood, *see* Gaywood River
River Nar, 18, 33, 71, 77, 140
River Nene, 18
River Ouse: 4, 19, 20, 31, 34, 35, 140; improvement schemes, 80; regatta, 108
Roads, 21, 22, 70, 77, 118
Rochefoucauld, de la, 12, 26, 35, 121
Rope making, 34

St Ann's Street, 72
St George's Gildhall, 6, 11, 17, 109, 137
St James' chapel: 1, 9, 61, 84, 85, 88, 91; collapse, 87; *see also* Workhouse
St James' Street, 1, 6, 9, 81, 114, 135
St John's church, 16, 100
St John's Terrace, 16
St Margaret's church: 88, 90, 92, 95, 100, 101; brasses, 60; early building, 4; endowment, 1; feast of, 1; graveyard, 77; great storm, 12, 75; library, 110; Reformation, 94
St Nicholas' chapel: 3, 32, 61, 64, 68, 77, 88, 95, 100; font, 88; library, 111; Reformation, 94; spire, 76, 136
St Nicholas' Street: 97, 136, 143; No. 11, 6
St Nicholas' House, 10
Salt, 1, 19, 23, 24, 46
Saturday Market Place, 1, 2, 46, 104
Savage, Frederick, 143, 144, 153
Sawtre, William, 88, 89
Schools: 113, 148; Gaywood, 136; grammar, 110, 113, 114; St Margaret's, 135; Sunday, 100, 115, 151; technical, 136, 148; writing, 114; *see also* Baptists, Methodists, Wesleyans
Shambles, 48, 52, 114
Shipbuilding, 33, 34
Shipping: 32, 65, 73, 76, 77, 78, 83, 100, 104, 125, 128; and emigration, 75; and plague, 77
Shops, 52, 112, 135
Smuggling, 30, 31
Soap making, 44

Society of Arts & Sciences, 151
Southgate Street, 13
South Gate, 8, 16, 33, 80, 126
South Lynn, 1, 13, 33, 42, 88, 106, 115, 128, 139, 140
Stanley, Lord, 14, 135
Streets: early, 1, 3; and health, 80; increase, 17; lighting, 17; and market traders, 48; old names, 42; pattern, 3
Sugars, John, 16

Theatres, 17, 109, 110, 136, *see also* St George's Gildhall
Thoresby, Thomas, 6
Thoresby College, 6, 10
Tower Street, 1, 98, 153
Town Hall, 10, 12, 48, 71, 86, 109, 121, 122, 128
Trade unions, 105, 146
Trinity Gildhall, 6, 11, 53, 75
Tuesday Market Place, 3, 11, 21, 35, 38, 42, 46, 49, 53, 54, 69, 72, 80, 84, 110, 121, 122, 123, 134
Turbe, Bishop of Norwich, 1
Turner family, 11, 13, 65, 132

Vancouver: George, 67; John, 67
Vermuyden, Cornelius, 18
Victoria, Queen, 56

Walpole: Horace, 71, 131; Robert, 12, 28, 65, 69, 71, 84, 130; Thomas, 132
Walsingham, 8, 9
War: 1745, 122; bombing, 136, 147, 150; Civil War, 26, 94, 126; Dutch, 125; and famine, 75; medieval civil, 118; prisoners of, 129; and shipping, 27, 33; Spanish, 128; W.W.I, 142, 144, 146; W.W.II, 137, 144, 148
Water industry, 39, 41, 80
Watergates, 10
Wesleyans, 16, 98, 99
West Lynn, 127, 136, 152
Whaling, 34, 36, 104
Whitefriars (Carmelites), 4, 89
Wigner, Thomas, 99
William and Mary, 97, 122
Wine, 23, 27, 30, 46
Wisbech, 139
Witches, 94
Wool, 23, 24, 28, 52
Workhouse, 81-7, 135, *see also* St James' chapel,

Yarmouth, 9, 24
Young, Arthur, 71